RAV KOOK

Rav Kook

Mystic in a Time of Revolution

YEHUDAH MIRSKY

Yale

UNIVERSITY

PRESS

New Haven and London

Frontispiece: Rav Kook, in Jerusalem during the years of his chief rabbinate.

Yale University Press books may be purchased in quantity for educational, business, or promotional use. For information, please e-mail sales.press@yale.edu (U.S. office) or sales@yaleup.co.uk (U.K. office).

Set in Janson type by Integrated Publishing Solutions.
Printed in the United States of America.

Library of Congress Cataloging-in-Publication Data

Mirsky, Yehudah, author.
Rav Kook : mystic in a time of revolution / Yehudah Mirsky.
pages cm. — (Jewish lives)
Includes bibliographical references and index.
ISBN 978-0-300-16424-4 (hardback)
1. Kook, Abraham Isaac, 1865–1935. 2. Rabbis—Biography. 3. Rabbis—Jerusalem—Biography. I. Title.
BM755.K66M57 2013
296.8'32092—dc23
[B]
2013026566

A catalogue record for this book is available from the British Library.

This paper meets the requirements of ANSI/NISO Z39.48–1992 (Permanence of Paper).

10 9 8 7 6 5 4 3

In memory of my father, Rabbi Professor David Mirsky zt'l

And in honor of my mother, Sarrah Appel Mirsky

כי באור פניכם נתתם לי תורת חיים ואהבת חסד, צדקה וברכה

Do I contradict myself?
Very well then . . . I contradict myself;
I am large . . . I contain multitudes.

—Walt Whitman

———————————

Our only resting place is in God.

—Avraham Yitzhak Kook

CONTENTS

TO THE READER

This volume offers a brief, accessible presentation of the
life, teachings, and legacy of Rabbi Avraham Yitzhak Kook,
a colossal figure little known in the English-speaking world.
It also tries to fill the crying scholarly need for a one-volume
study in English to go alongside the vast and growing body
of literature on him in Hebrew. It is addressed to readers new
to the man, the period, and his teachings, as well as to those
already familiar with them. This attempt to create a fellowship
of readers from disparate communities is more than fitting for
a book about a man who tried to do the same on a vastly more
consequential scale.

Unless otherwise stated, all translations are my own; in the
case of classical texts, I consulted several translations and tried
to offer the one best suited to the passage at hand. Transliter-
ating Hebrew into English is an inexact science, and I strove
for both consistency and readability while adhering to famil-

iar transliterations (for example, Yitzhak, Kook) and subjects' own preferences for the rendering of their names (for example, Haim Cohn). Sources for direct quotations are found in the notes at the end of the volume, and a bibliographic essay provides some basics of scholarship and suggestions for further reading. Rav Kook's writings are studded with allusions to a vast range of texts. His and others' allusions to Biblical, Talmudic, and other basic classical texts are italicized, and sources are given; the full range of his allusions, the vast scholarship on him and his thought, and much else are waiting for us to discover.

Introduction

The ceaseless prayer of the soul strives ever to
emerge from hiding into the open, to spread over all
the living energies of all the spirit and soul and the
forces of the body entire . . . So it is that all of Torah
and its wisdom is the ceaseless revelation of the
hidden prayer of the soul.
—Avraham Yitzhak Ha-Cohen Kook,
Pinkesei Ha-Reiyah and *Olat Reiyah*

THOUGH HE DIED IN 1935, Rav Avraham Yitzhak Kook (Rabbi
Abraham Isaac Kook) still towers in contemporary Israeli politics and Jewish spirituality; neither can properly be understood
without him. His controversial life and the colossal body of
writing he left behind offer powerful lessons and pose difficult questions. The contradictions of his life and thought are in
many ways the defining contradictions of modern Jewish his-

tory. The dream of synthesis on which he staked his life—today as elusive as in his time—still, for many, endures.

Rav Kook is today best known in the West—if at all—as the founding chief rabbi of modern Israel and the spiritual godfather of Religious Zionism. Yet these superlative biographical facts are in many ways the least interesting things about him. Rabbi, philosopher, Talmudist, communal leader, poet, mystic, and tzaddik, Rav Kook resists easy categorization. The endless play of light and shadow in his mind, at times fevered, at others serene, recasts the conventional ideas of his time in new and complicated patterns.

Born in 1865, Rav Kook lived through religious, political, and social revolutions in a wide variety of settings, all roiled in extraordinary ferment and uncertainty. He witnessed the throes of Rabbinic Judaism in the last decades of the Russian Empire, the new settlements of early twentieth-century Palestine, the Europe of World War I, and interwar Jerusalem. He engaged with the leading political, cultural, and religious figures of the time and became one of them. All these historic changes and human encounters registered on him with unnerving intensity. In his extraordinary lyric vision, fueled by the Kabbalah, Western philosophy, the rise of nationalism, and socialist universalism, the secular idealism of the early Zionists became fused into a great surge of human history toward its final resting place in God. To a disciple who asked for a summation of his philosophy, he replied that everything—humanity, the world, the divine itself—is rising.

His life was riddled with contradiction. The greatest theologian of Religious Zionism, he never joined the Zionist movement; a man who lived a life of the strictest ultra-Orthodox observance, he welcomed heresy as a cleansing bonfire whose embers would yield a new revelation. On the same day he might compose erudite and detailed legal opinions, reams of official correspondence, and shimmering mystical visions. In his writ-

ings, sometimes on the same page, one finds examples of pen-
etrating philosophical and human insight alongside evidence of
striking political and social naiveté. An ethical universalist who
saw socialism and even vegetarianism as vibrant and revelatory
stages in the moral redemption of humankind, Rav Kook imputed to the physical reality of the Jewish people and the Land
of Israel an essential sacredness that is shocking and at times
disturbing. He was a deeply dialectical thinker whose contradictions, and the attempts to resolve them, have fueled generations
of political and spiritual struggles down to the present day. His
writings have fired the settler movement, which has reshaped
Israeli politics, and have inspired the settlers' critics on the religious left. The messianic zeal of many settlers and their worship of the land are grounded in their reading of his teachings,
as is the ethical and universalizing reach of their more moderate counterparts. The rabbinic institutions he created in an
effort to unite the Jewish people and introduce reforms into
Jewish law have become strongholds of Orthodox chauvinism
and religious reaction in Israeli society today.

At the same time, he is central to the neo-mystic revivals of
the twentieth century and today. His celebrations of religious experience and social justice, of art and aesthetics, all from within
the deepest recesses of Rabbinic Judaism, thrill new generations seeking validation for their spiritual dissatisfaction, and
redemption not from without, but from within. In Israel today,
Rav Kook's writings are more widely read than ever, with new
volumes by and about him appearing every year.

Rav Kook stands in the pantheon of figures, all born in
the mid-nineteenth century, who laid the foundations of Zionism. Theodor Herzl projected Zionism as rescue. Ahad Ha-Am
preached Zionism as renewal. Micah Joseph Berdichevsky
proclaimed Zionism as revolution. Eliezer Ben-Yehuda taught
Zionism as resurrection, and Chaim Nachman Bialik showed

how a resurrected tongue could be brave and beautiful. Rav Kook—in tandem with his secular counterpart Aharon David Gordon—taught Zionism as redemption. It was left to their successors to disentangle—and sometimes flounder in—the crosscutting currents of these men's legacies.

Zionism was but one facet of Rav Kook's embrace of modernity. Throughout the eighteenth, nineteenth, and early twentieth centuries, a galaxy of Jewish thinkers grappled with the claims and textures of modernity. But almost none of them, and certainly not the traditionalists, opened themselves to the experience of modern life as expansively as did Rav Kook. He created a transformative reading of modernity that cast it as the bearer of the world's oldest and most authoritative truths, as revealed in the Bible and the Talmud and understood by the Kabbalah.

Kabbalah was crucial to him, both as a body of doctrines in whose complexity he found a template for the complexities of his times, and as a tradition of spiritual practice through which he brought into being new kinds of religious experience, fusing theology, philosophy, and a sacred reading of history into a deeply personal lyric mysticism.

He was, throughout, an Orthodox halakhist of a deeply traditionalist bent. And so the dramas of his life illustrate one of the most powerful and defining dramas of the history of religion as a whole: the complex and sometimes antagonistic relations between mysticism and the law, between the prophet and the sage. He was also a tzaddik, a saint, who worked on his character all his life, whose days were spent not only in public affairs and theological exploration but also in visiting the sick and the bereaved and looking after the poor. Central to his thought-world was messianism, an apocalyptic energy field that held in place the conflicting elements of his time. He saw in secular Zionists and socialists the unwitting heralds of the Messiah. This theodicy of history was deeply unsettling—and regularly infuriating—to the secular nationalists whom he cast as players in his messianic drama.

He lived through a crucial and wrenching shift in the meaning and moral valence of nationalism before and after World War I. Nationalism had been, before the war, a claim pressed by minorities against large multiethnic empires, but after Versailles it became a claim that minority groups asserted against one another. That shift to a new and increasingly violent reality became apparent during the last two decades of Kook's life, when he was at the height of his public activity and fame. It is unclear whether he grasped the magnitude or consequences of the change, or that in his celebration of romantic nationalism he was truly playing with fire.

Understanding the life of Rav Kook poses numerous challenges. The abundance, complexity, and variety of his writings; the range of Jewish legal, mystical, and philosophic traditions, and Western thinkers, on which he drew; and the political and cultural scenes to which he responded—navigating all these make for a daunting journey, one regularly rewarded by the wonder of his story and exhilaration evoked by his prose. His writings, composed in rich Hebrew, are interwoven with allusions to a vast range of texts from the Bible, the Talmud, Kabbalah, and modern philosophy. He is at once sui generis and very much a figure for our time. He thought and lived the contradictions of modern Jewish history with perhaps unequaled depth and passion. His hopes and visions for a restored Israel and a redeemed humanity remain. And the tragic results of their attempted implementation are, today, a chastening tale.

Confronting Rav Kook means grappling with a figure who embraced modernity, ethical universalism, and a deeply personal spirituality even as he held fast to the land, peoplehood, and the law. The richness of his output, the number of questions he took up, the multiple angles from which he addressed them, the sinuous turns in his thinking, the range of his interests (from deepest traditionalism to radicalism and panentheism)—not to mention the existence of his large, complementary halakhic corpus—make him a writer of substance in almost every area of Jewish thought. He is also a fruitful conversation partner for almost every modern Jewish thinker, as well as a challenging interlocutor on a range of topics, including theologies of culture and postsecularism, feminism and environmentalism, multiculturalism and human rights, process thought and postmodernism.

Souls of his magnitude do not come our way often. Sometimes, even now, one must brace oneself when faced with the full force of Rav Kook's passion. The more one tries to grasp him, the more he recedes, or perhaps ascends. Yet large as Rav Kook's life was, his work is even larger, with the life inseparably woven into it. In the classic terms of Jewish interpretation, the historical and biographical dimension is the *p'shat*, the prosaic and literal but indispensable gateway to the whole, which is filled with *remez*, *d'rash*, and *sod*, allusion, searching, and mystery.

1

"No Ordinary Rabbi":
Grieva, Volozhin, Zeimel, Boisk

He told me that his parents used to argue over
whether he would become an ascetic Mitnagdic
rabbi or a Hasidic master.
—Kalman Frankel, *Shemu'ot Reiyah*

LITHUANIA, *LITEH* IN YIDDISH, was, from the late eighteenth century onward, an intellectual nerve center of Jewish
life, an empire of the mind whose sway ran through the Russian Empire and touched the whole of European Jewry. In the
streets of its cities—Vilna (Vilnius), Kovno (Kaunas), Dvinsk
(Daugavpils)—and in its small towns and shtetls, the multiple
currents of tradition and change met, fought, coupled, and remade themselves in a peculiarly passionate kind of intellectualism, an icy rationalism ringed with fire.

That cerebral ardor coursed through rabbinic circles where
high Talmudism exerted a powerful pull, not least through the

educational influence and moral authority of the great yeshiva at Volozhin. Founded in 1802 by Chaim of Volozhin (1749–1821), the yeshiva, unlike a traditional *beit midrash*, had no formal ties to the local community and fostered an intense youth culture of full-time Talmudic study. A pioneering and vastly influential institution, the yeshiva reflected the interests, passions, and contradictions of its time. Through its doors passed many young men who later left their marks on all sides of the Jewish ideological barricades. Its cultural hero and presiding spirit was Chaim of Volozhin's master, Elijah ben Solomon (1720–97), known as the Gaon—the Genius—of Vilna. The Gaon held no formal rabbinic post and acquired magisterial authority by the sheer force of his scholarship and piety. His brand of fierce Talmudism, marked by a unique mix of intellectual independence, comprehensive knowledge of the whole of rabbinic literature, and adherence to the plain sense of the text, was a departure from prevailing modes of study and religious practice. Of course, Torah study had been a staple of Rabbinic Judaism for many centuries. Yet through the Gaon's teachings, and perhaps more importantly through his personal example, relentless and ascetic devotion to Torah study as the supreme religious act burned itself into the minds of his followers.

Though no less a Kabbalist than a Talmudist, the Gaon called for principled resistance to the mystically inclined Hasidic movement, then beginning its extraordinary rise. In Hasidism's celebration of ecstatic prayer and its theology of divine immanence, in which God could be reached from within the gross matter of the physical world, he saw a reckless dissemination of esotericism, careless denigration of study and detailed halakhic practice, and a dangerously optimistic faith in human nature's resistance to sin. In 1772, he declared Hasidism a heresy, thus becoming the first and archetypal Mitnaged—literally, "opponent," or more affirmatively, one who worships God with study rather than rapture.

Chaim of Volozhin, one of the Gaon's leading disciples, in an influential treatise titled *Nefesh Ha-Chaim*, endowed Torah study with unique spiritual power. Since, as the Kabbalah teaches, the Torah in its most spiritual form is the very blueprint of the world, only Torah study offers transcendence, true escape from the jailhouse of this corrupt and fallen world. He sought to put that vision into practice by creating at Volozhin, in present-day Belarus, a trailblazing yeshiva that would train, in a university-like atmosphere, an elite corps of Talmudists, drawn from a broad geographic area and taught by rabbis unencumbered by communal responsibilities. It was through the yeshiva in Volozhin and the new yeshivot it inspired that the reigning ideal of Mitnagdism—of Torah study as the supreme religious act—received its institutional articulation and exercised much of its hold over Jewish life in Lithuania and surrounding areas, including Courland (in present-day Latvia) to the north, Belarus to the east, and, eventually, Poland to the west. Although Hasidism was not to Chaim of Volozhin's taste, he concluded that a heresy it was not. There were significant numbers of Hasidim throughout the Mitnagdic heartland of Lithuania. They were largely followers of Chabad Lubavitch.

The founder of Chabad, Shneur Zalman of Liady (c. 1745–1812), was, like the Gaon, a distinguished scholar of both the Talmud and the Kabbalah. But unlike the Gaon, Shneur Zalman believed that the divine presence was immediately accessible, even in this world, through ecstatic prayer and focused action if one attained proper consciousness (hence "Chabad," an acronym for *chokhmah*, *binah*, *da'at*—wisdom, insight, understanding). Moreover, he believed that this consciousness could be taught to the masses—a distinctively Hasidic claim. His successors and followers, learned and philosophically minded, found a relatively congenial place in the highly scholastic landscape of Lithuanian Jewry.

Just six years after Volozhin's founding, in 1808, a teachers seminary opened in Vilna, sponsored by the local university, which sought to train young Jews in the ways of Haskalah, Enlightenment. As Haskalah moved eastward, it projected, as it had in the West, confidence in reason, general education, and progress. It internalized non-Jewish critiques of Jewish society's insularity and economic insufficiency while asserting its own continuity with elements of tradition, such as studying the Hebrew language and medieval philosophy.

Through the nineteenth century, these three movements—Mitnagdism, Hasidism, and Haskalah—vied for the soul of Russian Jewry, most of whom, of course, had their hands full with simply getting by. These currents flowed in multiple forms through communal politics and people's lives, and only sometimes followed the neat, schematic patterns favored by ideologues, partisans, and historians. Each philosophy represented the steady transformation of tradition; Haskalah most obviously, yet each projected a new form of authority and a newly privileged form of experience, since the familiar sway of the traditional rabbi had to contend at the time with the social criticism of the Maskil, the fierce intellectualism of the Mitnaged Talmudist and the mystic charisma of the Hasidic rebbe.

The eldest of Perel Zlota and Shlomo Zalman Ha-Cohen Kook's eight children, Avraham Yitzhak, was born on September 7, 1865, in Grieva (Griva), a small town in Courland, on the banks of the Daugava River. Grieva consisted of one avenue, less than two miles long, and several alleyways, home to 2,600 souls. Grieva's proximity to Dvinsk, a railway center on the other side of the Daugava, midway between Warsaw and St. Petersburg, gave it a slightly more urban flavor than usually prevailed in predominantly rural Courland, whose Jews were regularly unlettered. Jews numbered half of Dvinsk's population of some 23,000, roughly a third of which lived in poverty.

Shlomo Zalman, born in 1844, the son of a merchant and

alumnus of Volozhin, was orphaned at a young age and raised in the home of his stepfather, a local rabbi. His mother, Frayde Batya (nee Fellman), was the daughter of an early disciple of Chaim of Volozhin descended from a distinguished rabbinical line. Frayde's brother, Mordechai Gimpel Jaffe (1820–1891), another alumnus of Volozhin, was a distinguished scholar and communal leader. Shlomo Zalman studied at Volozhin too. After further studies, he married Perel Zlota, the daughter of a Chabad Hasid who had studied at Volozhin. They moved to Grieva, her hometown, where he taught the local boys and worked as a mendicant fund-raiser for religious institutions.

One can gather only a limited impression of Shlomo Zalman from the few mentions of him in the writings of his son and others. One obituary recalls his "love of truth and strong hatred of anything with a trace of lying or fakery" and his "gentle disposition and beaming countenance." Perel Zlota maintained her allegiance to Chabad. When the third Lubavitcher rebbe, the great jurist and theologian Menachem Mendel Schneerson, passed away in 1866 and his disciples divided up his relics, she received a button and some threads from his cloak, which she sewed into her eldest son's skullcap.

There was in Grieva a Chabad preacher, to whom Shlomo Zalman would weekly take his son Avraham Yitzhak for the third Sabbath meal, done in the Hasidic manner, accompanied by the singing of plaintive mystic hymns. Chabad youngsters were among his childhood friends, one of whom recalled that when Avraham Yitzhak would come to his house to sip a cup of tea, he would recite texts by heart as he drank. Avraham Yitzhak was an exemplary *iluy*, a rabbinic prodigy. These boys made their own nursery rhymes from Talmudic passages, astounded their elders with their powers of memory and concentration, and tended not to have many friends. In a culture that set extraordinarily high store by education, they were groomed from boyhood for leadership. Avraham Yitzhak, beyond his intellectual abilities, was highly emotional and early showed a lyrical sensibility and vivid imagination. His priestly lineage (hence, "Ha-Cohen") was a source of pride and a spur to boyhood dreams of one day serving in a rebuilt Temple.

Shlomo Zalman sent nine-year-old Avraham Yitzhak to Dvinsk for an intensive rabbinic apprenticeship with Reuven Levin, which lasted until he was fifteen. Levin, known as Rav Ruvele, was a much-revered and somewhat individualistic figure in Lithuanian rabbinic circles, a kind of "Talmudist's Talmudist" who never achieved quite the fame or communal authority of some of his contemporaries. In his youth, Levin had studied with the most Haskalah-minded of the Gaon's disciples, Menashe of Ilya. One of Levin's specialties was to find novel halakhic arguments for allowing *agunot* (grass widows) to remarry. When, in one such case, young Kook tried to outdo his master in argumentation and thereby undo his permissive ruling, Levin countered him with the Talmudic saying "With exactingness like that, we'll never be able to study."

Before and during Avraham Kook's early life, change was coursing through Jewish life in the Russian empire and in the elite rabbinic circles around him. The 1850s saw the emergence in the empire of traditional rabbis who had some secular learning. They were willing to approach social problems with new intellectual tools and gingerly to rethink traditional educational practices and long-held attitudes toward non-Jews and the nonobservant. When the leading Maskilic (Haskalah-oriented) journal, *Ha-Melitz*, opened its pages to them, the ensuing series of powerful and much-publicized exchanges on halakhic change ended up radicalizing rabbis and would-be reformers alike. The debate drove a wedge between radicals and the moderate rabbis, providing a powerful stimulus to the crystallization of separatist Orthodoxy, which became more self-conscious and ideologically mobilized than before.

When, in the 1860s, the agitation for halakhic change that had animated western European Jewish thinkers since the earlier part of the nineteenth century attempted to migrate eastward, it encountered a rabbinic culture fortified by the Talmudism championed by Volozhin: intellectually self-confident, capable, and prone to resist innovation. Moreover, whereas liberalism in western Europe tried to help individual Jews adapt to a surrounding society that was at least somewhat welcoming, in eastern areas what was required instead of piecemeal reform was a large-scale solution to the suffering of the masses.

Through the 1870s, Russian liberalism, such as it was, fell on hard times as the humanistic dreams of Alexander Herzen gave way to an atmosphere more akin to the fevered nightmares of Dostoevsky. Varieties of socialism and nationalism stepped in to offer solutions to the economic, political, and sociocultural disabilities of the Jews. By the 1880s, the cohort of Maskilic rabbis had effectively shifted their interests and thinking from working for moderate reform within Russia toward the nascent idea of rejuvenating Jewish life by developing Palestine, under the rubric of Chibat Zion, literally, "Love of Zion." A group of moderate and sympathetic Maskilic rabbis saw there a potential path to productivity and a measured adaptation to modernity.

This was the setting in which Avraham Yitzhak Kook grew up, and these men were among his relatives and teachers.

In 1880, at age fifteen, Avraham Yitzhak left home, in the custom of budding Talmudists, to study with a series of rabbis in small towns. During two years in Liutsin (Ludza), he divided his time between the *beit midrash* of a Hasidically minded Talmudist and the library of a cousin, a self-professed Maskil ("Enlightener") who regularly gathered around him youthful disciples. During his hours in the library, Avraham Yitzhak began to craft verse, including parodies of Maskilic verse. When, on his return to Grieva for the High Holidays, he brought his notebook of poems, his father did not hide his disappointment. The next year, he brought home a notebook full of Talmudic glosses.

The detailed reminiscences of his study partner of the time are revealing. Avraham Yitzhak dressed, wrote verse, and spoke in grammatical Hebrew, like a Maskil. Yet he also regularly expressed Orthodox attitudes severely critical of modernization and secular university education, and he did not know Russian.

He then spent another year in Smorgon (present-day Smarhon' in Belarus) studying, at his mentor Levin's suggestion, with a member of the Lithuanian rabbinic aristocracy. A lengthy, strikingly learned essay of his from that time on the claims and merit of natural science affords a glimpse into some of his preoccupations. The accomplishments of modern science are obvious, he writes, yet are no match for rabbinic tradition when it comes to grasping the ideas underlying the universe or the paths to human perfection.

On his return from Smorgon, in the spring of 1884, he met with Rabbi Eliyahu David Rabinowitz-Teomim (1842/3?–1905), a renowned Talmudist and rabbi of Ponevezh, who was looking for a husband for his eldest daughter, Batsheva Alta. In a memoir of his life, Rabinowitz-Teomim, known by the acronym Aderet, comes across as an immensely learned, gentle, and harried soul longing for the peace of the study hall and never able to reap the rewards of his intellectual talents. His life story, an unrelenting chronicle of bereavement, poor health, premature deaths (nine of his thirteen children died at young ages), bitter squabbles with rival rabbis for decently paying pulpits, and promises broken by capricious in-laws and rapacious congregants, sheds a harsh light on the dire socioeconomic circumstances of many Lithuanian rabbis of the time. Indeed, he was sometimes forced to the extraordinary expedient of going on strike, which consisted of refusing to answer halakhic questions. In this respect, the nascent socialist stirrings of the time seem not to have passed Aderet by.

When it came time to find his eldest daughter a husband, he asked around and heard about young Kook, who, aside from being an upstanding young man and a pious scholar, had fine parents, to whom Aderet's poverty did not matter. He suggested a meeting in Riga, and his reaction to his prospective son-in-law was immediate and moving: "And when I laid eyes on him and spoke to him for several hours, my soul cleaved to him, I loved him profoundly, as I got my first glimpse of him and his extraordinary talents and piety and (saw) that he would become a mighty cedar."[1] After the prospective couple were introduced in Dobvelen (Dubulti, Latvia), where Aderet regularly went to take the waters, the betrothal agreement was signed in Dvinsk in the fall. Avraham Yitzhak Kook set off for a year and a half's study in Volozhin.

In Volozhin, Avraham Yitzhak was thrust into a more dynamic yeshiva environment than he had known before—perhaps the most dynamic one anywhere. Some 250 talented young men came to Volozhin from all over Eastern Europe for intensive study year-round, generating a youth culture of extraordinary intensity. "When I first entered the yeshiva and looked around I was astonished by what I saw," another student later recalled. "In all my life, never had I seen a yeshiva of comparable grandeur and beauty, a broad, long study hall, bookstands arrayed along its length and width from end to end with only a narrow aisle between them, the tables tapered along the sides so that the Talmud folio of one not touch that of the other standing in front of him."[2]

At Volozhin, Avraham Yitzhak became a disciple of the dean, Naftali Zvi Yehudah Berlin (1816–1893), known by the acronym Netziv, who combined staggering erudition, keen analytic powers, and a felicitous writing style with administrative acumen and charisma. He was in many respects the truest inheritor of the Gaon of Vilna's textual revolution, incorporating the whole of ancient rabbinic literature, well beyond the Babylonian Talmud, into the curriculum. Unlike the Gaon, Netziv did not try to harmonize the various texts, but allowed each its own distinctive voice. Also unlike the Gaon, he seems to have had little truck with Kabbalah. But unlike most Lithuanian Talmudists, he had a passion for the Bible. And he deeply engaged in his own way the critical textual and historical studies of the time.

Though nearly all the students were of Mitnagdic background, there were a few Hasidim; one was none other than Micah Joseph Berdichevsky, who later emerged as the enfant terrible of the Hebrew literary renaissance. Far from being a typical Lithuanian, or "Litvak" (as much a marker of cultural orientation as of geography), Berdichevsky was the son of a Hasidic rebbe. He arrived in Volozhin after being driven from the home of his father-in-law for reading Haskalah literature. Yet Berdichevsky sat all day in tallit and tefillin, as did his classmate Avraham Yitzhak Kook. Berlin recognized that Berdichevsky was "of a different world."[3] He also sensed something special about Kook—whom he called *mayn Avraham Izci*—and urged students experiencing crises of faith to talk with him.

Haskalah and its literature were in the air at Volozhin, in the dormitories, and at times inside the folios of Talmud over which the students pored day and night. Indeed, a fellow student named Zelig Reuven Bengis noticed that Kook would, during his Talmud study, repeatedly look down at some papers on a shelf of his study stand. Thinking that Kook was stealing glances at Maskilic literature or newspapers, Bengis reported his fears to Berlin, who told him to leave Kook alone, saying, "He's a tzaddik." Unable to restrain himself, the student eventually caught a glimpse of Kook's mysterious papers: "And what did I find? Pieces of paper, handwritten with the Name of God."[4]

Even then Kook was hard to pin down. Was he a Maskil or a tzaddik? He studied from seven in the morning until midnight and prayed with an intensity that was at variance with the cool intellectualism of his peers. Unlike the mostly clean-shaven students, he had a beard; yet like a Maskil, he spoke in Hebrew. He was known as "the prodigy from Dvinsk."[5] While Chaim Soloveitchik, the other leading Talmudist on the faculty, sometimes engaged Kook during the preparation of his lectures, he nonetheless urged his disciples to "beware of the pious lad from Grieva."[6] To Soloveitchik, a thoroughgoing Mitnaged and a genius of abstract, elegant textual analysis, "pious" was no compliment.

Avraham Yitzhak spent a year and a half in Volozhin. Before leaving, he received rabbinic ordination from Berlin's brother-in-law, the eminent scholar Yehiel Mikhel Epstein. He kept it a secret from his father-in-law out of both modesty and a budding scholar's embarrassment at obtaining the professional license of a community rabbi. Indeed, the job of a communal rabbi was, in late nineteenth-century Lithuania, a grueling, thankless, and unenviable situation, and no young Talmudist as promising as Avraham Yitzhak, now Rav Kook, would seek such a position if he did not have to.

Avraham Yitzhak married Batsheva Rabinowitz-Teomim in the spring of 1886. He moved to Ponevezh, where he resumed Talmudic studies with his father-in-law, Aderet, and studied Kabbalah with a local rabbi. Financial troubles descended almost immediately. Aderet's salary scarcely sufficed for the rent even when it was paid, which was not often. He, his wife and children, and son-in-law were all soon living for free in cramped quarters in the courtyard of a local hospital. They took turns sleeping on the six chairs and hard benches that were nearly all their furniture.

This was an impossible situation, and with the encouragement of the revered tzaddik, scholar, and family friend Israel Meir Kagan (known as the Chafetz Chaim), Rav Kook went looking for a rabbinical position and found one in Zeimel (Zeimelis), two and a half miles from the border of present-day Latvia. It had 1,000–1,200 inhabitants, a little more than half of them Jews, who were farmers and tradesmen.

A Sabbath visit to the town in the winter of 1888 proved successful, and the townspeople elected him as their rabbi. This was, for Aderet, a bittersweet moment: "And in my heart I chuckled at their dreams, and told them that they could be sure that in a few years they would be boasting of his fame . . . And I wept with a bitter heart that because of my sins he had been forced to accept a rabbinic post in the springtime of his days."[7]

Before moving to Zeimel, Kook published his first articles, which centered on his master, Netziv, defending his piety against Orthodox critics and praising his modernity to general readers. The first appeared in January 1886 in the staunchly reactionary journal *Mahazikei Ha-Dat*, where Netziv's Bible commentary, *Ha'amek Davar*, had been criticized as insufficiently respectful of the ancient rabbis. Flexing his literary and rhetorical muscles in a withering attack on his master's critics, Kook seized the opportunity to lay out his own ideas on some mounting preoccupations, the status of the Aggadah—the extensive, nonlegal, more literary, and theological discussions in the Talmud—and the philosophical teachings of Maimonides. His second foray into print, in the fall of 1887, was a three-page essay on, again, Netziv, this time an encomium rather than polemic, in a Maskilic journal, *Knesset Yisrael*. While the first ar-

Rav Kook in the early 1890s, during the time of his first
rabbinic post, in Zeimel. Photo courtesy of Beit Ha-Rav Kook.

ticle praised Netziv as a staunch traditionalist, here Kook high-
lights Netziv's responsiveness to changing times and his inno-
vative, even "critical," scholarship. Sensing a hint of hero worship, his classmate Berdichevsky detected in Kook an implicit
ambition to succeed his master.

Several traditionalist rabbis had, in the preceding decades, begun to take their own place in the robust journalistic and periodical culture of the time. In the 1880s, this burgeoning Orthodox intelligentsia further asserted itself, and Rav Kook planned to take his place among them. In 1888, at age twenty-three, he published the first issue of a projected monthly periodical titled *Ittur Sofrim*, a Talmudic phrase suggesting both scribal ornamentation and literary license. Ornamented it was, with letters of approbation and articles by distinguished rabbis: Netziv and Aderet of course, but also Yitzhak Elchanan Spektor of Kovno, the most commanding legal authority of the time, who noted that he hoped the journal would not devour too much of the young editor's time.

The editor's ambitions for the journal were considerably larger than the conventional Talmudic and halakhic discussions that made up most of the contributions. In a lengthy opening essay on the art of writing, Kook wrote that his journal sought to restore the lost face-to-face exchange of the ancient Oral Torah and thus to heal the fissures in Jewish society. In another essay in the first issue, he laid out a program to rationalize and systematize the institutionally and intellectually decentralized framework of Halakha, deliberately evoking Maimonides' monumental and systematic efforts at codification in the twelfth century. His closing essay, which appeared under the pen name AY"H Sofer (taken from Isaiah 33:18, and also an acronym for "Avraham Yitzhak Ha-Cohen, Scribe"), explores the nature of prophecy. In Russian radical circles of the time, especially the writings of Vladimir Soloviev, whose writings engaged many Jewish intellectuals, the prophet beckoned as a moralist, political liberator, national oracle, and artist par excellence whose experience of revelation could speak even amid the ruptures and rationalism of modernity. Prophecy was engaging Kook, too, and again his touchstone was Maimonides, whose naturalistic view that the philosopher could become a prophet through his own efforts had long seemed at odds with the Bible's depiction of prophecy as something bestowed through God's will. Kook offered his own solution: the prophet's inner life is indeed the sum of his efforts, but the power of verbal expression is given to him, or withheld, by the untrammeled will of God.

The second issue of *Ittur Sofrim* appeared later that same year, 1888. Most of the issue was again taken up with Rav Kook's own writings, and again he explored Maimonides' systematizing of Halakha and his doctrine of prophecy. He also penned an essay on ethics. Perhaps reflecting his financial travails and first impressions of his new flock in the shtetl, he wrote appreciatively of the religious merit of ordinary people who, unlike rabbis and scholars, had to survive, physically and morally, in the unforgiving world of the marketplace. Again, he used the pen name AY"H Sofer, here a striking assertion of literary identity as well as a provocation: *ayeh sofer*—"where is the writer" who will rise to the challenges of the time? His nom de plume left the question explicitly open and implicitly answered: here I am.

The second issue of *Ittur Sofrim* was the last. In the spring of 1889, Kook's wife Batsheva died at age twenty-two of what seems to have been pneumonia. At the urging of Aderet, who could not bear to lose his son-in-law, and faced with having to raise his and Batsheva's baby daughter, Frayda-Chana, Kook quickly married his wife's cousin Raiza Rivka Rabinowitz-Teomim. He continued to mourn his first wife, writing elegies to her years afterward. He expressed his grief in a letter written after his second marriage: "I was forced to cease the work of *Ittur Sofrim* due to the illness of my wife . . . and since then I have been very broken and much time has passed with great cares and sadness in my heart."[8]

His twenty-fourth birthday found him bereaved, driven by economic circumstance to an insignificant rabbinic post, his ambitious journal undone too quickly. Humbled and perhaps a little lost, this self-confident, somewhat brash young man turned inward. In the next dozen years, he published very little, though he wrote a great deal, turning from his large project of reforming halakhic practice and redefining prophecy toward exploring moral and spiritual self-cultivation. All the while, he worked to explain and justify, to the tradition and to himself, his own inner life, his passions, his sometimes-radical ideas, and his place within the passions and revolutions of his times.

The small-town rabbinate left him much time for study and reflection. He and Raiza Rivka had three children together: a son, Zvi Yehudah, and two daughters, Esther Yael and Batya Miriam. There were communal duties, of course, which he approached with pious asceticism. Like many small-town rabbis, he received a good portion of his salary in the form of salt for resale, though he insisted that it be measured in glass scales so that he would not get a grain more than he had earned. When the merchants balked, he chose to forgo that portion of his pay. He devoted much time to local charities and welfare societies. He wrote halakhic opinions, delved deeper into the Kabbalah, spending time with the renowned Kabbalist scholar Shlomo Elyashiv, rabbi of Shavil, and kept reading the books and periodicals of the day. And he continued to write.

A brief commentary he wrote in 1890, at age twenty-five, on a number of seafaring Talmudic legends, known as "The Tales of Rabbah bar bar Channah," brims with citations to a broad range of Kabbalistic texts and commentaries, and vibrates with his anxieties. Taking the sea as a symbol of wisdom, he writes that the challenge facing the would-be sage is how to navigate the contending seas of practical wisdom and contemplative bliss, of natural science and revealed Torah, without running aground on the shoals of insolent arrogance and faux spirituality. In the tale of an anonymous Ishmaelite trader who imparts his wisdom to a rabbi wandering in the desert, he sees a glimpse of an ideal sage: He draws on all that he finds in his travels and has an intuitive grasp of the soul, rooted in the immediacy of the senses and unburdened by the intellect's questions and uncertainties. He is a rambling figure, "wandering the roads to see God's work and wonders, and he knows the ways of virtue and its paths befitting each man in his own right . . . and shows him the path to his perfection, for the paths are not equal for every man."[9]

It was not long before Rav Kook would set out on a journey of his own.

In 1891, a Warsaw publishing house released a slender, thirty-six-page volume bearing the title *Chevesh Pe'er* (*Turban of Beauty*, taken from Ezekiel 24:17), by an anonymous author who identified himself as Cohen Da'ato Yafah, "A Priest of Immaculate Mind." The book is an excited polemic on the mitzvah of tefillin, or phylacteries, in particular their proper placement high on the forehead. This mundane point of religious practice is taken to far lengths by the anonymous author, for whom improperly placed tefillin are a frontal assault on rabbinic authority and a tripwire for divine wrath, whose first victims will be complacent rabbis and their wealthy patrons. This strange tract did not fail to attract notice. One well-regarded rabbi of the time observed that the volume "has shaken the world," adding that "the author's intentions are pious, but he has defamed God's people and may God forgive him."[10]

Shortly after the volume was published, Avraham Yitzhak Kook left Zeimel for a solitary journey of some 155 miles through Lithuania and Belarus, bypassing the haunts of his youth— Liutsin, Smorgon, Volozhin—and making the acquaintance of several mystics, wonder workers, and unconventional rabbis. All along the way, he promoted and preached on the tefillin tract, acting, he said, on behalf of its author, who preferred to remain anonymous and who was, of course, him.

To be sure, the Gaon of Vilna had laid great stress on the

meticulous observance of tefillin protocol and encouraged his followers to wear them all day long. Rav Kook wore them all day too, as did some other Lithuanian pietists, and his tefillin wearing likely played a role in his own meditations. But that is hardly enough to explain this strange episode. The sermons he preached cast a bit more light. In them are two themes that appeared with gathering force in his writings through the decade: the primacy of mind as the link between God and man—he depicts tefillin as vessels of *da'at*, understanding or consciousness, an association with roots in Kabbalistic ethical literature—and the relationship between Jewish and gentile morality, itself a function of gradations within the sphere of mind.

In his sermons, he recurs again and again to tefillin as embodying the intellect and the mind (referring to them by both the philosophical term *sekhel*, intellect, and the Kabbalistic *mochin*, consciousness), literally pressed onto the body: "The power of divine mind that is in tefillin shines the rays of the light of the mind to the body—to the heart and brain and thus the mind works upon the will."[11] The improper placement of tefillin, therefore, confuses the boundary between body and mind and, interestingly, between the nations and Israel. The former are governed by nature—indeed, their ethics, genuinely binding on their own terms, are those of natural law. Israel, by contrast, lives by the divine Torah, which alone can unite the body with the mind, the human with the divine.

There was historical precedent for Rav Kook's pilgrimage. In 1236, the great Rabbi Moses of Coucy was moved by a vision to journey through Franco-Germany and parts of Spain to preach against the neglect of tefillin. Kook worked from that historical script, with a twist. He went nearly incognito, staying clear of the people and places that had known him as a brilliant prodigy, presenting his impassioned tract as that of another, giving sermons whose erudition and intellectual subtlety would make them unlikely to register on many of his listeners. After enacting this tangled mix of humility, rage, introspection, and wanderlust, he made his way back to Zeimel and began to keep a spiritual diary. In one of his early entries, he wrote, "It seems one cannot acquit one's obligations as regards the duties of the heart without preparing a book of one's own."[12]

His nascent ideas flowered in a collection of sermons he gave from 1894 to 1896 and then compiled, in the (ultimately futile) hope of eventual publication. He titled it *Midbar Shur*, the "Desert of Shur" of Exodus 15:22, and, in a pun on a line in the Zohar, and on his own name ("Kook" meaning in Yiddish "to look"), the "Desert of Vision." *Midbar Shur* is preoccupied with the achievement of *shlemut*, the classical Hebrew term for the Greek philosophers' eudaimonia—happiness, flourishing, perfection—of the individual and, in religious terms, the cosmos. In this text, the task of perfection proceeds through a series of concentric dualities—nature and choice, matter and form, action and thought, heart and mind, humanity and Israel —that resolve and realize themselves in the great Divine Will of whose workings they are a part. Self-perfection aims not to repress the creature, individual or national, but to bring its own divinely implanted telos to perfection.

There are two kinds of perfection. The first, which is closer to natural virtue and the estate of all humanity, leads to the re-alization of one's own nature, as, in the words of Ecclesiastes, "God has made man upright" (Ecclesiastes 7:29). The second kind of perfection is the particular patrimony of Israel—the transformation, through the Torah and commandments, of one's human nature into something angelic or even divine. Indeed, Israel's very body is the matter for the Torah's form. Israel must remain distinct from the nations, as mind remains distinct from matter. And that distinctiveness is morally justifiable only by virtue of Israel's vocation for all mankind.

His drive to strike a balance between Jewish and universal ethics, the former's distinctiveness and the latter's genuine moral force, seems to indicate that the ethical radicalism and appeal of revolutionary movements in Russian Jewry touched him too. But beyond the anxieties of Jewish identity, a deeper and richer set of ideas is at work here as well. Thus he writes that while natural morality is God-given, it is not godly, not divine, since, on its own terms, it is not rooted in human recognition of the Divine Will, a recognition necessary *for God's own perfection* through Israel, a seemingly radical idea that is at the center of major schools of Kabbalah.

Throughout *Midbar Shur* echo the ideas of a thinker who influenced him greatly, the eighteenth-century mystic and philosopher of Padua known as Ramchal, Rabbi Moshe Chaim Luzzatto. Ramchal died in 1746 at age thirty-nine, streaking like a comet across the life of his times and leaving a long trail behind. An astonishingly erudite, prolific, and protean figure, he figured as a heretic in the minds of his enemies and as a near-messianic figure among his disciples. Later Jewish Enlighteners adored Ramchal's plays and other literary works, written in pellucid Hebrew. Rabbis saw his tract *Mesillat Yesharim* (*The Path of the Righteous*) as an indispensable guide to attaining true piety, and Kabbalists revered and pored over his mystic writings—especially his treatise *Kalach Pitchei Chokhmah* (*138 Apertures to Wisdom*), in which he systematized, philosophized, and rendered into elegant Hebrew prose the fantastically mythic and deeply obscure terminology of the Lurianic Kabbalah.

Isaac Luria (1534–1572), known as ARI for Ha-Elohi Rabbi Yitzhak, or "the divine Rabbi Isaac," stood at the head of a circle of gifted and creative mystics in sixteenth-century Safed. Luria synthesized the disparate cosmological, metaphysical, and theological doctrines that preceded him into a mythic vision of primordial creation as a great drama of divine withdrawal and resulting catastrophe that set in motion all cosmic history. God, as it were, contracted Himself, leaving in the empty space thus created vestiges of divine light in "vessels," nodal points of boundless divine energy contained by a corresponding principle of restraint. Unable to contain the divine light, the vessels shattered, scattering sparks of divine goodness and crude husks of shattered vessels, which together compose the forces of good and evil pulsating through the universe. The contest between these forces takes place over and over through eons, on multiple levels of being—not least, the human will—en route to the ultimate cosmic and metacosmic repair and restoration, *tikkun*.

Luzzatto translated the explicit, shockingly mythic imagery of Luria and the Zohar, the colossal thirteenth-century opus of Jewish mysticism, into a Neoplatonic synthesis of metaphysics, ethics, and a sacred history of the world. The Gaon of Vilna taught that Luzzatto's allegorical reading of Luria was the truth, and the study of Luzzatto's writings became a touchstone of Lithuanian Kabbalah.

Luzzatto discerned two forms of divine providence, that within which human beings consciously discover their own wills, for good or ill, and the hidden "providence of unity," an invisible hand guiding humanity and all creation to its ultimate perfection. The tikkun is made even more heartbreakingly perfect by its being a restoration, retrieval, atonement, and repair that heals the fissures within God Himself.

With Luzzatto in hand, Rav Kook develops a seemingly innocuous point toward the end of *Midbar Shur:* "holy" is all that is near the great apotheosis of the tikkun. Accordingly, "profane" is that which has not yet woven itself into the fabric of the final tikkun. Could the seemingly profane be sacred, and the seemingly sacred, profane?

Years earlier, in a letter to Aderet, he had hinted that such a thing was possible. Perhaps, he wondered, the great rebellions against rabbinic authority then occurring were in fact the plagues of rebellion that the Mishnah (the canonical third-century text that is the cornerstone of the Talmud) indicated would herald the coming of the Messiah? Such a comment was a run-of-the-mill observation of Jewish moralists. But when overlaid on this new insight on holiness as proximity to apotheosis, it yielded a dramatic idea. If the seemingly apocalyptic collapse of traditional Jewish society was indeed the first step of the messianic age, perhaps rebellion, so near the sacred telos, itself was holy.

In 1896, Rav Kook left Zeimel and took up a rabbinic post in Boisk (Bauska), a small city of ten thousand people, forty miles from Riga. He had been befriended by Boisk's late rabbi, Mordechai Eliasberg, a luminously conciliatory personality amid the fractious internal politics of Russian Jewry. At his death, Eliasberg was eulogized by the Orthodox and secularists alike. A trace of his influence can be seen in an unpublished essay by Rav Kook in 1894, urging an end to fractiousness and calling for "peace to the people."[13]

Unlike Zeimel, Boisk had a substantial German-speaking minority, and many of its inhabitants, including some Jews, were moderately well-off, educated professionals active in public affairs. The town had a government-appointed official rabbi, with whom Rav Kook got on well and whose intellectual son he befriended. Here, too, most of his time was taken up with rendering halakhic decisions and undertaking pastoral work. He established a small yeshiva, and he tried to engage younger working people through classes and a youth movement. This more cosmopolitan setting afforded him a wider angle on the different ideological currents swirling around and within him.

Yet the study hall was never far from Rav Kook's mind, and a chief preoccupation in the mid-1890s was a controversy rocking the yeshivot of Lithuania, Ukraine, and Russia. The bone of contention was Mussar. Literally "morality," or "ethics," Mussar was the name of the movement inaugurated in mid-century by Yisrael Lipkin of Salant (1810–1883), another alumnus of Volozhin. Yisrael Salanter sought to challenge modernity from without and spiritual stagnation from within through regimens of strenuous moral self-cultivation, a uniquely Mitnagdic spirituality that would fill the vacuum left by Lithuanian intellectualism, without recourse to Hasidism or Kabbalah.

In the 1880s and 1890s, Mussar became a flashpoint as it began to make its presence felt in many yeshivot (though it never took hold in Volozhin). The study of medieval and early modern moralistic tracts, which was a staple of Mussar, was departure enough from the conventional Talmud-centric curriculum. What critics found intolerable was the way the texts were studied. During sessions in the study hall and in separate chambers called "Mussar houses," students would engage in paroxysms of self-exhortation, shout a line or two of text over and over, flail about, and gesticulate in frenzy. A student at the Mussar stronghold of Slabodka recalled the mix of study and hysteria: "If a stranger suddenly were to appear in the Mussar house and hear with his ears and see with his eyes the shouts, the sighs, the grimaces, the fists pounding the walls, he would justly think he had come to an insane asylum."[14]

To make matters worse, Mussar adherents installed *mashgichim*, "moral tutors," to supervise the students' religious lives, an affront to independent-minded students and cerebral Talmudists alike. Things came to a head in 1897 when students in leading yeshivot revolted against what they saw as Mussar's encroachment on their intellectual and personal lives. Prominent rabbis published declarations against Mussar, prompting a wave of polemics for and against in the press and debate in traditional society. Eventually, a sort of equilibrium emerged: Mussar remained in some yeshivot, and its most vociferous advocates and foes retreated to their respective corners.

Rav Kook, sitting in Boisk, was riveted by this drama. He had found himself moving well beyond the precincts of Lithuanian Talmudism. His search for interiority had taken him through one body of work after another, and none ultimately satisfied him. Philosophy alone, he wrote in an unpublished reflection, was too cerebral and unconnected to action. Hasidism was vital and spoke to the inner life, but by reducing metaphysics to psychology missed the point—the urgency—of the true *tikkun*. The way of the Mussarniks offered little more than a transitory spiritual high, shorn of Hasidism's warmth and color, though they were right to focus on disciplining the life of the mind and one's ethical fiber. Something in Mussar was deeply precious, and something about it went too far. Luzzatto's works offered a synthesis of philosophy, mysticism, and self-cultivation, but how could it be integrated with all those traditions?

Rav Kook wrote furiously in his notebooks. One must study Mussar, but from a text that he will write himself, articulating the teachings closest to his own soul. Such is the nature of wisdom. In a comment that would have raised eyebrows in most Lithuanian yeshivot, he wrote that Halakha is akin to natural science, in that it provides knowledge but not wisdom. Only the individual, he says, can figure out for himself his particular path in serving God, the ways in which he can avoid the snares of this world "in accord with his own nature, state and mind."[15]

This is no mere bit of pedagogy, but a reflection of the deepest truths of metaphysics: "The foundation of *tikkun* is to organize every thing and every power, be it in the soul or the world, justly in its place . . . *God made man and the world righteous* [after Ecclesiastes 7:29], with all the powers and means necessary for wholeness of body and soul, to do good and attain understanding, and one who undoes the order derived from His governance ravages and destroys."[16]

To believe in God is to believe that one's soul and character are God-given and must come to self-realization, not only for one's own sake but also for that of humanity and of God Himself. This takes work: "sifting" the raw material of one's own soul, recognizing the good, and, as Luria put it, "sawing off" the bad.

In Zeimel, Kook had begun a commentary on *Eyn Ya'akov*, a popular sixteenth-century anthology of the Aggadic, or non-legal, portions of the Talmud, and he continued it in Boisk. He wrote hundreds of pages intended to channel the energies of Mussar into study instead of ecstatic recitation, interpreting the Talmud in the terms of medieval Jewish philosophy and pietism. He called it *Eyn Ayah*, literally "the falcon's eye" (Job 28:7), and with the acronym, "the eye of Avraham Yitzhak Ha-Cohen." If, for Mussar, the religious life was a lonely battle with the devil and flight from God's wrath, in *Eyn Ayah* it was a lifelong effort at self-cultivation that would bring one's morals and mind into alignment with the divine ethos structuring and sustaining the universe.

Writing on the Aggadah was a complicated choice. Its unsystematic, often anthropomorphic, and regularly hyperbolic—at times fantastic—tenor had for centuries made it a focal point of polemics, apologetics, and various strategies of reading. Long looked down upon by scholars for its seemingly simple nature, in contrast to the bracing complexities of Talmudic legal passages, the Aggadah's popularity among laymen did little to enhance its status in the rabbinic fraternity, or that of people who wrote on it.

Although begun as an alternative Mussar text, *Eyn Ayah* came to be less structured and more expressive than his diaries, even if not as unbridled. Rav Kook's argument, explicit in his foreword and implicit on every page, that the desire to study the Aggadah is as legitimate as the study of Halakha, reflects his drive for a richer, more expressive religious vocabulary, as well as an acceptance of the stirrings of each student. His need to justify his own study of and love for the Aggadah is thus part of the larger drama of the age.

In 1897, the same year that the Mussar controversies came to a head, another movement stepped onto a much larger stage and began to catch Rav Kook's attention: Zionism.

Modern settlement of the Land of Israel, and religious involvement with that enterprise, predated Theodor Herzl and the Zionist movement by decades. In a departure from traditional immigration for the purpose of dying in the land's physically desiccated but spiritually fragrant shade, religious Jews began arriving in the early 1800s for the express purpose of building institutions. A number of them were disciples of the Gaon, who saw in Luria's and Luzzatto's teachings the idea that redemption could be hastened by earthly means. Later in the century, a number of moderate rabbis supported Chibat Zion and its programs for socioeconomic uplift through settlement and education.

Herzlian Zionism was a different story, in its Western European cosmopolitanism, its perception of Jews as collective players in the new transnational political game, and its embrace of secularism and acculturation as the very vehicles of rescue. Not many traditional rabbis were willing to engage with Zionism and with Herzl—the utterly deracinated and assimilated Viennese journalist and playwright who seemed as far as one possibly could imagine from the traditional image of the Messiah. And those who did, gingerly, did so because his seemed to be the best ideas around for relieving the disabilities of the Jews. Indeed, Herzl, keenly aware of his need for some sort of rabbinic imprimatur and a traditional base of support, was able to keep rabbis involved in the Zionist movement precisely to the extent to which he was able to keep the cultural Zionists at bay. Led by the great essayist and intellectual Asher Ginsberg, known as Ahad Ha-Am (1856–1927), and championed at the Zionist Congresses by the young firebrand Chaim Weizmann, their interest in Zionism was precisely for the spiritual and cultural answers it would provide, not only, as Ahad Ha-Am put it, for the problem of the Jews, but also for the problem of Judaism. A number of Orthodox rabbis attended the early Zionist Congresses; some were cautiously encouraged, while others were appalled and became some of Zionism's most articulate opponents.

Surprising as it may seem in light of his later path, Rav Kook took almost no part in the early stirrings of Jewish nationalism. He refrained from signing rabbinic petitions supporting or opposing Chibat Zion and was friendly with advocates on both sides. The Land of Israel scarcely figures in his writings of the time—unlike the Jewish people, who almost always do. His first reaction to the news of the First Zionist Congress was to compose an essay, unpublished until 1920, which saw Zionism's possibilities in light of his legal preoccupations. The significance of Zionism, he wrote, was in the realm of halakhic change. The law had to be modified, but the Reform movement was wrong in its accepting exile as an eternal necessity. Perhaps Zionism could restore the ancient Sanhedrin court and thus create the possibility of real, and legitimate, halakhic change. Yet that was a far cry from the terms of rabbinic support for Zionism, such as they were at the time.

While Rav Kook kept these particular thoughts to himself, his rabbinic peers had begun to notice that he was marching to the beat of a different drummer, as did his early disciples. One was Binyamin Menashe Levin, a stormy Talmudic prodigy from Telz (Telsiai, in present-day Lithuania). They met in 1899 when Levin was managing an inn at a resort town on the Baltic frequented by local rabbis; the regular manager, a Hasid, had absconded with the till. The other rabbis staying at the inn,

Levin later wrote, subjected Rav Kook to a public grilling on
Talmudic minutiae, which he not only passed but also turned
into an impromptu lecture, to the consternation of his inquisi-
tors. "His beliefs and ideas," Levin writes, "were strange to his
fellow rabbis, who were, to be sure, masterful Torah scholars
. . . but whose beliefs and opinions had not taken wing, and
they remained like children . . . And there was a special charm
to him in his extraordinary humility and his proceeding with a
particular grace among all men."[17]

Rav Kook and Levin took regular walks along the shores of
the Baltic. Levin's description of their conversations conveys
what seems best described as the synthetic workings of Kook's
mind:

> To the questions and contradictions with which I would at-
> tack, he wouldn't, like most, respond with answer after an-
> swer, but would begin to encompass the sphere of the ques-
> tion from all sides, from idea to idea, stringing thought to
> thought and image to image, near and far, until all would
> come together . . . By the waves, rising, falling, and rising
> again, his spirit would rise upward and he would precede his
> high-flown answer thus: The waves of questions and doubts
> that we always encounter, they have a center, from which the
> changes and transformations in our spirit flow and burst out.
> Our task is none other than to encompass all those waves
> and their turnings and seek their center, and then we will
> find that all were but the outcomes of that one great central
> question, and deep in the very depth of that question the
> many others will dissolve by themselves.[18]

Taken with Levin, Rav Kook invited him to come to Boisk,
where he moved in with the Kooks and tutored their son, Zvi
Yehudah. Levin introduced Rav Kook to his former teacher in
Telz, Shmuel Alexandrov, a Talmudist and anarchist, and the
two proceeded to carry on a lively correspondence on Buddhism, the writings of Soloviev, and more. That two Eastern

European rabbis with no formal secular education would even know about these things and be able to discuss them at length is less surprising than one might think, given the rich Hebrew and Yiddish periodical culture of the time.

In the mid-1890s Rav Kook had keenly followed the youth revolts of the yeshivot. At the turn of the new century, he was still preoccupied by youth revolts, but his angle of vision widened as he began to think deeply into the surge of young people who cast aside religious beliefs and practices for socialism and Zionism, some of whom, like Berdichevsky, had been his classmates. Berdichevsky and Kook moved in tandem during those years, undertaking similar activities and responding to the same developments, with Kook at every step of the way trying to stay within the rabbinic fraternity and developing increasingly dialectical ways of doing so, and Berdichevsky time and again shattering the vessels.

A fellow, younger alumnus of Volozhin, Chaim Nachman Bialik, was starting to trace a course elliptical to both of them, away from Halakha and toward a Hebrew literary renaissance that would reassert historical continuity, a secular reenchantment fueled in large part by a lyrical discovery of his own subjectivity. In 1902, he wrote, "I didn't just come upon light/nor inherit it from my father/for from my slab and crag I hollowed it out/and quarried it from my heart."[19] For his part, Rav Kook, especially in the acceptance of himself that came with his explorations of Aggadah, a subject that engrossed Bialik more and more, was learning that he too could quarry new truths from his own heart.

In the years 1901–4, Rav Kook published a lengthy series of essays, entering the lists as a genuine supporter of Jewish nationalism, but with some reservations and on his own distinctive terms. He contended that Zionism could not hope to succeed if it remained divorced from religion. Though the essays appeared in *Ha-Peles*, a resolutely Orthodox rabbinic journal, they were explicitly addressed to secular Zionists and socialists (and implicitly to rabbis who might want to try and talk to them), and they display both arresting insight and genuine naiveté. For instance, he wrote that because national renewal dictated a national aesthetic, secular activists should grow traditional beards and earlocks. More to the point, he was deeply exercised by the inaccurately reported pronouncement from the First Zionist Congress that "Zionism has nothing to do with religion," and he refused even to countenance the possibility that Herzl was keeping religion out of Zionism precisely to keep it from imploding.

While working on the essays, he corresponded with his former father-in-law, Aderet, who had moved to Palestine to be deputy chief Ashkenazi rabbi of Jerusalem. Rav Kook wrote him that the nationalism of their day was akin to philosophy in Maimonides' time, a tissue of foreign ideas to be reworked into something holy. And he indeed read nationalism through the lenses of medieval philosophy. In the first essay, "Te'udat Yisrael u-Leumiyuto" ("Israel's Mission and Nationhood"), Kook categorically denies that Jewish nationalism (which he refers to by the Hebrew *leumiyut*) is akin to non-Jewish nationalism, because the former is guided not by passion but by the mind, and thus knows that its true vocation is an ethical mission for the benefit of all humanity. Without the restraining hand of tradition, he wrote in the *Ha-Peles* essays, Zionism would degenerate into what he derisively referred to as *nazionalismus*, which was nothing but self-loving chauvinism and an easy pretext for immorality and xenophobic violence.

Addressing the revolutionaries' claim that traditional Halakha obstructs moral progress, he wrote that, on the contrary, the mitzvot light the way to the perfection of the future—a time when the animals will have been transformed into humans, and humans into angels. Thus kashrut is meant to prepare us for vegetarianism, a great step forward in the moral perfection of the human race—but must not be done before its time, for the complacency and self-satisfaction it might bring. Indeed, he wrote, one could imagine a bloodthirsty tyrant who prided himself on his vegetarianism, eerily presaging Hitler.

Recalling his reflections on Mussar, Rav Kook wrote that every single religious life is part of the broader religious life of humanity and the mitzvoth as we know them now. And so—finally cycling back to the question of burgeoning Jewish nationalism—only by keeping the Torah and the mitzvot, in all their details, could one participate in Israel's historic mission for the liberation of all humanity. This, he argued, is why political Zionism's eschewal of religion was doomed to failure, because in so doing the movement alienated itself from the deepest wellsprings of Jewish identity in the past and Israel's historic mission in the future, an alienation for which no act of diplomacy, however skillful, could compensate. And that is why the Jewish soul had to be poured into the organic body of Jewish nationalism without delay. No merely religious party (such as the Mizrachi, formed in 1902 as a faction within the Zionist movement) could do the job—the movement had to be converted as a whole.

Political and economic issues do not figure in these writings, and anti-Semitism, which he takes as a given, scarcely interests him at all. He explores Zionism solely for its cultural possibilities, which are in turn inextricably tied to morality and spirituality. His interlocutors here are the cultural Zionists of Ahad Ha-Am, for whom national spirit, understood as ethical consciousness, was the defining feature of Jewish identity throughout history.

An unfinished volume that Rav Kook worked on at the time, aimed at young heretics and freethinkers, expands on the ideas in the essays. He accords other religious traditions a significant place in the civic and religious history of the world, in the past, present, and the redemptive future. He suggests that one may accept the findings of biblical criticism and still keep faith with tradition.

In his notebooks, written for nobody but himself, he went even further, exploring the multitudinous ideas rushing through his head. He developed a dense, increasingly private idiom, one bristling with allusions to the texts through which his train of thought was passing. He was, like most rabbis, obsessed with the mass abandonment of traditional belief and practice spreading through Russian Jewry. Unlike nearly all his rabbinic peers, Kook saw here a spiritual drama with much to teach those who, like him, stayed within the fold. In a deliberate echo of Kant, he wrote that inasmuch as we cannot perceive ultimate truth, "it is in our representations," the images and pictures in our minds, "that we live and sense."[20] He continued: "The hues in which reality comes to be represented, throughout time, are the garments of reality in relation to man."[21]

He is echoing not only Kant but also the Kabbalah. "Hues" are a synonym for the Sefirot (literally, "enumerations"), the nodal points of divinity emanated downward and outward from the unknowable infinitude of Eyn Sof (literally, "the endless") into the worlds of time and space; in the most central Kabbalistic teaching, the Sefirot constitute the deep structure of all of being. "Garments" refer to the outermost layers of ideas and souls. Thus, he continues, contemporary heretics are right to say that the literal truths of tradition and scripture, the veils, cannot be the truth. Where the heretics stumble is in failing to provide an alternative that can recognize the distance between human and divine truth and yet still, like the Torah, serve as a basis for ethics.

One day as Kook and Levin walked on the outskirts of Boisk, they began to discuss a recent article on the literary merits of the Song of Songs, the Bible's lengthy—and richly sensual—love poem, ascribed to King Solomon. The canonization of the erotically charged Song had challenged and stimulated rabbinic interpreters since antiquity. Rav Kook began to riff on the famous comment of Rabbi Akiva, recorded in the Mishnah, that "if all scripture is holy, the Song of Songs is the holy of holies" (Mishnah Yadayim 3:5). Levin produced a pencil. Kook sat down on the ruins of the town's old wall and began to write: "Literature, painting, and sculpture aim to actualize all the spiritual concepts impressed deep in the human soul."[22] Art has a duty to bring every last "etching secreted in the depth of the thinking and feeling soul" to full expression.

King Solomon and Rabbi Akiva both grasped—as do the artist, mystic, prophet—that love, in all its forms, is divine. All selfhood, individual and collective, is the outward vibration of the divine. That pulsating divine energy, with all its contradictions, was coming to the fore as the history of the world neared a messianic climax and final restoration. Even seemingly bad things must come to expression, yet "when they are still in their raw state, they are defiled and evil and must be defended against by the force of good, with the Torah and the fear of God."[23] Traditional Judaism's relationship to the rebellions of modernity was not to be strictly antagonistic, but dialectic.

These ideas strained the tradition to its very limits. He had, by this point, come to stand in an exquisitely tensile relation to his times, and he continued to do so for the rest of his life. Unlike his rabbinic peers, he not only understood but also in some ways deeply identified with the revolutionary religious and political currents around him. Unlike the revolutionaries, he remained deeply committed to the tradition—its ideas, structures, and laws—and to its promise of at least the possibility of genuine sanctity and transcendence. And he believed that all-out religious rebellion would in the end destroy the world. Nietzsche, he wrote in his diary, was like Shabtai

Zvi, the seventeenth-century pretender whose immature messianism unleashed a flood of antinomianism and shook Jewish
society to its marrow. But, he added, a slim membrane stands
between that radicalism and the coming of the Messiah.*

Scrawled on the first page of the notebook containing
these last reflections, in his son Zvi Yehudah's hand, we find the
words "The Last in Boisk," for indeed, in the spring of 1904,
Rav Kook left.

Several years earlier, a visitor from Jerusalem had come to
town. Yoel Moshe Salomon was a descendant of one of the families that had immigrated to Palestine nearly a century earlier
to live out the this-worldly messianic teachings of the Gaon. Salomon's grandfather and father had each spent their lives building institutions in Palestine, and he himself had established a
printing press and a newspaper. He had also been a founder of
both West Jerusalem and the first agricultural colony, Petach
Tikva. In 1902, Salomon was on a committee seeking to replace
the recently deceased rabbi of Jaffa, the ancient coastal town
that had become the de facto urban center of the new Jewish
settlements in Palestine. Salomon was much taken with Kook,
who mixed deep Talmudic learning and halakhic authority with
wide reading, a conciliatory personality, and striking receptiv-
ity to new ideas. Salomon approached Aderet to ask whether he
could speak to his former son-in-law, and then set about creating a coalition on behalf of the relatively unknown rabbi of
Boisk. After several years of negotiating and coalition building
among his backers, Kook received his appointment.

His choice of Palestine was by no means obvious. He had
been looking to leave Boisk, preferably for a yeshiva. Religious
Zionists were perplexed by his decision because he had not
been involved with them or their work. Moreover, Jaffa was,

---

*The "slim membrane" is likely his reworking of a Kabbalistic concept,
kelippat nogah, "the luminous shell" at the very border of good and evil.

as a friend admonishingly wrote him, "a metropolis of desolate sin."[24] There is no record of exactly what motivated him to take the position in Jaffa, but a number of factors likely came into play: the unquestioned sanctity of the Land of Israel and the biblical commandment to live in it, the opportunity to step onto a larger stage, the chance to be reunited with his still-beloved former father-in-law, a sense of adventure, and the stirrings that in those same years were bringing to Palestine a tumultuous generation whose awakenings moved in him too.

Shortly before the Kooks left, Rav Kook was visited by Rabbi Yitzhak Nissenboim, a fluid writer and orator long active in Chibat Zion and then in the Zionist movement. He and Kook had never met: "I knew what a large role a rabbi like this would play in the development of the Yishuv [the Jewish community of Palestine], but I was not terribly interested in this rabbi. He had taken no part in Chibat Zion, or, later, Zionism. He had not written important books, so what would I have had to do with him? So I decided to be in the new rabbi's home and get a proper sense of him."

He left an arresting record of his visit: "I spent three days in the city of Boisk and spent several hours each day in the rabbi's home. We discussed various matters in halakha, the Aggadah, and life questions. I saw before me no ordinary rabbi, following well-worn paths, but a man of the spirit, paving his own way. He had not found it yet, but was searching for it, in all the length and breadth of Judaism. He was diving into the seas of the Talmuds, Midrashim, philosophy, Kabbalah, Hasidism, and the new Hebrew literature, and bringing up precious stones with which to pave his way."[25]

The Kook family left Boisk for Palestine on April 24, 1904, with a large group of townspeople accompanying their carriage for some while. Eventually, Rav Kook stopped, stood before them, and gave one last homily. Citing a well-known rabbinic dictum that one ought to take leave of a friend with a word from the Torah, he said the real pain of separation is the interruption in the shared study of the Torah, which life sometimes demands. But because our inner connection remains, we are never truly separate from one another. God, he said, has commanded us to leave for the Land of Israel, but we do so with the faith that we will all, in redemption, meet again.

After traveling from Boisk to Riga, Dvinsk, Vilna, Odessa, Istanbul, Izmir (Smyrna), and Beirut, on Friday, May 13, 1904, he came ashore in Jaffa, bending low, as pious Jews had done through the ages, to kiss the ground.

2

The New Will Be Holy: Jaffa

Jaffa, a small community . . . but very strange. All
shuddering, boiling and bubbling. Taut and ready.
All kinds of parties and streams, directions and
inclinations. Wars among them, of words, of course
. . . Everything is floating, changing, shifting form.
And there's a rabbi, a genius, rhetorician and a bit
of a poet, so different from the rabbis you've known
or even appreciated in your life. Yet when it comes
down to it, you can't really grasp him either.
—Joshua Radler-Feldman (Rebbe Binyomin),
"From the Weave"

Two great Jews live among us today in the Land of
Israel, Rav Kook and Yosef Chaim Brenner.
—Berl Katznelson, in Shimon Kushnir,
Ha-Roeh Li-me-Rachok

THE KOOK FAMILY WAS MET at the Jaffa pier by local notables, representatives of the agricultural settlements and the religious establishment in Jerusalem. Carriages brought the Kooks to their new home on Alroy Street in Neve Zedek, the first Jewish neighborhood built outside the Old City of Jaffa. On the Sabbath, Rav Kook spoke in a local synagogue—not in Yiddish, but in fluid Hebrew—on the theme of loving truth and peace. Early on, he made the rounds of the groups and communities whose needs he would be expected to accommodate—merchants, agricultural pioneers, Chabad Hasidim, Lithuanian ascetics, traditional Sephardim—and took his first trip to Jerusalem. There, he visited the holy sites and on the Sabbath spoke in the Old City's Churva synagogue, the religious and cultural center of Jewish Jerusalem.

Though the geographic border marked by the Jaffa port was clear enough, the cultural boundary was far from obvious, and changing. The ancient, historic city was becoming the urban hub of the burgeoning agricultural settlements forming the cutting edge of change in Jewish Palestine. In the quarter century preceding the Kooks' arrival, Jaffa's Jewish population had grown fivefold, to five thousand, and it would reach thirteen thousand in the following decade, out of a total population of 45,000. Many of the new Jewish Jaffans were modernists, and some, out-and-out freethinkers. They built new neighborhoods and new institutions—a vocational school, a Hebrew-language high school, a lending library—much to the disapproval of the city's staunch traditionalists. Kook's predecessor as rabbi, Naftali Hertz Halevi, a gentle Lithuanian pietist and Kabbalist, had arrayed himself alongside his colleagues in the Jerusalem rabbinate as a foe of modernizing trends. Kook's candidacy had appealed to those seeking a more forward-looking alternative. At the same time, his sponsorship by the unimpeachably devout Aderet, and his own rich learning and obvious piety, reassured the traditionalists, at least initially. But the Ashkenazi rabbis of Jerusalem kept an eye on him.

Those rabbis and their society, which were referred to, first by the modernizing immigrants and then by themselves, as the "Old Yishuv," the old Jewish Settlement, were in mounting crisis. The Old Yishuv took its modern shape in the early decades of the nineteenth century with the immigration of latter-day disciples of the Gaon of Vilna. The Gaon's ideological program had two facets: enthroning Torah study at the very pinnacle of religious life, and hastening the Messiah's advent by human action. Each idea yielded its own sort of successor in Jerusalem: the staunchly traditionalist Perushim—literally, "the separate ones" or "ascetics,"—who devoted themselves to sacred study, and the religious clans, like the family of Yoel Moshe Salomon, who steadily built up new institutions, enterprises, neighborhoods, and agricultural settlements.

Through much of the nineteenth century and into the twentieth, the Old Yishuv was led by the venerable chief rabbi of Jerusalem, Shmuel Salant (1816–1909), whose unshakable piety, humility, humor, and sound financial and communal judgment made him a stabilizing force and conciliatory leader. In the late nineteenth century, the Old Yishuv leadership was fortified by new arrivals—Lithuanian veterans of ideological combat with Haskalah, and Hungarian rabbis who had won official recognition in their home country for their secession from the organized, modernizing Jewish community. They were led by the Litvak Talmudist Yitzhak Yerucham Diskin (b. 1839), whose father had created a self-described "zealot" faction in Jerusalem, and a slightly younger rabbi and protégé of Hungarian separatists, Yosef Chaim Zonnenfeld (b. 1849).

The Old Yishuv, with its piety, economic dependence on charity from abroad, and rule by rabbinic authority, stood in stark contrast to the New Yishuv, which was burgeoning in the Galilee region and the areas around Jaffa. Around 1900, a series of economic crises and migration waves, along with population growth and a failure to build significant yeshivot, called the fundamental legitimacy of the Old Yishuv into question, forcing this most conservative of cultures to deal with seemingly unavoidable, threatening change.

The year 1904, when the Kooks arrived, marked the beginning of what Zionist history calls the Second Aliyah, migration (literally, "ascent") to Palestine. Zionist historiography registers five such waves from the 1880s through the late 1930s, each with its own characteristics. But the Second looms large, not least for bringing in many highly charged ideologues and revolutionaries who went on to play decisive roles in all that followed (David Ben-Gurion being the most famous). Most of the twenty thousand Jews who arrived between 1904 and 1914 were, like migrants everywhere, trying not to remake the world, but simply to find a better life. But those few thousand who did want to remake the world, and stuck out the multiple hardships of migration, formed a powerful core.

The Eastern European activists of the Second Aliyah brought with them their identity struggles and their ideologies, including secular nationalism, social democracy, Marxist revolution, and romantic ideals of self-realization. Unlike Herzlian Zionists, they were driven more by socioeconomics and questions of identity than by politics and diplomacy. Countercultural, they were antagonistic toward traditional Judaism, mixing Haskalah, the anticlericalism of the labor movement, and Russian radicalism. Though overwhelmingly Yiddish speaking, they were committed to creating a new, Hebrew culture as a vital alternative to the withering Jewish identity of the diaspora. Accordingly, Micah Joseph Berdichevsky spoke of their being "the last Jews or the first Hebrews." Their socialism was couched in the language of Jewish national identity and prophetic ideals of social justice. Indeed, the ways in which they rejected tradition reflected a deep, even if deeply argumentative, engagement with it. Their preoccupations were revolution, Zionism, generational conflict, a search for new community, relentless self-criticism, commitment to labor, bachelorhood, the Land of Israel, and men and women working together.

What made them come? Before departing from Russia, the future labor leader Berl Katznelson, then twenty-one, wrote to his brother, capturing these youngsters' mix of hope and desperation:

> I want to go to Eretz Yisrael. I want to do something . . . I want to live somewhere. It's a small spark, but I don't have it in me to snuff it out. I'm drawn to all those stubborn ones, not, of course, the stubborn talkers, the professional Zionists, propagandists and noisemakers . . . but to the stubborn workers of all kinds, laborers, teachers, business clerks and artisans, who have thrown it all away to try and start a new life. To be rid of exile, to live an experiment . . . for myself, ourselves, for our Jews, I want us to have some other corner, a different life, to escape this suffocating air.[1]

Rav Kook migrated at age thirty-eight, somewhat older than most migrants. These intellectually minded, religiously rebellious Jewish youth mattered to him deeply. Before long, he found himself in crosscutting ideological battles to his left and his right, between the Old Yishuv and the New. Thinking his way through pushed him and his ideas in new and increasingly complicated directions.

Rav Kook was, in those early weeks, flooded with new impressions. And as he wrote in his journal, he chose to open himself to all of them: "All the moods that pass over one, down to the details, and all their most varied and most delicate occurrences, all are meant to fill out the form of one's self, and through them create the impress of one's own acts, thoughts and feelings . . . No impression passes over a man, but for a purpose. . . . And this is the raising of the sparks."[2] That "raising" is the Kabbalistic term, central to Hasidism, for the redemptive discovery of divinity in everything.

This gesture of opening himself to a new, dynamic, bewildering reality led to everything that followed. To be sure, in the Old Country he had been curious, observant, sensitive to the stirrings of the time. But now he took that a step further, opening up experientially as well as intellectually—and reading his own reactions as a disclosure and source of knowledge. What began as an opening to experience made for a flood of impressions and equally tidal reflections. Four and a half years later, he wrote to a colleague still in Europe:

> Thank God who made me this kind of self, a spirit and soul living and feeling all the different movements and agitations with all their birth pangs and travails, but also with all the strength of their life force and faith in redemption, the things all palpably meet in me, and I must deal with them in deed and action, and endure all the breakers of the different waves and the height of their pounding. And hear the hidden, secret voice within them.[3]

On July 3, 1904, just two months after Rav Kook's arrival in Jaffa, Theodor Herzl died of cardiac sclerosis, in Austria, at age forty-four.

Herzl's early death was shocking and electrifying. In Boisk, Rav Kook had toyed in his journal with the idea that Zionism might be a manifestation of Messiah ben Joseph, an obscure figure in rabbinic tradition, prefiguring the better-known Messiah ben David. The Talmud says that in the first act of the messianic drama, Messiah Ben Joseph would die. And now, Theodor Herzl was dead.

A memorial service was held in the Jaffa branch of the An-
glo-Palestine Company, a bank with close ties to the Zionist
movement and the economic citadel of the New Yishuv. Rav
Kook spoke, along with his Sephardic rabbinic counterpart and
two Zionist leaders. He wrote Aderet that he knew there would
be objections to his eulogizing the freethinker Herzl, but concluded that it was nonetheless his responsibility to convey
to the New Yishuv that he, and the Torah, cared for them.
His address, though studded with citations to rabbinic texts,
went well beyond politesse, moving associatively to a startling
conclusion. Messiah ben Joseph, he said, is meant to bring deliverance to the body in preparation for the ultimate deliverance, brought by Messiah ben David, to the soul. Messiah ben
Joseph—like the great gentile leaders, a master of war and
statecraft—lays the earthly, material foundation for the eventual reign of the spirit. The two Messiahs' mutual estrangement
reflects the bitter estrangement of matter and spirit throughout
history. Messiah ben Joseph may die to make way for the spiritual kingdom, but his tragic death itself drives home the error of
our ways, our fatal inability to wed body and soul. The union of
ben Joseph and ben David will fuse matter and spirit, body and
soul, releasing Israel's spiritual gifts outward into the world.

"And lo," he concluded, "the Zionist vision has been revealed in our time, as the footsteps of Messiah ben Joseph."[4]
It was time for Joseph and Judah to be united once again. The
great outbursts of heresy and impiety in the present day were
bitter, necessary steps toward the messianic era. They would
teach the Israel of the spirit how to live and flourish in this
earthly world.

He never mentioned Herzl by name. It is far from clear
that the figure of the assimilated Viennese playwright, an irre-
ligious freethinker, could have borne the extraordinary, nearly
Christlike freight that Rav Kook's sermon lay on his shoul-
ders. But beyond that, Herzl the man was nearly beside the

point; Rav Kook's evolving messianism was not about a personal Messiah. It was about processes originating in God's attempts, through human action, to reconcile His eternity with the world He created. The process was deeply dialectical—the flourishing of the body was the essential prerequisite to the flourishing of the spirit. And in that affirmation of the body, the person of Theodor Herzl disappeared.

Not long after, Rav Kook made his first expedition to the new agricultural settlements of Rishon Le-Zion, Rehovot, Nes Ziona and Gedera. He was pleasantly surprised to see that the farmers were sympathetic to religion and respectful of religious law. In addition, he spoke with young people who, as he described them to a correspondent, "are, for our sins, ruined in thought and word."[5] It was all very new. Passing through the fields, he pointed and said: "Look! A Jewish cow!"[6] Once, on the way to Rishon Le-Zion, he told a traveling companion, "I could kiss every stone in this land—and even the mules on the way."[7]

Back in Jaffa, he plunged into a crush of activity, adjudicating in rabbinical court and doing informal mediations; answering halakhic queries; helping local charities and welfare institutions; officiating at civic ceremonies; and receiving visiting dignitaries and new arrivals. Much of his time was spent dealing with the new agricultural colonies of independent farmers, trying to bring their rabbis into his orbit without treading too much on their local authority. In the settlements and in Jaffa, he was charged with building synagogues and ritual baths, supervising kashrut and kosher slaughtering, a lucrative trade whose practitioners often failed to appreciate the strict standards imposed on them by the new rabbi, and who at times pilloried him for interfering with business. He worked to uphold standards of public decency, an effort that did not endear him to Jaffa's pimps and madams—and so his friendship with the brawny young men of the local football association occasionally came in handy.

It naturally fell to him to be the public scold when it came to the observance (or desecration) of the Sabbath, especially since many of the younger new arrivals preferred to spend their Sabbath evenings in the café and their Sabbath days rowing on the Yarkon River. His only authority there was moral, and while his rhetoric reflected disapproval, it likewise conveyed his real admiration for the young secularists' immigration to Palestine. He tried to put a human face on religious observance. For instance, when a physician refused to travel to a patient on the Sabbath, out of fear of reprisals from the more stringent Orthodox, Rav Kook walked alongside the man's carriage the whole way. This unconventional mix of piety and responsiveness won him admirers and hearts.

On top of all this, he spent much of his time visiting the sick, counseling the distressed (to the point of performing the occasional exorcism if nothing else would do), and tending to the poor. He regularly gave away his household possessions, and signed as guarantor for paupers' loans until his family convinced the local loan society to stop honoring his signature.

Engulfed as he was by people, Rav Kook was often lonely. He made friends with some of the local Breslov Hasidim (followers of Nachman of Breslov) and moderate Maskilim, but there were not many whom he felt could understand him. Many of his deepest exchanges were with correspondents—friends and students—still in Europe. He continued his exchanges with Shmuel Alexandrov on Eastern religions, Russian philosophy, natural sciences, ethical universalism, the relationship between intellect and emotion, and the spiritual possibilities of anarchism.

He corresponded at length with two disciples from Boisk: Binyamin Menashe Levin, who had moved to Berlin for academic studies; and Moshe Zeidel, a budding scholar of Semitics to whom he wrote long, fatherly letters, answering the young man's sincere queries on everything from ethically questionable mitzvoth (meant to educate humanity gradually) to the theory of evolution (proof of humanity's inevitable progress) to Bible criticism (irrelevant to the Torah's deep meaning and significance). As time went by, Rav Kook confided to his young correspondent that he longed for intimate, tender conversation with a small band of people who could understand one another and the magnitude of the spiritual tasks ahead.

He found one soul mate in particular. Ya'akov Moshe Charlap was a native Jerusalemite, born in 1882 to a distinguished rabbinical family. From a young age he practiced a regimen of self-mortification and endless study, and had by his early twenties already attained some standing among Lithuanian Kabbalistic circles in Jerusalem. In the spring of 1904, he went to Jaffa on doctor's orders. On the morning of the Shavuot holiday, he prayed in the Sha'arei Torah synagogue, where he heard Rav Kook, himself just a few weeks off the boat, offer a sermon and recite *Akdamot*, the long and complex eleventh-century Aramaic poem central to that festival's morning service. Charlap later wrote: "Twenty-one years old *(sic)* I was, and here, I heard how the Rav recited *Akdamot* before the congregation, atremble and weeping, and I was shaken to the foundation of my soul. From that moment on I clung to him with fierce love, and was his student and disciple forever . . . I felt seized by a God-flame, all my corporeality scattered and gone, and my soul, bound with the Rav's, rising to the very highest worlds."[8] Not long after, Charlap returned to Jerusalem. In 1909 he became rabbi of Sha'arei Chesed, a New Jerusalem neighborhood, whose 115 families represented a retiring, pietist side of the Old Yishuv. He made frequent trips to Jaffa to see Rav Kook, and they would go for walks along the coast and sit and talk late into the night.

There developed between the two of them a deep and extraordinary bond. Charlap came to regard Rav Kook as *Tzadik*

Ha-Dor, the saint who, in Kabbalistic and Hasidic doctrine, takes upon himself the uplifting of his time, and whose soul channels God's energies into the world. For Rav Kook, Charlap embodied a gentle Old Yishuv spirituality that he encountered all too seldom. He felt himself able to share with Charlap some of his most far-ranging speculations, particularly about the ultimate nonexistence in God of the dimensions of time and space, and the ultimate erasure of the distinction between spirit and matter. He was perhaps able, by encouraging his younger, sadder colleague, to ameliorate some of his own melancholy. And Rav Kook shared with Charlap his deep frustration with the Old Yishuv and its guardians, who simply did not understand that one can live, spiritually, in the Land of Israel only by cleaving to the People of Israel, sinners and secularists included.

A little less than a year after his arrival in Jaffa, Rav Kook made his first sally into the emerging culture wars, opening the seams that he would be navigating for decades to come. The crux was a heated exchange with Eliezer Ben-Yehudah, the former yeshiva student and renegade intellectual who likely did more than anyone else to resurrect Hebrew as a spoken language. Born Eliezer Perlman in 1858, Ben-Yehudah became a radical secularist and an equally radical cultural and linguistic nationalist. He moved to Jerusalem in 1881, and by 1905 he had founded several newspapers and associations for the advancement of Hebrew, initiated a massive, multivolume historical dictionary of the Hebrew language, and antagonized the traditional religious establishment for decades. The other leading cultural nationalists—Ahad Ha-Am, Bialik—disdained him as a soulless linguistic mechanic, though none of them could compete with his ability to create, from scratch, Hebrew words.

In March 1905, Ben-Yehudah fired a volley in one of the last skirmishes around the Uganda Plan, the hotly debated proposal that Zionists relinquish claims to Palestine in exchange for a charter in British East Africa. The subject of this particular column in his newspaper *Hashkafah* (Outlook) was the allegation that he and other supporters of Uganda did not care about Jewish history. Ben-Yehudah was scornful of the so-called "Zion Zionists" who opposed Uganda, but no less dismissive of Uganda supporters who felt the need to proclaim their attachment to Jewish history. "Another great and terrible argument of the 'Zion Zionists,'" he wrote, "is that 'they, the Ugandists, are turning their back on our entire history.' How much cynicism in this argument?! Men who have turned their back on the past accusing others of doing the same thing! For let there be no illusions. The only ones who haven't turned their backs on the past are 'the committee for the investigation of sins' [a sobriquet for Ben-Yehudah's pious tormentors in Jerusalem]. All of us, all of us, have turned our backs on the past, that is our glory and splendor!"[9]

This was too much for Rav Kook to bear. Ben-Yehudah had laid the issue squarely on the table. It was one thing for Orthodox rabbis to claim that Zionism was heresy, but here was a leading figure of the Hebrew revival proclaiming a radical rupture with the past, not in sorrow or anger but in exultation, and on behalf of all Zionists and perhaps all modern Jews. Talk like this would push young Zionists further away from tradition and make rapprochement with Orthodoxy impossible.

Indeed, Rav Kook's reply, published two weeks later in Ben-Yehudah's newspaper, was titled "An Open Letter to Our Young Brethren Dwelling [*sic*] the Holy Land." What exercised him was his conviction that Ben-Yehudah, whom Kook refused to name, was talking not only about them, but also about him: "That a writer should dare to witness in the name of the entire community, that we all have turned our back on our past . . . this is rare chutzpah."[10] Rav Kook would not take a position on the Uganda debate, noting that there were good people on both sides (indeed, the Mizrachi were also Ugandists, and Rav

Kook himself had, in Boisk, entertained the possibility), and he chastised Ben-Yehudah for his smug certainty: "It is a bad sign for any party if it thinks that it alone has the source of life, all the wisdom and righteousness, and all others are empty breath and herding the wind." Talk of turning one's back on Jewish history, he continued, was a cheap counsel of despair that played to the crowd, "but differs from the best thoughts of the thinkers of every people and tongue, who . . . know the value of our great spiritual work in the world and the beauty of our inner life, which didn't stop even during times of greatest persecution."

Running throughout was a bold call to his young readers. If Ben-Yehudah had been speaking only for himself, Rav Kook would not have argued with him. But since he was speaking about the "young brethren," Rav Kook's hope was that they would answer him too. He signed with a new flourish: "Avraham Yitzhak Ha-Cohen Kook, servant to a holy people on the holy ground."

The immediate effect of this open letter on its intended readers was unclear. What, the young rebels likely wondered, did this rabbi want from them? For his part, Ben-Yehudah wrote in rejoinder that in speaking of "us," he had meant only avowed freethinkers like himself. And yet, he argued, "the great Rabbi Kook's" declaration that no one group has a monopoly on the truth was itself unwitting proof that the rabbi himself had "turned his back" on the authority, and certainties, of rabbinic tradition. The fact that he looked and dressed—and observed Halakha—just like the rabbis of the Old Yishuv made little difference.

Another set of readers agreed. Seventeen leading rabbis of Jerusalem penned a carefully worded open letter to "The eminent rabbi and genius, man of many gifts etc. celebrated saint our master and teacher Avraham Yitzhak Kook," which was published in Yisrael Frumkin's traditional organ *Havazelet*. They wrote: "At first glance his sallying forth to answer this man [Ben-Yehudah] is very strange."[11] Why should a man of such obvious piety and learning even deign to engage this wretch or his kind? Rather than simply denounce or ignore the hated Ben-Yehudah and all that he represented, the new rabbi in Jaffa had taken the trouble to argue with him—and with an unmistakably sympathetic eye toward the man's readers, whom he addressed as "we." Because Rav Kook is a recent arrival, they wrote, he touchingly thinks that Ben-Yehudah is merely a rotten apple, "unlike us, who well know his audacity and profound heresy." The Jerusalem rabbis were reactionaries, but they were not stupid. In closing, they thanked Kook for his "worthy intention"—in rabbinic parlance, an implicit rejection of his deeds.

Fault lines were starting to emerge. The new rabbi was placing himself between his clerical peers and the heretical young, celebrating both camps' commitments to tradition and change, in terms that made obvious sense to neither.

Another heretic was on Rav Kook's mind: Spinoza. Like other Zionist thinkers, he was fascinated by this first modern Jew for his rebellion, his political reading of the Bible, and his total identification of God with nature—the natural world to which the Zionists were trying to return. Spinoza's excommunication, Rav Kook wrote in his journal, was providential.[12] Had Spinoza continued to be a respectable member of the community, his ideas might have taken root and been even more destructive. Yet a Jew he was, and his pantheism could not entirely be discarded. Moses Mendelssohn, the father of the Jewish Enlightenment, Rav Kook wrote, began the work of purifying Spinoza, but did not finish. The Ba'al Shem Tov, the founder of Hasidism, continued that work, not knowing that it was Spinoza he was purifying, drawing his knowledge, as he did, from its inner source. The work of purifying Spinoza continues. Spinoza's fusion of God with nature was close to the truth, but not quite. There was more work to be done, here in the Land of Israel.

Rav Kook's reunion with Aderet was short-lived. Just under four years after arriving in Jerusalem, the sage and father figure passed away on February 8, 1905, at age sixty-one. He had come to Palestine to serve as deputy to the aged Salant, who outlived him by four years. His appointment by Salant was a hard-earned laurel after decades of humiliation and grief, a final recognition of his learning and piety. Aderet was an ungainly fit in the Old Yishuv, and his clumsy attempts to introduce his own standards of scholarship and probity into that labyrinthine society served only to alienate everyone. He died as he had lived, eminence just out of reach, awing his intimates with his erudition and spirituality, even on his deathbed.

The following year Rav Kook published a small volume in his memory, followed by a second volume of brief essays. Taken together, they convey how far his ideas were starting to take him. The first work was titled *Eder Ha-Yakar*, a play on the "precious sum" of Zechariah 11:13, and on Aderet's acronym, Eliyahu David Rabinowitz. In truth, the book is scarcely about Aderet himself, whose moral virtue and personal benevolence are referred to time and again as the model for a new kind of rabbi whose intellectual and historical horizons, as limned by Rav Kook, would be far broader than one imagines Aderet's could possibly have been. The chief subject of the book, which draws largely on his earlier essays in *Ha-Peles* and unpublished writings from his Boisk years, is the intellectual, moral, and spiritual challenge to tradition posed by modernity. Rather than give up hope or adopt a reactionary stance, traditionalists are urged to respond to contemporary conditions with new projects of their own. Moreover, they need to recognize that neither the freethinkers' intellectual and moral critiques of the tradition, nor their ethical criticisms of the contemporary rabbinate, are unfounded. The answer to the moral critique is the kind of virtue and piety exhibited by Aderet, whom he describes as "a natural Jew in the full sense of the term," for whom "the Hebraic harmony emerging from the entire praxis of the Torah in all its branches sounded in the very depth of his self." The answer to the intellectual critique, which takes up the great majority of the work, is to widen the angle of religious vision— not by imitating current fashions in Western culture, but by absorbing the best in literature, philosophy, and contemporary scholarship and adapting it to the collective national-spiritual vocation of Israel. He urges Hasidim, Mitnagdim, and moderate Maskilim to bury their hatchets—which, he says, in many ways they already have—and make common cause to win over the hearts of the young.

Later that year he published another slim volume, *Ikvei Ha-Tzon* (*The Tracks of the Flock*), its title taken from the Song of Songs 1:8: "If you lose your way, O fairest of women, go ye to the tracks of the flock and herd your goats by the shepherds' tents." The true shepherd trusts his flock and tries to understand where it is that they are trying to go. In *Eder Ha-Yakar*, he suggested ways that his rabbinic colleagues could address the stirrings of the new generation. Here, he offered, based on his own intense experiences, a sympathetic reading of youthful rebellion. *Ikvei Ha-Tzon*'s six lyrical, at times ecstatic, essays trace an arc from the conflicted realities of the time to a pious devotion to the sublime.

The volume opens with the essay "Ha-Dor" ("The Present Generation"). There is, he writes, no denying the pervasive sense of crisis: mass defection from tradition, compounded by pogroms and persecution. And yet there is hope, of a paradoxical sort: "Our generation is wondrous, a generation full of puzzlement. One is hard pressed to find anything like it in all our history. It is composed of opposites, darkness and light groping about in confusion. It is low and degraded, and great and exalted; it is entirely guilty and entirely innocent."[13] The younger generation made a huge impression on him:

> Dreadful sorrows and travails have made [this generation] determined and fierce . . . It can't be stooped and bent even if it wanted to . . . A generation like this, which is willing to die bravely for what, to its mind, are noble ideals, among them the sense of righteousness, justice, and knowledge that it feels within it, can't be lowly. Even if its goals may be utterly wrong, its spirit is exalted, great, and awesome.[14]

The key to understanding the generation is provided by the famously cryptic Mishnah Sotah 9:15: "*be-ikveta de-Mashicha chutzpah yisgei*"—"in the time of the footsteps of the Messiah, chutzpah will swell."

This revolt against authority is more than a sign of messianic apocalypse. To Rav Kook, many young people disrespected authority because they had somehow risen above it, and the absence of an intellectual program to match their undoubted moral passion was the source of their confusion, bitterness, and cynicism. Their rebellion was itself a sign of their "thirst for thought, and reason, and with it for richer, more drenched feeling, fresh, and alive."[15]

Hardened by the sufferings of recent times, these young people would not return to tradition out of fear of God, but they might return out of love. What sort of love? That spirit of enlightenment that the ancient sources call *the air of the Land of Israel* (Babylonian Talmud [BT] Bava Batra 158b). That is, the spirit, within individuals and within nations, that has moved beyond conflict, fusing ideals and selfhood, attaining equanimity and freedom, accepting both the necessity of endless striving and the fact that our ultimate ideals are never truly realizable on earth, but only in God.

The exilic Torah of the diaspora no longer suited "the generation of the footsteps of the Messiah." They were filled with love, justice, and power; the task of rabbis was to bring them to self-awareness. Rather than seeking to stifle these young people, spiritual leaders should be empowering them, precisely via the Torah that they earnestly—and even justifiably—despised. With those lines, Rav Kook fundamentally rewrote the terms of Orthodoxy's self-understanding. That which seems to make some people very bad Jews is precisely that which makes them perhaps the greatest Jews of all.

The final essays lay out a vision of the unity of religion and philosophy, and of spiritual renaissance, precisely in the physically parched and spiritually conflicted Land of Israel. He begins by taking on Spinoza, whose sublime equanimity in equating God with nature did away with the very possibility "of audacity as of humility, of sanctity as of joy, of purity as of a life of wanting to do something true."[16] Spinoza's vision reflected "a great light . . . broken and crooked," which, when "scoured, burned white hot, and smelted," will reveal that the ideals embedded in the world and in ourselves are the true motive force behind all human life and culture. The soul, he continues, desires ultimate selfhood, which is God. Left to its own devices, that yearning can be translated only into bare feeling or, at the most, into philosophy and its handmaidens, a decent social order and placid theology. Misalignment between the religious feeling that seeks to exceed all bounds and the rational theology that seeks to channel and constrain it breaks the levees, flooding the boundaries. This oceanic religious feeling is shared by all humanity—but only in Israel does it animate an entire nation, which reworks all social, political, cultural and economic life into vessels, "a Torah of life."[17] In ancient times, the Israelite kings, by imitating their gentile peers, forfeited divine ideals and, thus, their ethics. The national-divine ideals of the Jewish soul went underground for centuries ever after.

The youth rebellions of this (premessianic) time are but "the demons of the twilight."[18] Once the youth recognize that their own deepest ideals are those of the Torah, they will choose to serve God, which, contra conventional religiosity, does not mean servitude. It is instead the actualization of divine ideals—the manifold ways in which the infinite and eternal God makes Himself present in the world and in the mind. Ideals are ethical principles, epistemological categories, aesthetic stirrings, the zeitgeists shaping world history. They are, finally, the Sefirot, the points of divine energy at the heart of Kabbalistic doctrine, whose interactions structure all of God's manifestations in time and place, and thus all of being: "The divine ideals, the ways of God, His desires, emanations, Sefirot, attributes, paths, roads, gates, and countenances, some of whose ideal contents are also engraved and fixed in the human soul, which *God has made righteous* [Ecclesiastes 7:29], and the greatest desire hidden in the depths of the soul is to bring that hidden light to realization."[19] By recognizing that all we know, even our very selfhood, is but an attempt to describe the interactions of divine energies as they vibrate in our lives, our minds open to the possibility of infinitude and God.

Serving God, then, expresses the Jewish people's love for justice and longing for the divine ideals, as individuals and as a collective, which are implanted in their very nature, and in turn mandate the cultivation of their own physical nature. It is precisely because gentile nations do not have this unity that they can even conceive of a distinction between religion and ethics, and that the forces of progress need to make that distinction in order to clear a space for morality. But that distinction is fatal, for ethics must always draw from a higher source, "the supreme mind." Israel's mitzvot are mere reflections of the great light emanating from the future, the destination of the moral progress of mankind. The divine ideals illumine "the shining unity" of all creation; it was the detachment of divine ideals from Israel's nationhood that made possible in turn "the unity wrapped in idolatry," that is, Christianity, and then Spinoza. The darkness of the Middle Ages made the ideas of God and freedom seem incompatible, and the idea of worshipping God its own monstrous form of idolatry. Now that mankind had discovered the idea of evolution—from the very lowest to the highest—and Israel is returning to its land, the divine ideals are reemerging, casting onto the world the light of ethics and freedom.

This great openness and freedom was still, Rav Kook argued, to proceed through tradition. A year after his arrival, there had opened in Jaffa an avowedly secular Hebrew high school, which became famous as Gimnasiyat Herzliya—as destructive for him as a Christian mission. Though he had written creatively about Bible criticism, he found the school's entirely unchurched manner of teaching it too "disgusting"[20] even to describe. He tried, in vain, to get Gimnasiyat Herzliya not to organize school trips on the Sabbath and to undo the promiscuous mingling of boys and girls in the classroom. While acknowledging the high school's benefits to the Hebrew revival and national identity, he thought it still "sinned greatly against the spirit of Israel in its rendering all sacred into secular."[21] His ambivalence vividly came out when once walking past the school with Charlap. Rav Kook said that one had to recite two traditional blessings on the spot: "Blessed is He who restoreth the widow's estate," and "Blessed is He who will uproot idolatry from our land."[22]

He knew that a return to the traditional schooling of the shtetl was certainly not the educational answer. Moderate traditionalists responded to Gimnasiyat Herzliya by founding an alternative school, Tachkemoni, which taught secular subjects in a manner consonant with moderate Orthodoxy. Rav Kook threw his support behind them, asserting authority on hiring, curricula, and the overall spiritual atmosphere. The Jerusalem rabbis of course disapproved, regarding, as they did, the staff of Tachkemoni as little better than "unmannered Sabbath desecrators and heretics."[23]

The school succeeded on its own terms, but eventually disappointed him on all counts. In 1913 he wrote that there was in it "a little Torah, a little piety, a little Enlightenment, but a broad living spirit, sacred originality, that will beat with a strong heart on the spirit of national renaissance grounded in the sacred—that is missing."[24] He was looking not for bourgeois Orthodoxy, but for something as strong and even destabilizing as the secular revolutionary spirit of the times.

He had ideas about training rabbis, too. Two and a half years after his arrival, Rav Kook began to weave plans for a new yeshiva, combining traditional Talmud study with philosophy, Kabbalah, and literature—along with foreign languages and secular learning. When it opened, he taught Talmud, rabbinic commercial law, and medieval Jewish philosophy. He was unable to raise the funds to match his ambitions, and it remained a small institution, on the top floor of the synagogue that housed the local Orthodox elementary school (which also, in a departure from the norm, provided vocational education).

His educational ideas were spelled out in a long and instructively fruitless correspondence with an esteemed older scholar, Isaac Halevy. A Lithuanian Talmudist, Halevy had written a massive semicritical history of rabbinic Judaism that sought to vindicate tradition and beat nascent academic Jewish Studies at its own game. In early 1908, Halevy posed to Rav Kook a series of questions on the state of Jewish education and the rabbinate in Palestine.

The Eastern European rabbinate, Rav Kook answered, ensconced in what was still very much a traditional society, was no model for the New Yishuv, or even for the Old. Jerusalem could not produce great rabbis, because of crushing poverty, infighting, and an exaggerated fear of Haskalah, arising from a mix of piety, indigence, and isolation from the rest of the world. The result was that the freethinkers educated their children for success in life, while the religious left their children totally unprepared for living.

Over the following months, they corresponded back and forth, with Halevy asking again and again why the Palestinian rabbinate could not simply stand up on behalf of tradition. With mounting frustration, Rav Kook wrote him that one could not send rabbis out to serve communities that saw no need for them. Moreover, he wrote Halevy in the late spring of 1908, some of the new generation's criticisms and even revulsion at the thought of old-style rabbis were well deserved:

> The living movement of the New Yishuv, the joie de vivre and vigor, mental expansion, and national pride afoot in [it] cannot bear the stooped back, the wrinkled sad faces sowing fear and downheartedness, the straying gaze of despair and hatred of life, the strange Eastern garb, which, when joined to an air of oppressive poverty, spreads a spiteful fear on one used, even a little, to European ways. None of these could be accepted without anger by the New Yishuv, and when the most common type among alumni of the yeshivot of the Old Yishuv is precisely of that type, the opposition against the acceptance of communal rabbis is enormous.[25]

Because Rav Kook shared much of the New Yishuv's critique of the Old, he was seized with a vision of what rabbis and Judaism might be. He thought that Halevy, who had gone so much further in facing modern scholarship than almost anyone he knew, would understand him. But in the end, Halevy could not. It was largely in the circles of disciples and admirers growing around him in Jaffa that Kook found more receptive, and generally younger, ears.

There were, in those years, some older immigrants too. Aharon David Gordon arrived, like Rav Kook, in 1904, at age forty-eight. A moderate Mitnaged by birth and education, he worked for decades as an administrator of the estates of Baron David Gunzburg, perhaps Russia's leading Jewish philanthropist, who was also a scholar of medieval philology and a patron

of the arts. A largely self-taught philosopher, Gordon abandoned traditional religious belief and practice, but held on to
its reach and pathos. He found himself set aflame by a vision
of resurrection by return to the vital energies of the peasantry
and the land. After settling his affairs, he made his way to Jaffa,
which he found, as he wrote in his first letter back to Europe, "a
degraded Asiatic city," in no small part because "the locals have
not yet risen to the level of the nature of the Land of Israel."
And what was that nature? It was, he continued, "hope . . .
great and fruitful labor that gives birth to great forces." He
soon left Jaffa to work on a farm. "Labor has afflicted us," he
would say, "and labor will heal us."

Another older figure, one with whom Rav Kook found a
common language and close personal ties, was a writer, Alexander Ziskind Rabinowitz, known as Azar. An admired contribu-
tor to the Hebrew periodical press, he struck a balance in his
writings between Haskalah and faithfulness to the still-pious
masses. An active Zionist and associate of Ahad Ha-Am, Azar
moved from Ukraine to Jaffa in 1906 at age fifty-two, quickly
becoming a fixture of its burgeoning literary community. He
was drawn to Rav Kook and began to record his table talk:

> Just as there are laws in poetry, so is there poetry in laws.[26]
>
> The idea of freedom of thought has become debased
> and castrated, since it's used by slaves of one thought to war
> against slaves of another.[27]
>
> So long as [heretics] are engaged with ethics and ex-
> panding the good, that is a quest for God.[28]

He also began introducing Rav Kook to the young writers of
the Second Aliyah.

In the spring of 1908, a would-be writer from Galicia,
Shmuel Yosef (Shai) Czaczkes, arrived in Jaffa. On his first Shabbat in the city, curiosity took the twenty-one-year-old to the

Sephardic synagogue, where, he later wrote, an announcement read that a guest sermon would be delivered by "the giant among giants, the clear light of the skies, the complete scholar, more beautiful than the saints, *a kindness to Avraham and Yitzhak will rejoice*, the goodly named scholar Rabbi Avraham Yitzhak Ha-Cohen Kook."[29]

When the young rabbi spoke, the young Galician had a hard time following his Lithuanian-accented Hebrew and the rush of his ideas. Czaczkes noted that the congregation seemed "not like people listening to a sermon, but like listeners to songs and hymns from a sacred mouth, such that the soul listens as much as it can." As for the rabbi himself, "a wondrous and humble majesty seemed to hover over him." Kook seemed, he thought, like something out of Rembrandt.

Not long thereafter, Azar introduced the two, and the young writer began to visit the Kooks' home. Like many new arrivals, he seethed with anger at the rabbis of the time; he came to see in Rav Kook the hope of something better, even if it was likely doomed. Later that year, Czaczkes published his first story, "Agunot," a stunning, mythic tale whose title means "chained women," the grass widows, whose tragedies are a bone lodged in the throat of the halakha. The work came out under his new pseudonym, Agnon.

In 1906, Rav Kook's son Zvi Yehudah, age fifteen, left for Jerusalem to study at a yeshiva in the Old City. While there, he became interested in the teachings of Nachman of Breslov, with which his father was familiar. Indeed, in those years Rav Kook kept a volume of prayers based on Nachman's teachings in the bookstand at his synagogue seat. Yet when Zvi Yehudah sent his father a volume about Nachman, he received in return a gentle admonition: "The inner character of this great man needs greatly to be studied, but for that one needs a healthy heart, and good mental hygiene . . . and a sound connection with other perspectives for and against these views—and then things will shine as they should."[30]

Rav Kook understood the pull of Nachman—his passionate embrace of contradiction, his willingness to fling away the intellect for the sake of belief and illumination, his seeing the spiritual conflicts of his time coursing through his own seething soul—and, characteristically, sought both to let that impulse run free and to contain it too. That dual motion structured his own life and thought again and again.

Although a highly visible public figure, Rav Kook was very lonely. In the winter of 1908, he wrote to his brother Shmuel: "Yes, in my spiritual matters you know that my desire is very great and for my sins I accomplish nothing. I have nobody with whom to speak from my heart, neither young nor old, who comes close to getting the point of what I wish for and this wearies me greatly."[31] He added that Zvi Yehudah, observing correctly that his father's journals were badly in need of editing, had begun to copy them as a first step toward possible publication. He concluded: "*I cast my burden onto the Lord* [after Psalms 55:23], be it in matters of the flesh or the spirit."

In the fall of 1907, Zvi Yehudah, sixteen and back in Jaffa, sent a copy of his father's *Ikvei Ha-Tzon* to an up-and-coming writer. "My father," Zvi Yehudah wrote in the cover letter,

> is one of the scrupulously observant rabbis. Beside his genius in Torah he has merited the designation *Tzadik*—yet with that he is a free scholar and philosopher, unbounded, in the full sense of the word . . . With a torn and seething heart he sees and ponders the rupture of his beloved people, torn to pieces, and sees the source of all evil in people not knowing each other . . . With his pen he publishes and publishes his ideas in every direction . . . He talks and talks with everyone worth talking to, talking and writing from the dawn.[32]

The letter was addressed to Yosef Chaim Brenner, who, though just twenty-six, had already emerged as one of the most interesting writers of the time. Brenner was living in London, editing a literary periodical with a friend, Yehoshua Radler Feldman, who went by the pen name Rebbe Binyomin and soon decamped for Palestine. Their journal, *Ha-Me'orer* (The Waker), never had many subscribers, but in the one year of its operation, it was the premier Hebrew literary periodical of the day.

Brenner grew up in the Pale of Settlement, on the cusp of Chabad Hasidism and Mitnagdism, eventually rejecting both in favor of Enlightenment. Yet he never entirely abandoned Hasidic pathos and longing. That, along with deep empathy for the suffering of the Jewish masses, and a painful clarity about their long-term chances for physical and cultural survival, made him the tortured secular saint of Hebrew letters. He and his circle were—along with the sort of religious intellectuals that Rav Kook was hoping to cultivate—the real intended audience of *Ikvei Ha-Tzon*. But Brenner's pitiless, nearly ascetic lucidity about the depth of Jewry's predicaments and the spiritual crises of his time would not let him be drawn into the rabbi's mystic theodicy of his and his generation's rebellion and longing.

In 1909, Brenner moved to Jaffa and joined the editorial board of the country's most influential newspaper, *Ha-Po'el Ha-Tzair* (The Young Worker). That same year, Rav Kook founded a journal, *Ha-Nir* (The Furrow); his brother Shmuel handled the business end. It contained articles by Kook, Azar and Rabbi Shem Tov Gefen, an idiosyncratic polymath who was developing an anti-Spinozist, neo-Kantian mystical philosophy of science that he termed *adamantanut*, "earthness."

Rav Kook published two essays, "Derekh Ha-Techiya" ("The Path of Rebirth") and "Telamim" ("Furrows"), arguing the necessity of Israel's national rebirth for the spiritual good of humanity, and pointing out that modern heresies are but the expression of the great spiritual dross that the rebirth of Israel will cleanse. He also wrote a brief critique of contemporary literature as being insufficiently steeped in the Jewish classics.

Brenner wrote a devastating, sarcastic review. Intentionally or not, he used the same description of Rav Kook that Zvi Yehudah had included in his letter to him:

> Now we see that even the most *scrupulously observant*, even the closest to the path of faith, in the end, if he doesn't want to be judged a total zero, simply must, on collision with free thought and sensual living, be tossed from thought to thought . . . to preen with the great names whether he needs to or not, to sound the alarm: O Generation, see, we also know about Spencer, Schopenhauer and Ibsen! And above all, perfectly to avoid logical conventions, because of the straightforward conclusion of simple ideas about the history of human progress, faith and religion—ideas he reluctantly accepts.[33]

Rav Kook's "path of rebirth," he continues, "is essentially a path to nowhere, the fruit of the mind of a foggy, metaphysical soul . . . Why all the verbiage, rabbi, why?"

> Let us grant him, our master Avraham Yitzhak Ha-Cohen, that after all, his confused assumptions and incoherent visions are nothing other than the fruit of a soul torn in two despite the external optimism, drowning in the world of light.

And yet, he added, *Ha-Nir* was not just another Orthodox, reactionary publication:

> At times one senses in its writers—and especially in certain lines of Rav Kook—that we are dealing here with people of soul, storming, seething—a puddle, but with a tempest roiling its waves.

As for Rav Kook, he was "an outstanding character among the rabbis of Israel."*

Literary pursuits aside, most of Rav Kook's time was taken up with rabbinical duties, especially rendering halakhic decisions, many pertaining to living in the Land of Israel. In 1907, he published *Etz Hadar* (*A Stately Tree*), a treatise on the desirability of Palestinian *etrogim*, the citrons taken up in the prayers of the Sukkot harvest festival, over imported citrons—a relatively uncontroversial position, though he buttressed his legal arguments with larger philosophical ideas. Some of his rulings on other matters proved explosive, earning him, finally and formally, the wrath and enmity of the rabbinic watchdogs in Jerusalem.

His first serious quarrel with them began innocently, on a matter that ordinarily might have stimulated scholarly disagreement but not much more: the use of sesame oil on Passover. So central is Passover to Jewish identity, and to Passover the absolute prohibition on leaven, that over the centuries Jews took great precautions to avoid even the barest trace of it. In the Middle Ages there developed a practice among Ashkenazim also to refrain from eating *kitniyot*. A Talmudic term best translated as "legumes," it indicated almost anything that might look or taste like grains or act as leavening, such as rice, buckwheat, or sesame.

In the early fall of 1909, Rav Kook's Jaffa rabbinical court certified that the sesame oils produced by a local factory were indeed kosher for Passover, because production processes introduced by this modern factory made leavening impossible. Almost immediately, the Hasidic rabbinical court of Jerusa-

---

*Azar sent a copy to Ahad Ha-Am, who was exercised by the journal as a whole, and Shem Tov Gefen's eccentric essay in particular. He sent Azar a withering letter, offering barbed advice on how best "to make an impression on educated people."

lem sent him a letter, making no legal arguments but asserting that, modern factories or no, sesame oils had to remain forbidden. Even if the oils were technically permissible, they wrote, rabbinical responsibility meant zealously guarding tradition, especially in changing times. Moreover, they asked, how could he have issued so bold a ruling without first consulting them?

After answering the technical legal issues, he addressed the larger, policy questions: we will not win the trust and loyalty of the younger generation by prohibiting that which we know to be permitted; new technologies create new realities and thus demand new rulings; this is an opportunity to encourage the New Yishuv, and within the bounds of Halakha. And, finally, since when has one city's rabbinical court ever submitted its rulings for approval to the court of another?

A heated correspondence ensued. Large issues were at stake in this seemingly recondite debate—attitudes toward changes in society and technology, the adoption of halakhic policies favorable to the New Yishuv, the judicial independence of the rabbis attuned to that growing constituency—and both sides knew it. At one point, Rav Kook suggested that they all come together to formulate joint policies and agreed-upon jurisdictions for the new social and legal realities aborning in Palestine.

That was too much. Seeing that they could not bring this Jaffan upstart to heel, the Jerusalem rabbis issued a declaration two weeks before Passover, stating that sesame oils were as forbidden as ever, that technologies had not changed a thing, that they were *the* authority, and that woe betide anyone who would contaminate Jerusalem at Passover with sesame oils. In a gesture mixing contempt and the barest measure of professional courtesy, they did not mention Rav Kook by name. His last letter to them was, finally, angry. "It makes no sense to institute new stringencies on the basis of weak nitpicking . . . The early and later authorities simply could not have imagined this."[34] On issues that the classic authorities had left open or could not have foreseen, Kook wrote, we must decide for ourselves, and I need not consult with you.

It may seem that the Jerusalem rabbis were making a mountain out of a molehill, but they correctly sensed his independence and his willingness to embrace new solutions. It was one thing, and disturbing enough, for young Kook to publish his literary and philosophical musings on the need for change. It was another to see him weave them into the fabric of the law and bend that great edifice toward the new, godless entity taking shape in—and threatening to take over—the Holy Land. Their next big argument with him was imminent, and the stakes would be much higher.

The year 1910 (5670 in the Jewish calendar) was, according to traditional calculations, a *shemittah*, a Sabbatical year. According to biblical law, every seventh year the land was to lie fallow—unplowed, unsown and unworked. The law had itself lain fallow for centuries, since Jewish agriculture in the Holy Land was nearly nonexistent. Now that had changed, and so, come the Sabbatical years, what were Jewish farmers to do?

In 1889, leading Lithuanian rabbinic authorities had ruled that, since the biblical Sabbatical laws applied only to land owned by Jews, agricultural settlements could sell their lands to non-Jews for the Sabbatical and then continue to work them. But in the intervening years, Jewish agricultural enterprises had grown in number and scale. Avowedly Orthodox settlers of Petach Tikva and the moderate Maskilim of the First Aliyah were now joined, and perhaps outnumbered, by out-and-out modernists, secularists, and socialists, all of them committed to building a new society—the people about and for whom Rav Kook had written *Ikvei Ha-Tzon*. Maintaining the Sabbatical year according to the ancient guidelines would spell ruin for the traditional farmers and make it clear to the New Yishuv that when it came to squaring its enterprise with tradition, rabbinic leaders had nothing to say.

Rav Kook threw himself into the challenge, undertaking to promote both the legal sale of lands to non-Jews and a round of educational work on the significance of the Sabbatical year. He quickly found himself under assault by the rabbis of Jerusalem—who forthrightly prohibited the consumption of any Jewish agricultural produce grown during the Sabbatical year—and a number of leading Eastern European rabbis as well. He was denounced in articles, open letters and the time-honored Jerusalem medium, florid and biting wall posters (known as *pashkevilim*).

Rav Kook laid out his views in a book, *Shabbat Ha-Aretz* (*Sabbath of the Land*), 120 pages long when published and, amazingly, written in just over a week. (Zvi Yehudah, then eighteen, helped him edit the volume, one of the first of his many editorial forays into his father's works.) In the volume, he annotated and updated all of Maimonides' exhaustive legal rulings on the Sabbatical year; more importantly, he laid out his own argument for extending the *heter mekhirah*, "the permissive sale," throughout the Land of Israel.

His chief arguments, buttressed with his usual erudition and no small degree of intellectual daring, were as follows: since most Jews were not living on the Land of Israel, the biblical prohibitions were not in full force; thus, in technical halakhic terms, the contemporary Sabbatical year was not of biblical but rabbinic writ, a second-order obligation providing greater room for leniency; in pressing and unfamiliar circumstances there is well-established precedent for stretching the law or relying on minority views; residence in the Land of Israel is itself a mitzvah of the first order, and so to perform the mitzvah of the Sabbatical year at the cost of genuine socioeconomic injury to those living in the land is to set the Torah at cross-purposes with itself.

He made clear that the sale did not relax all the prohibitions of *shemittah*, and that he preferred that Jews observe the Sabbatical year no matter what. But reality could not be ignored: "In our days, when the basis of the Yishuv is commercial agriculture, and preventing this commerce would destroy all its livelihood and future standing . . . it is downright obligatory to maintain the permissive annulment through sale."[35] And that was a future he wanted to preserve. As he wrote in the preface to the volume: "For *this is from God* [Psalms 118:23], that He has given his people a furrow on His sacred soil, to be a *Petach Tikva* [an opening for hope, and the name of the first Jewish agricultural settlement; Hosea 2:17]."[36]

Interestingly, Rav Kook's master Netziv had ruled against the Sabbatical sale in 1889—precisely because he saw in nascent Jewish agricultural efforts the stirrings of redemption and the restoration of Jewish national life in its fullest, including halakhic, sense. In parting from his master and most of his colleagues on this large question, Rav Kook showed the stirrings of his own growing historical consciousness. As he wrote his disciple Moshe Zeidel: "We must see life in two dimensions, as it is, and as it should be. Absolute righteousness is always rooted in how things should be, but provisional righteousness, which touches more on acting in the present, is built on how things actually are . . . The two are connected, like alternating horizons on a long journey."[37] God save us, he wrote again a few days later, from those who would confuse ideals with reality.[38] The balance between the two, he wrote in the preface to his treatise, is a reflection of "this time [when] we as yet have nothing whole—but the time has come for the rebirth of the Torah directed to the rebirth of the land."[39] The mitzvah of the Sabbatical year being of second-order, rabbinic status at that time, he held, was itself a reflection of the liminal historical moment through which the world was passing.

When Rav Kook's arguments appeared in print, his opponents' polemics and threats grew sharper. He entered into a lengthy, spirited, and fascinating dispute with Ya'akov David Wilovsky, who went by the acronym Ridvaz. A distinguished Lithuanian scholar twenty years Rav Kook's senior, he had moved to Safed from Chicago in 1905. On the eve of the Sabbatical year, he bought a small parcel of land precisely so that he could let it lie fallow. The author of a brief treatise arguing against the possibility of sale, he wrote Rav Kook that this "sale" was so entirely fictive that it did not affect the Land of Israel's status. How then had the sages of the 1890s allowed it? They had been fooled, he wrote, in a tissue of historical invention, by heretical Zionists who cynically pleaded poverty and desperation. And, he suggested, they were fooling Kook too, or maybe just threatening his livelihood. Ridvaz offered what he thought was a better alternative: Jews should raise funds to support God-fearing farmers.

Rav Kook answered that, while grievously wounded by Ridvaz's imputations, he was still convinced of the rightness of his course: "I know for certain that if this sale is not performed, many, many will transgress all the Sabbatical prohibitions with no warrant at all; and the evildoers will exult to say that all is permitted, freely to uproot Torah commandments with no question, and one can't grasp the sheer destruction of the sacred Torah and defamation of God's name to emerge from this."[40] He would gladly encourage farmers willing to observe all the prohibitions, "peacefully, respectfully, and lovingly, for His blessed name and those who live on her and work her soil, not by threats or strange terrors, shouting or fighting." He did indeed work to raise money to support Jewish farmers who chose not to avail themselves of the permissive ruling, and strongly protested to the managers of Baron Rothschild's agricultural settlements when they forced the permissive sale even onto devout farmers who wanted to go without it.

Undeterred, Ridvaz kept writing to Rav Kook for years afterward, hoping somehow to convince him of the error of his ways. Rav Kook answered time and again in a mix of exasperation, respect, and serious engagement with a principled opponent whose indefatigable questioning forced him to clarify his own self-understanding as rabbi of the New Yishuv. A Litvak to the core, Ridvaz was utterly unmoved by mystical attempts to find the light in everyone and everything.

In the spring of 1913, Rav Kook restated his views to Ridvaz as plainly as he thought he could. Israel's sanctity and divine connection derived from a distinct holy soul passed on from one generation to another, and from the Jews' own Torah and good deeds. In the present, protomessianic times, many souls were deeply deficient in the Torah but powerfully connected to their essential Jewishness—hence their devotion to the Jewish people and the Land of Israel. This is the generation that the Zoharic literature calls "good within and rotten without."[41] They are, he says, *chamoro shel mashiach*, literally, the donkey on which the Messiah will ride into Jerusalem, according to the prophet Zechariah (Zechariah 9:9). The Zohar said it would be "ugly from without, and good within" (Tikkunei Zohar §60); playing on the word *chomer* ("matter"), he called this generation the one that would lay the material foundation for the spiritual redemption to come.

In that controversy as in others to come, Rav Kook did his best to maintain his equanimity. When Ridvaz lay gravely ill later that year, Charlap wrote and suggested that Rav Kook not only pray for him, but forgive him as well. He replied, "He has no need of forgiveness from me, *through both me and him the Highest is acclaimed* [Mishnah Sotah 40a]."[42] When Ridvaz died, Rav Kook wrote to an associate that "grief at our great loss at the departure of that tzaddik . . . makes it hard for me to think with peace of mind."[43]

The *shemittah* controversy crystallized Rav Kook's view of the New Yishuv and his place in it. The enterprise was sacred on its own secular terms. Its ultimately provisional secularism could, at the present historical moment, make its own claims as an essential feature of Israel's rebirth, a rebirth that would free Israel and the world from the constricting notion of religion itself. And it was his responsibility to bring that secular revolution to self-consciousness, to accommodation, and, ultimately, to union with the tradition it was struggling fiercely to reject.

The idea of a new literature drew him time and again. It was there, he wrote Zeidel in the fall of 1908, that "the old will be renewed, and the new will become holy."[44] (The Hebrew original bears a spirited pun—*ha-yashan yitchadesh, ve-he-chadash yitkadesh*). He encouraged his disciples and associates to create new journals wherever they were—Meir Berlin, the son of Netziv living in Berlin, established *Ha-Ivri*, and Binyamin Menashe Levin, then at university in Bern, established *Tachke-moni*, where, in 1910, Rav Kook published the essay "Dewdrops of Light."

Building on some of the ideas in his Eastern European essays, he wrote that the mitzvot of today are a means to the higher ethics of the future, which will reach beyond Judaism toward all humanity and even to the animal and natural worlds. Yosef Chaim Brenner responded again with scorn and a dash of appreciation generously laced with irony. It was, he wrote, "like all his writings, riddled with confusion and contradiction."[45] Acknowledging that Kook did "yearn for synthesis," Brenner gave credit to "this excellent rabbi" for making "some points that are excellent in their way, much like the *Torat Ha-'Olah* [the work of the great sixteenth-century authority Moses Isserles], that scholastic-Kabbalistic-philosophic work . . . which, in its time, likewise tried to unite what can't be united."

At the time of the *shemittah* controversy, Rav Kook wrote an essay that appeared, finally, in 1912 in Levin's journal. In "Li-Mahalakh Ha-Ideiot be-Yisrael" ("The Procession of Ideas in Israel"), he presents a dialectical philosophy of Jewish history structured along a series of theses and antitheses whose collective synthesis is redemption. Israel came into being to light the way for humanity via the creation of a society where the universal God idea—at work in every people—would animate all. That holistic vision was tried during the First Temple, but failed because personal morality had not yet sufficiently developed. That failure led people to think of God, above all His ethical teaching, and the nation, as two distinct rather than complementary matters.

The Second Temple period was meant to restore nationhood in its fullest sense by fostering the development of personal spirituality. As the Hebrew Bible's profoundly collective notion of immortality became individualized, the God idea was displaced by the religion idea—a smaller, narrower conception, sustainable in exile. It was, so to speak, the constriction and privatization of the God idea that made it available to the world as a whole.

Indeed, with the Temple's destruction and Israel's exile, the God idea had nowhere to go, and so ascended above the bounds of any one nation to the heights of yearning for justice and pure thought. From those heights, the God idea has sent out rays of light, to the benefit of the entire human race, but without a real foothold in the life of a nation and government. The God idea in its fullness, and as naturally expressed in Knesset Yisrael (the classic term for "the sacred community of Israel," and in Kabbalah one of several names for the meeting point of God and the world), renders life self-evidently good on its own terms, with no further need of justification. Idolatry, by contrast, has no divine root and knows no rest. It is anger personified because it cannot imagine anything more ultimate than this world and all its sorrows.

In this cascade of alienations—Israel from its natural foundation, the God idea from this world, the natural world from the world of the spirit—ethics becomes divorced from nation-hood and people are left with "religion . . . an occluded, arti-ficial concept." It yields dreary fanaticism, despair, or the thin aesthetic gruel of "religious feeling." The nation too had de-generated into "the idea of the state," which, he says, in a swipe at the social contract, is ultimately nothing more than a glori-fied insurance company. People justly demand a deeper ethical commitment than what the narrow idea of "religion" can pro-vide. All these antinomies were blessedly and finally heading to their ultimate, healing resolution. Israel, relieved for millennia of the need for "statecraft and its quarrels," and a spectator to global affairs, now sought to resurrect its healthy, natural ener-gies and return to the world stage; as it did so, it would harvest the best energies of world religions, of nationalism, of univer-sal ethics and the spirit: "We are preparing to receive them all."

In this essay, Rav Kook offered a kabbalistically inflected reading of Nachman Krochmal's *Guide for the Perplexed of the Time*, posthumously published in 1851, which offered a Jewish revision of Georg Wilhelm Friedrich Hegel. The philosopher of Jena had famously relegated Judaism to an early stage in the development of *Geist*, the spirit animating all history. Indeed, the very overcoming of Judaism was what freed the spirit's march into history. Krochmal argued that Hegel (and for that matter the Berlin Haskalah) had it exactly wrong: the nation, the *Volk*, is the setting within which spirit and knowledge of God arises. There can be no spirit without national culture, and Israel's mitzvot are the vehicles whereby the spirit is actu-alized in the consciousness of the believer. Contra Hegel, the *Volksgeist* is not a secular principle, but a synthesis of spirit, na-tion, and religion. And so, again contra Hegel, the Jews are not transcended by spirit; rather, they already bear within them-selves its highest actualization. Israel's history proceeds in dia-lectical cycles, but it is free of the mortal pattern by which all other nations rise, flower, and decline. Finally, contra Hegel, but closer to another German philosopher, Johann Gottfried Herder, it is the nation, the fusion of body and spirit, and not the state as such, that represents the highest realization of the spirit.

Two other early theorists of Jewish nationalism, Moses Hess and Ahad Ha-Am, identified Jewish nationhood with ethics—as an alternative to tradition. Ahad Ha-Am in particular, in an important essay of 1904, "Flesh and Spirit," articulated the contrast between the earthy Torah of the First Temple and the ascetic, spiritualized, and individualized Judaism of the Second. The latter fostered the ethical core of the Jewish national spirit, which would take religion's place (and he rejected political Zionism as an alienated simulacrum of First Temple earthiness). For Rav Kook, by contrast, the fusion of spirit, ethics, and Jewish national identity are of the essence of tradition. And in one of his departures from both traditional thought and Jewish modernists like Ahad Ha-Am, he read the concrete workings of modern history as their own form of revelation within a great and subtle divine plan. The Torah and its mitzvot, even the rituals and their seemingly nonrational aspects, will, in the fullness of time, reveal themselves to be the bearers of universal morality via the embodied spirituality of Israel.

This integration of Hegelianism with Kabbalah is not as surprising as it may seem, once it is recalled that Hegel himself was influenced by the same Neoplatonic currents that shaped the Kabbalah. Hegel's God is immanent—not in the timeless natural world, as he is for Spinoza, but in the historical world, in its conflicts and attempted resolutions, which are the medium through which Absolute Spirit comes to realization in the great philosophical opus of human history.

The antique, Neoplatonic, Kabbalistic vision of spirit straining through matter toward self-realization was deeply appealing to modern thinkers for whom God was no longer as securely in heaven as before, if indeed He was there at all. Of God's existence and place on heaven and earth, Rav Kook had no doubt. But he understood why some would doubt, both because of the small-mindedness and dogmatism of conventional religiosity, and because God Himself is far more deeply enmeshed in the material world and its many and multiple occlusions than humans can imagine. There is in that vision a touch of sadness, and yet great hope, because it is the darker clouds that hold potentially the greatest light.

Forging his local rabbinate was not easy. Rav Kook found himself repeatedly accused by the Old Yishuv and the New of being allied with the other. It was his very ecumenism that created the opening for these charges.

Even as he tried to create a new, responsive rabbinate, he would not and could not cease to be a traditional halakhist. Thus, in 1909 he opposed the creation of a Hebrew Magistrate's Court (literally, Hebrew Court of the Peace), whose equitable arbitrations would be an alternative to both the Ottoman legal regime and traditional rabbinic law. The secretary of the forum promoting the new court was none other than Shai Agnon, who later wrote that Rav Kook unwittingly helped spur its founding by his unfamiliarity with the legal requirements of contemporary commerce. In a number of cases, Rav Kook managed to bring down upon himself the wrath of legal forums of the New Yishuv, for being insufficiently progressive, and the Old Yishuv, for even sitting and adjudicating among heretics in the first place.

The Jaffa town council saw Kook as essentially a civil servant in its employ, one whose independent-mindedness was inappropriate and certainly inconvenient. He of course saw things differently. In this revolutionary situation—building a new Jewish people and perhaps a new Judaism in the Land of Israel—he, of all people, emerging theologian of the revolution, was not about to serve as a mere bureaucrat, and certainly not as a contractor for the collection of local satraps, bourgeois professionals, and land speculators sitting on the Jaffa town council.

The creation of Tel Aviv on nearby sand dunes in 1909 expanded Rav Kook's writ while adding to his problems, as Jaffa–Tel Aviv became a secular urban center. He did not succeed in stopping that development, nor is there any reason to believe that he could have. Perhaps his greatest success in this case was his ability to maintain himself as a traditional rabbi deeply sympathetic to the new Palestine.

In 1910, he urged the creation of a religious council that would regulate and manage religious affairs generally, parallel to the town council; a year later, participants in a town meeting agreed. Though Rav Kook was not a member of the religious council, before long the town council came to see the new body as a threat, for its very existence as an alternative center of power and for the enhanced leverage it provided Rav Kook, whose efforts to mediate between the two councils proved futile. The largely autocratic old guard had its hands full with the new, upstart democracy rising in Tel Aviv, and a council of untamed religionists was the last thing they needed.

Kook's disdain for the idea of a rabbi as a civil servant colored his relations with his Sephardic counterparts too, heirs to generations of maneuver and deference within the Sublime Porte (government) of the Ottomans. He was, in many ways, sympathetic to the Sephardim and respectful of their traditions. Still, the old system, he wrote to Isaac Halevy, had turned most of the official Sephardi rabbis into glorified clerks, the position that much of the Jaffa council hoped he would occupy. When the town council proposed in 1911 that Ben Zion Uziel, a brilliant, gentle scholar, be appointed Sephardic chief rabbi of Jaffa to serve alongside Rav Kook, the latter was not pleased. Though the two managed to cooperate on social welfare, education, and other matters, tensions remained. In 1913, Uziel tendered his resignation, which the council refused.

Rav Kook did not have much to do with the Arabs of Jaffa. Like many halakhists, he did not regard Islam as idolatrous, and was more sympathetic to it than to Christianity. When, in 1911, *Ha-Ivri*, the newspaper edited by Netziv's son, Meir Berlin, by then a leading activist in the Religious Zionist Mizrachi party, published a sketch in which Arabs were given the blanket designation "the enemy," Rav Kook took him to task. Not only did talk like that give ammunition to Jews' foes and irritate the Turks, he wrote him, it ignored the many Arabs of goodwill. Kook urged Berlin to desist from that sort of thing, "whose benefit is zero, and damage, incalculable."[46] Instead, he suggested, promote "the paths of peace and brotherhood, which we encounter among the genuinely practical men of the Yishuv, and among the Arab inhabitants of the land, of course (I mean) the best of them."

In the fall of 1913, Rav Kook had an idea for an initiative that would bring some peace between the New Yishuv and the Old and, he hoped, enhance his standing with both. A year earlier, he had asked Ben-Zion Yadler, a respected rabbi and preacher in Jerusalem, to serve as his representative and supervise the observance of agricultural *halakhot* (such as tithes) in the agricultural settlements of Samaria and the Galilee region. As the project progressed, Rav Kook began to consider a program of regular rabbinic visits to the new settlements, not only for halakhic supervision but also for preaching, teaching, and religious revival. At first he thought he would travel by himself, in the company of local rabbis from Haifa, Tiberias, and Safed. But as he made preparations, he learned that one of the Jerusalem rabbis wanted to come too, none other than the rabbinic judge who had by then emerged as one of his chief critics, Yosef Chaim Zonnenfeld.

They were, in the end, a band of ten: Rav Kook and an assistant, Charlap, Yadler, Zonnenfeld and his son, the local rabbis, and a representative of the mission's funders. They set out from Jaffa on November 19, 1913, and were on the road by carriage, horse, and mule for just under a month. The delegation made twenty-six stops in all, going as far north as Metula. Everywhere they went, they asked the local community for a written statement about its members' religious lives and their willingness or unwillingness to accept rabbinic supervision.

The reception was, not surprisingly, warmest in the venerable cities of Tiberias, Haifa, and Safed and in the settlements of the moderate First Aliyah, such as Zichron Ya'akov and Hadera. There, the rabbis were respectfully and at times gratefully received. The locals were inspired to refurbish or even build synagogues and to allocate time and monies for religious education.

Things went differently in the settlements of the Second Aliyah, where kosher food was often not to be had at all and services were nonexistent, even, or especially, on Yom Kippur. Rav Kook regularly told their hosts that he and his colleagues were coming not only to exert their influence but also to be influenced in turn. But the gaps were great. At Merhavia, near Haifa, which numbered about fifty workers, the rabbis conducted a memorial service for two Jewish laborers recently murdered by Arabs, one at Kinneret, the other at Deganya.* The rabbis were well practiced at eulogies, but not for out-and-out secularists, who died actively defending the no-less-novel enterprise of secular Jewish agriculture in the Holy Land. Zonnenfeld, perhaps reflecting his own uncertainty about what to say, cited a verse from the biblical ceremony for the funeral of an anonymous corpse, *our hands did not shed this blood and*

---

*The victim from Deganya, Moshe Barsky, was killed while fetching medicine for his friend, Shmuel Dayan. In commemoration, Shmuel named his firstborn son Moshe Dayan.

our eyes did not see (Deuteronomy 21:7), a confession entirely in keeping with the traditional quietism of the Old Yishuv.

Rav Kook, characteristically open about his conflicts, tried to have it both ways. After expressing discomfiture at eulogizing unrepentant sinners, he said that nonetheless he did want to honor these heroic fallen of Israel. That was too much for some in the audience to bear, and one of the workers rose to denounce rabbis in general and Rav Kook in particular. The evening dissolved in arguments.

At Poriyah, a settlement of thirty-five workers nestled on a hillside southwest of Tiberias, overlooking the Sea of Galilee, something extraordinary happened. As the rabbis and the workers were eating dinner in the communal hall, shots rang out. Three Arabs, it turned out, had tried to steal some sheep. The workers apprehended them, took written statements, gave them some food and a bed for the night, and sent for the Turkish police. Afterward, the workers gathered around the fire for singing and dancing. Rav Kook, overcome with emotion, wrapped himself in a watchman's cloak and headdress, danced with them, and went for a horseback ride. On his return, he and some of the other rabbis continued dancing. Zonnenfeld sat by the fire and offered, not sermons, but stories about life in Jerusalem.

At daybreak, Rav Kook addressed the group, again charting his own course between the Old Yishuv and the New. The land would be won by mitzvot, he said, by Sabbath and kashrut, but no less by working the land. After thus validating the enterprise of the New Yishuv, he pleaded with the workers to take upon themselves the religious observances they associated with the Old. Donning a watchman's cloak and headdress once more, he began to dance and sing.

Although the rabbis registered some gains, the trip was, on the whole, less than successful. Try as they might, they could not talk the young revolutionaries into embracing precisely what they had come to Palestine to reject. As for Zonnenfeld, his month on the road likely deepened his grasp of how deep a challenge he, and all that he stood for, faced from the New Yishuv and from his unorthodox colleague from Jaffa.

Mordechai Ben Hillel Ha-Cohen, a businessman and disciple of Ahad Ha-Am, emigrated from Belarus to Palestine in 1907 at age fifty-one. He briefly engaged Brenner as his personal secretary. Pursuing a mix of business and literary interests, he was among the founders of Tel Aviv and a member of its town council from its inception. Ha-Cohen's memoirs, published in 1928, offer a fascinating glimpse of how Rav Kook struck a sympathetic but canny man of affairs:

> One never heard idle chatter from him. On the contrary, you felt that his words, in person or print, were just missing their full expression, and that he was offering you just a little of what he had. . . . God created him with a pure heart, and he was full of love for all among his people, with him there were no sinners. . . . Add to that the virtues of a man who knows the meaning of ethics and culture, responsibility and obligation, and then you will well understand why and how [he] attained his place as the rabbi of Jaffa.[47]

Yet Rav Kook was something of a provincial when it came to officialdom. Ha-Cohen writes that while Rav Kook "had a weakness" for the "glory of the rabbinate" and was dazzled by the institution's possibilities in the new Palestine, "his office was sorely deficient; the idleness of the *beit midrash* buried its professionalism, which requires order and routine." Above all, it was his conciliatory instincts and worldview that most highlighted the defects of his virtues: "Rav Kook is not a man of war, nor can one depend on him in a decisive moment, because some other influence will come from who knows where and sway him in the other direction. . . . He has the soul of a poet . . . And yet his soul is alert, alive, sweeping others in."

Indeed, even Eliezer Ben-Yehudah buried the hatchet. By 1913, the lexicographer, at work on his monumental historical dictionary of Hebrew, was sending Rav Kook etymological queries out of respect for his erudition and, perhaps, the realization that he might indeed be some kind of bridging figure after all.

In 1913, Rav Kook's circle attempted another journal, *Ha-Tarbut Ha-Yisreelit* (The Israelite Culture), which featured essays by Azar, Charlap, Zeidel, and a young religious poet electrified by Kook's ideas, Yosef Zvi Rimon. It most prominently featured "Zer'onim" (Seedlings), a collection of brief essays by Rav Kook, largely culled from his journals, although two were largely written for the journal itself. Taken together they laid out his sense of himself and the germ of his enterprise.

The first, "Thirst for a Living God," begins:

> The spirit can find no footing but in the divine air. Knowledge, feeling, imagination, and desire, and their external and internal motions, all make it necessary for men that there be, precisely, God. Then they will attain their fullness, their equilibrium and equanimity. If man seeks even a little less than this greatness, he is instantly wrecked like a ship at sea. Clashing, storming waves cast him ever from rest; tossed from wave to wave, he will not know himself . . . Our only resting place is in God.[48]

God is, of course, above and beyond the world and anything humans can think, feel, or imagine. The gateway to Him is

> the divinity that is revealed in the world, the world in all its beauty and splendor, in every spirit and soul, creature and crawler, every sprout and flower, nation and kingdom . . . the ideas of every writer, imagination of every poet and thoughts

of every thinker, feelings of everyone who feels, and the stormy courage of the brave.[49]

Yet still, where in all that romanticism is the connection to God? It lies within, in somehow making contact with the ultimate source of the spirit's longings, the great divine lights secreted in one's own soul.

How to live by those lights is the subject of the second essay, entitled "The Sage over the Prophet" (after BT Bava Batra 12a). Poets, he writes, powerfully depict life in all its beauty and despair. But their imaginative powers are of little use when it comes to improving life in this world, and for that we have physicians, judges, architects, engineers, businessmen, and other men of affairs. The prophets were the poets of the ethical and spiritual life of Israel and all mankind. But they too could not penetrate the gritty details, where good and evil live. Only one prophet could do that, and that was Moses, who "knew God face to face" (Deuteronomy 34:10), while his "shining speculum" (BT Yevamot 49b) enabled him to see all the details and thus to give the law. After him, a division of labor took hold: "the work of broad perspective was given to the prophets, and the work of the details to the sages."[50] Indeed, it was the sages who finally succeeded in eradicating idolatry, a task at which the prophets so crucially and tragically failed. Prophecy has long since vanished, but it will return—indeed, contemporary dissatisfaction with rabbis, scholastics, and men of details is a messianic ferment, a longing for prophecy. In the end, the breadth of the prophets and the practical wisdom of the sages will meet, "and the soul of Moses will appear once again in the world."[51]

Brenner, by then living in Jerusalem, wrote appreciatively about the journal's literary quality, Rav Kook's included.* "These

---

*He wasn't alone. Agnon shared the manuscript of his novel *And the Crooked Will Be Made Straight* with just two people, Rav Kook and Brenner.

are men of culture in the full sense of the word," Brenner wrote. "Whether it is Israelite culture in its Orthodox-Judaic sense or not is open to debate, but that this is true literary culture, of that there is no doubt."[52] But he bitterly rejected Rav Kook's casting of all existence as the expression of spiritual yearnings and suggested once again that for all his efforts to bring the revolutionary spirit of the times into some religious vision, he was more at odds with the tradition and his own rabbinic mystic persona than he chose to admit:

> The exalted—and I stress that word in all responsibility—worldview expressed in all the "seedlings" of Our Master Rabbi Avraham Ha-Cohen Kook in this book is, for those of us *who stoop to live and look* [Psalms 113:6], nonsense. "Our resting place" is not "only in God," and what is more, we don't know a resting place and don't even look for one anymore . . . And what is more, we don't believe his professed tranquility. The one who wrote "Souls of the World of Chaos" and "Suffering Cleanses" [two of his other essays] provides evidence that the soul contortions of the heretics and "destroyers" are not foreign to him at all—to the contrary.

Rav Kook, Brenner wrote, was trying to square as many circles as he could, "but with syntheses like these, *limping as they go* [after Genesis 32:32]"—as did Jacob after his struggle with the mysterious angel—"we are better off wandering in the antitheses of the dusk!"

It was Brenner and all he represented that Kook had in mind when he wrote about "souls of chaos" whose revolutionary spirit vaulted them over and above religion. Brenner, whose rebellion he saw as the harbinger of the new revelation and redemption; Brenner, who embodied the chutzpah that would trigger the advent of the Messiah; Brenner, whom he wanted to convince of his vision of the new heavens and new earth, the

Some of Rav Kook's literary interlocutors during the Jaffa years.
Sitting from right: Shai Agnon and Azar; *standing from left:* Yosef Haim
Brenner and David Shimoni, 1910. Photo courtesy of Lavon Institute for
Labour Movement Research, Israel.

new Jerusalem, taking shape in Jaffa and the Land of Israel.
And Brenner refused to be seduced.

Rav Kook knew what Brenner thought of him, and talked
it over with Azar.

He spoke well, the one who said my soul is torn. Of course
it's torn. We can't envision someone who isn't torn. Only
the inanimate is whole. But a human being has contradictory
longings, a permanent war is waged within him, and all his
effort is to unify the antinomies in his soul by an encompassing idea in whose greatness and sublimity all is gathered
and brought to utter harmony. Of course this is just an ideal
toward which we yearn—no mortal can reach it—but by our

efforts we can draw closer and closer to it, and this is what the Kabbalists call "Unifications."[53]

It was indeed through the Kabbalah and its vision of a multi-layered world that Rav Kook sought to understand the increasingly powerful and contradictory currents coursing through his times, his soul, and the soul of the world. This labor of understanding—and labor it was—took place out of public view, in the fastness of his study and his journals.

3

The Mists of Purity

Great rivers splash in my heart. Great and wide
fountains are opening before me . . . My language is
too short and weary to reveal the smallest bit of the
freshness of the light of spiritual life that fills me up.
All my bones say, O God who is like You [Psalms 35:10],
and I shall sing of Your strength and chant Your grace,
kindly, at morning [Psalms 59:17].
—Avraham Yitzhak Kook, *Shemonah Kevatzim*

As TIME WENT ON, Rav Kook's journals began to take on a
life of their own. Beginning around 1910, he took a long hia-
tus from writing essays, engulfed as he was by the torrent of
his thoughts. The private notebooks became his own house of
learning, and the text he was studying was his own increasingly complicated soul. He recorded his theological explorations, his religious experiences and attempts to understand

them, and the traces of experiences too great for words. He kept journals throughout his life, but eight notebooks written from 1910 to 1919 stand out for their length, passion, complexity, vigor, originality, rhetoric, and intellectual power. They are the mother lode from which his disciples excavated his most canonical works. Their publication in their original form in 1999 made clear how hard a job that was.

Spiritual diaries are rare in the history of Jewish mysticism, and his turn to this intensely subjective, sprawling genre speaks volumes about his independence and the tenor of his thought. Much of the drama in the notebooks—as in his corpus generally—is the meeting of multiple intellectual and spiritual traditions. At this nexus, Rav Kook formulated his answers to long-standing questions in Jewish philosophy, addressed new questions, and articulated a living theology.

His erudition and wide reading are on display throughout, but the spine of his theologizing was the Kabbalah—for him, not simply another set of doctrines, but the inner truth of the world and the key to living. Yet he was a philosopher still, and to that end the Kabbalah offered a language and ideas with which one could live and work within multiple—and conflicting—truths, and on different and, ultimately, complementary levels of reality.

Again and again he goes at his preoccupations, circling basic problems over and over in a flood of rhetoric, and almost never in the same way twice. His language is obsessive, regularly florid, and often startlingly beautiful.

> What do I see in a vision? I see the supreme thought, the thought that encompasses all, the thought that contains the force and innards of everything. I see how all the great streams splash out from it, and from the pools proceed rivers, and from the rivers brooks, and from the brooks floods, and from the floods, currents, and the currents too, divide into smaller channels, and the channels divide into a mass

of thousands of multitudes of *thin-veined branches*,* arteries. And if one is narrow, it holds on to the current, and if the current before it is narrow, it holds on to the flood, and if the flood is narrow, it holds on to the stream, and if the stream is narrow, it holds on to the river, and if it is too narrow for the river, it takes hold of the God-stream filled with water, which is tied to the thought that has no narrows, and there is the place of the watercourses *great and wide* [Psalms 104:25]. And the final abundance, dripping down from the thin-veined branches, flows this way from the first source of the supreme thought, above which any eye would be too faint too look, and *God said I will dwell in mist* [I Kings 8:12].[1]

This chapter traces the essential cluster of ideas at work in Rav Kook's notebooks from 1910 to 1914. They are a heady, volatile mix of concepts that regularly pull and strain against one another within one man, an ultra-Orthodox rabbinical authority trying to hold them all together.

Everything is alive. Nothing is inert. A seething dynamism pulses through everything, and everything is part of an eternal, organic whole. All is animated, illuminated from within by God, who vibrates in each and all with absolute, radiant, and loving presence; and everything is rising. All that is, was, or will ever be is of God, a personality beyond all personality living in all three persons—he, you, and I. The eternal God manifests Himself in historical time in the universal yearning for goodness, love, beauty, and truth, all of a piece with His own yearning for self-expression. We are the field on and through which that divine yearning strains for self-realization. The resolution of that longing is holiness; the place where the soul comes to rest is the holy, as near as we can get to the endlessly beating heart of God. In the words of a classic Zoharic passage, "there

---

*The word he uses, *konkanot*, alludes to a Talmudic homily (BT Hulin 91a), in which the word signifies *reykanin shel Yisrael*, the bumpkins of Israel.

is no space that is empty of Him, neither above, nor below" (Tikkunei Zohar §57). As the prophet said, "the world is full of His presence" (Isaiah 6:3).

But if God is truly everywhere—to the point that He nearly obliterates the very concept of "where"—what room is left for anything that is not Him, for human personality or will? How to square the great, jagged diversity of life with the all-encompassing circle of a living, animating, infinite God?

Much of Western theology developed around this central problem of God's immanence and transcendence, His dual presence on earth and in heaven. Rav Kook's journals are one long attempt to wrestle with this conundrum—not only as a philosophical problem but also as a complex vision coursing through his times and his own soul: "I am full of love for God. I know that that which I seek, that which I love, is not called by any name. How could one name that which is more than everything, more than the good, more than the essence, more than being? And I love, and I say, I love God."[2]

There is divine light in everything, and it is on the move: "The inner light shining in all of being, must build its world. It runs its course heedless of its connection to the surrounding light outside it, full of worlds . . . for inside it is fixed a heavenly longing, to join the incalculably greater surrounding light."[3] The divine light in all things strains upward, toward the source that is also its destination. The "inner" and "surrounding" lights to which he refers are the *yosher* and *iggulim*, literally, "linearity" and "spheres"—which figure prominently in the rich symbolism of Lurianic and Chabad teachings—whose interactions constitute a sacred geometry of immanence and transcendence. For Ramchal, *yosher* is the divine plumb line inserted deep into the world, along which we ascend as we are inexorably drawn back to our divine source. And *yosher*, as any reader of biblical Hebrew knows, also indicates fundamental, natural ethics and human decency.

Yosher is the most central thing in being, according to Rav Kook; the *iggulim* are secondary.[4] That is to say, living freedom, absolute freedom, from the fount of being, the freedom inherent in the very idea of God, whose moral dimension has created being, is everything. Divine immanence, not transcendence, is the central feature in His, and thus the human, drama. This immanence is freedom, in that it strives to burst all boundaries and be most truly itself. This centrality of freedom is one of Rav Kook's major departures from the familiar terms of Orthodoxy. The sort of freedom he means is, in the classic formulation of Isaiah Berlin, "positive freedom," not so much the freedom from restraint as such and more the freedom to realize one's innermost drives, aspirations, and selfhood.

Necessity—and its implicit cruelty—is ultimately an illusion, and not only for humans: "We already can ascend to the height of unity with life as a whole, and onward from there with vegetative and mineral being, with the epitome of life, with the spark of living light within them. They effect us, and we effect them."[5] Yet human morality is but a pale reflection of the divine morality that it seeks to imitate and that is so complete it has no need to choose from within a divided self.

What, then, is holiness? It is that which reveals the ultimate unity of things, in all their diversity: "With the abundance of holy spirit we feel how the divine spirit of life flows through everything, all the ways of life, all the wills, all the worlds, all the thoughts, all the nations, all creatures, all the *halakhot* of Torah and mitzvot, the practical, the intellectual, and the emotional, and all that proceeds from there, and from all the imaginations and affects of the soul to which they give birth."[6]

This holiness is far from conventional piety. It is in the nature of revelation to unsettle, cut against the grain. Because God lives within time as much as beyond it—and perhaps more within it—to seek God is, inter alia, to attend to the life of one's times, including the cascading heresies of modernity.

In *Ikvei Ha-Tzon*, he wrote about messianic chutzpah. In the notebooks, he took this even further. The heretical idealists were no mere miscreants; to the contrary, they were souls from *olam ha-tohu*, the world of welter, waste, and chaos of Genesis 1:2, into which God first said, "Let there be light," the world in which, as the Lurianic myth taught, souls and beings collapse and shatter from their own uncontainable longing.

> The souls of the world of Tohu are great, very great.* They seek much from existence; they seek that which their vessels cannot endure; they seek a very great light. . . . Their living ferment does not rest. They are revealed in the impudent of the time, all the more in an end of days, an era before the birth of the world . . . before the birth of a law above the laws . . . They kick and rage, break and destroy . . . there is no rest. These storms will bring bountiful rains, these dark fogs will prepare great lights, *and from the pitch darkness, the eyes of the blind will see* [Isaiah 29:18].[7]

"A law above the laws": even the deepest morality is neurotic, a will divided against itself. The new law will be the norm of nature, what he calls "the splendor of the supernal Adam," at the time being glimpsed in the ideals of social justice and Jewish solidarity for which the revolutionaries of the Second Aliyah were sacrificing themselves. ("The inner soul vivifying the socialist doctrine," he wrote, "is the light of the practical Torah."[8] On attaining self-awareness, it will be the foundation of the Torah. Anarchism, he continued, is rooted even higher on high, in the very ideal of *devekut*, cleaving to God, and conversely is further today from its sacred self-consciousness, and wild.) The struggles of modern heretics—principled,

---

*The great sixteenth-century mystic and philosopher Moses Cordovero (*Pardes Rimonim, Sha'ar 'Arakhei ha-Kinuyim*, §22), identified the chaos of *Tohu* with the cosmic principle of *Binah*, insight, the third of the Sefirot, the metaphysical womb of both repentance and freedom. Cordovero added: "It has no form of its own" and is "a question without an answer."

idealistic, antibourgeois, ethical nationalists willing to sacrifice themselves in the jails of the tsar and the harsh swamps of Palestine—make a new revelation all its own, dissolving the familiar division of religious and secular, the spectrum separating out the wavelengths of the divine light.

With these ideas, Rav Kook fundamentally rewrote the terms of Orthodoxy's self-understanding. The seeming sinners were, in their commitment to the Jewish people, the land, and social justice, closer in themselves to the messianic restoration than were pious Jews.[9] The latter, though, were greater in their spirituality; in the messianic apotheosis, the two groups would reach and heal each other. In the liminal time they were living through, the external and internal were reversed. Conventional, obviously faithful Judaism is but the truth of exile; the seething rebellion of the age is the truth of redemption, the emergence into the light of that which has been hidden. And that which has been hidden is that which has been the truest thing all along. Driving the reversal, impelling, pushing it through and forward, is the great longing, finally moving toward its final resolution, in the holy.

Why did the new revelation have to come through chutzpah? Because only a spontaneous, un-self-conscious drive can break through all the necessary accretions, compromises, and halfway measures of exile on earth, through the labyrinthine channels of action, patterning, creation, and mind that structure the endless manifestations of the divine. Chutzpah is akin to what the masters of Chabad referred to as *dilug*, skipping, vaulting over seemingly unbridgeable gaps—nonbeing and being, nothingness and existence, man and God—a skipping that lands on its feet because in the end it is all the same ground. That ground has many words, and one of them is nature, thought and lived through to its deepest intentions: "Holiness itself is the strengthening of the divine longing and spiritual light in human will and nature."[10]

There is a term for the divine light pulsing through nature: the Land of Israel. As Rav Kook puts it: "The holiness within nature itself is the holiness of the Land of Israel; the Divine Presence that went into exile is the ability to maintain holiness in opposition to nature. But that combative holiness is incomplete; its higher essence must be absorbed into the higher holiness, which is the holiness within nature herself."[11]

In those years, Aharon David Gordon, Rav Kook's secular counterpart, was calling from his kibbutz for Jewish regeneration through nature as the life-giving alternative to the disembodied Jewishness of exile. Rav Kook, like Gordon, sought redemption in and through nature, but characteristically wanted not to abandon the centuries of exile but to assimilate them into the dialectic of self-realization that is holiness.

What did nature mean for Rav Kook? It was a synonym for the state of being what one most truly is; which is why it is also, paradoxically, a synonym for freedom, whose expression in action is the will: "Those who argue over nature and human freedom forget that the spirituality of man and the world also has a nature, and seeks her freedom. And the freedom of spirituality and her naturalness are the foundation of morality and the Torah."[12]

We usually apply the term *nature* to the physical world (for example, trees, oceans, solar systems) because it is so obviously and powerfully itself. Nature is serenely confident and self-knowing, vigorous and forceful, exact. But it is blind, wild, a slave to necessity, and devoid of will, intention, or self-consciousness. Left to its own devices, it goes nowhere. Properly understood, it holds the key to redemption: "We will draw from nature its vigor, strength, its exactitude, endurance, and persistence, its moderation and self confidence . . . but we will free ourselves of its blindness, wildness, slavish necessity, negation of intent, and lack of idealism. And then we go upright, *marching on the high places of the earth, inheriting a legacy uncon-*

strained [Isaiah 58:14 and BT Shabbat 118a], *dressed in strength and grandeur, and laughing at the last day* [Proverbs 31:25]."[13]

The vessel of self-realization and knowledge is the will, ours and God's. Indeed, the world and all of being are nothing but His will, in places bent, braided, restrained, and contracted to make possible the wills of others. Yet still God's will lives in everything—animal, vegetable, mineral, and spiritual—and that is why each and every thing in its own way wants to rise. The will has a rich history in Kabbalah. The Zohar says "the will of wills . . . is the revelation of every beginning" (Zohar 3:129b). The Renaissance sage Menachem Azaria of Fano wrote that "His name and His infinite Will are one"; a bit over a century later, Luzzatto asserted that His will, a limiting principle on infinity, is what we seek to understand.[14] This will, Luzzatto said, can manifest itself as forethought, wish, desire, purposive action, a conclusion in the mind, conciliation, and even a gracious countenance, "and this truly is a great secret indeed."[15]

The Kabbalistic conception of the will is arrestingly all-encompassing, and, it must be admitted, a little strange. Is the will truly all there is? Arthur Schopenhauer (1788–1860), the German philosopher, thought so, seeing in the world nothing but a will to power. Rav Kook criticizes Schopenhauer by name and says that a will wrapped up only in itself will indeed be blind and destructive. But opening our eyes and looking beyond ourselves reveals something else: "All those whose spiritual eyes are open see not only a will, blind and deaf, but one *full of wisdom and insight* [Isaiah 11:2]."[16]

By "wisdom and insight," *chokhmah* and *binah*, he is alluding to the second- and third-highest rungs of the Sefirot, the deep structure of being, coming right after the first emanation of the divine out of infinitude. *Chokhmah*, wisdom, the second emanation, is the first crease in the great unknowable infinite, since wisdom is that which articulates limits and teaches us how to surmount them. The very existence of wisdom points to the prior, primordial will, of streaming infinitude, which it seeks to limit.[17] The primeval Fall was none other than the divine will's tragic inability to maintain itself in its descent into time and space, and that failure is the root of all our sorrows: "The worlds fell with the fall of the Will, man fell in the depth of sin, his will was diminished and dirtied, all went dark, and small, pathetic and gloomy."[18] More than an interesting interpretation of the Fall, this is the difference between Rav Kook and other celebrants of the will—Schopenhauer, Nietzsche, Rousseau—for whom the human will as such, as it is now, is redemptive. That is a deadly illusion. The redemption of the will requires first the Torah and mitzvot, and ultimately the redemption of Israel. Rav Kook continues:

> And the blighted will, to its light will be returned, when strongly expressed in the will of the nation. His nation, *the great nation whose God is near it* [Deuteronomy 4:7] . . . when it takes hold of selfhood, will gather within it the entire soul of man . . . It will banish the evil, mendacity, filth, fears, shame, death itself, from the world . . . And this divine courage *lo is standing just behind our walls, the voice of my beloved, here he comes, skipping on the mountains, capering on the hills* [Song of Songs 2:9, 8].

Israel's national rebirth will vanquish death itself.

In laying out his theory of prophecy, Maimonides outlined a structure of the human person: the body; the mind, capable of contact with the divinely ordained intelligences governing the world; and mediating between them, the faculty of the imagination, whose alchemy transforms abstract ideas into tangible images, and material images into embodied ideas. Mosaic prophecy was unique—and uniquely law giving—in that it bypassed the imagination.

First in his Eastern European writings and then again in

his notebooks, Rav Kook dwelled at length on this Maimon-idean picture of the self. Subtly but crucially, he introduced a new term and new range of associations, *regesh*, intuition, sentiment, feeling, alongside, and at times synonymous with, imagination, at times even above it, in the place where mind or intellect might be: "Here's the order: One must purify and strengthen the body and all its energies; then comes the faculty of the imagination and all its branches . . . then feeling and all its ramifications, and atop them the clear mind and all its ramifications. And the light of higher listening, which comes from the sparkling, highest holy spirit, comes atop them. This order is not only the case with individuals, but also for an entire nation at different periods in the course of its life."[19] What is this "light of higher listening"? It is the alchemical work of the mind, which smelts all the dross of multifarious and contradic-tory senses and impressions into a rich, unified whole.

The end result, the summit, the highest meeting of mind, imagination, and feeling, is silence, the only possible resolu-tion to the multitude of voices, the aural correlative of infinity: "The supreme holiness is the holiness of silence, the holiness of being, when man recognizes himself and his individual in-teriority vanishes, and he lives a life of commonality, the life of all." Yet the master of inner silence, he continues, is no recluse: "He doesn't consecrate himself, separate and distinct. He is alive, and his entire life is the holy of holies, the very life of life. His heartbeats, bloodstream, soul-longings, vision, and gaze, true life all, in all of them and through them, surge a life of God-courage."[20]

The master of silence, Rav Kook continues, has a hard time with what the Kabbalah calls *tzimtzum*, the necessary contrac-tions of focus without which prayer, study, moral reasoning, and civilized life are impossible, without which existence itself is impossible, because he wants everything and nothing—he wants freedom. Then, in a breathtaking move, Rav Kook writes that the contemplative master of silence is but a more perfected version of the masters of chutzpah:

> The chutzpah of the Messiah's footsteps comes from an inner longing for the supreme holiness of silence, and in the end it will come, for Israel is destined to stand closer in than the ministering angels . . . The sons of the boundary-defying impudent will be prophets of the highest level, higher than Moses and shining with the splendor of Adam.* The entire Tree of Life, in all the depth of its goodness, will be revealed in and by them. Bringing this supreme light to the world, requires the work of the tzaddikim, full of the higher *chesed.*[21]

Who, or what, for Rav Kook, are the tzaddikim? Who are the real saints?

The tzaddik is, in the Bible, the Talmud, and other classic sources, the just and pious man, the saint. In the Kabbalah, the tzaddik is the living embodiment of the ninth Sefirah, called *yesod*, the principle of life-giving transmission, expressed, inter alia, in human sexuality. The tzaddik, in his Torah and mitzvot —and his teachings—transmits life to the world. Hasidism put the tzaddik, his inner and outer life, at the center. The Hasidic tzaddik not only sought spiritual communion with God, but also worked to draw divine energies and knowledge down to earth and to his community. As the Ba'al Shem Tov put it, he fashioned "a path and channel to draw (divine) abundance to the world."[22] For Hasidism, the tzaddik's spiritual task was to focus spiritual energies in a time and place, drawing divine energies down for the commonweal, thus deepening and quickening divine immanence. This belief was of a piece with another central doctrine, *ha'alat nitzotzot*, "the raising of the sparks" of holiness scattered throughout creation, via work and worship

---

*The "splendor of Adam" refers to the transfiguration of humanity and the dissolution of the binaries of body and soul. The Hebrew word *chesed*, which is difficult to translate, denotes loving-kindness and grace.

through corporeality, grasping the spiritual core vibrating at the heart of matter and thus achieving *bitul ha-yesh*—the dissolution of substance, of suchness, the restoration of matter to its origins in God.

Nachman of Breslov went further. The true tzaddik is acutely aware of not only his own spiritual ascents and descents, achievements and failures, but also the spiritual stirrings, longings, and crises of his own time, which he registers within himself and even takes upon himself. The tzaddik is in deep communion with his immediate followers, of course, but equally and perhaps even more with souls wracked by doubt and drawn to heresy. That dark plain is where he does, for himself and others, his richest work. Rav Kook avoided Nachman's famous exploration of the bounds of reason and madness, along with his doctrine of "the casting off of the mind," as the prerequisite to revelation. But he too took upon himself the work of experiencing and reconciling the conflicting spirits of his people and his times.

What, then, is the work of a true tzaddik in fragmented modern times? Putting things together, in his acts and in his mind, he "unifies within himself all the opposites, and all the good scattered in the world."[23] Indeed, a hallmark of the greatest tzaddikim is that they love the world; they see the light everywhere, and their aesthetic sense is keen.[24] They are virtuosi of synthesis and inclusion.[25]

The tzaddik needs some primal chaos and disorder to keep off complacency. But he has further knowledge of the ultimate unity both underneath and above the disorder. His powerful, often sorrowful experiencing of the pains of others and this world, his riding in his own regularly tortured soul the waves and troughs of the zeitgeist, are the necessary conditions of his saving knowledge.

The tzaddik is what Hegel called a world-historical person,

who knows in his bones the very essence of the World Spirit, "the universal unconscious instinct of men," and also knows, before all others, where, in the present historical moment, the World Spirit wants to go—and he shows others the way. The true tzaddik draws onto himself the evil within all people who cling to him in good faith, transforming their evil into good. Sometimes he falls, the better to appreciate the darkness.

The tzaddik has panoramic vision. The higher his soul ascends, the more he senses the unity of all things, turns to them in love, and becomes, in Rav Kook's words, a kind of healing consciousness to those around him: "And these very ones are the *tzadikei yesod olam* [foundational tzaddikim of the world], who acquit the whole world and shine the light of kindness onto every creature, who love to justify the creatures and hate to condemn them. It is they who are the true students of our father Abraham, who walk in his ways."[26] There are many kinds of tzaddikim. Some conform to conventional religion, magnificently, whereas others rebel, magnificently; some are paragons of wholeness, and others, of contradiction.

Rav Kook saw himself as a tzaddik, and in all likelihood as the tzaddik of his time, *Tzadik Ha-Dor*. That Hasidic concept becomes, in his hands, a stunning rebuke to conventional Orthodoxy and the conventions of his rabbinic peers. *Tzadik Ha-Dor* is *Matzdik Ha-Dor*, the one who justifies his era, takes its sins within himself, and transmutes their dross into gold: "And so the pure tzaddikim don't decry evil, they add justice; they don't decry heresy, they add faith; they don't denounce ignorance, they add wisdom."[27]

The tzaddik is not the Messiah (and Rav Kook did not see himself as the Messiah)—but he has glimpsed some of the Messiah's own light. The higher tzaddik affects the work of the Messiah, which is the undoing of the Fall. With the accomplishment of that "repentance of nature," no nation will be jealous of another, and man will be brother to all his brothers, God's creatures all.[28]

Rav Kook was aware of the moral pitfalls of nationalism. His Eastern European writings bear the imprint of Moses Hess, Vladimir Soloviev, and others who saw nationalism's justification only in its ethical mission to humanity. Like Nachman Krochmal (under the impress of Herder), he saw nations as the vessels of spirit in history. Ahad Ha-Am had declared ethics to be the defining feature of the Jewish national spirit, still alive within an ultimately disenchanted world. Rav Kook agreed on the centrality of ethics, but he was nothing if not a seer of enchantment.

Of course, the ease with which nationalism can degenerate into violent, self-loving chauvinism is a constant temptation. At its best, Israel's nationalism obtains its pride of place precisely because of its acute understanding of the tensions between nationalism and ethics, of the subtle but crucial distinction between loving oneself as a part of God's creation and loving oneself out of an illusory superiority over others.

Rav Kook's nationalism has three key features: a passionate connection to the Jews and a belief in their centrality to both the world and God's purposes within it; an argument that nations are the vessels in and through which people are formed, are educated, and engage with the world; and a vision in which the nation, an essentialized entity, along with the natural world and the human body, is an indispensable foundation for the spirit and for the consummation of God's self-realization in and through the world.

This valorization of the nation runs perilously close to self-love and its ravaging moral effects. Rav Kook noted that while individuals can undo their self-love without fatally weakening themselves, groups cannot. The Swiss philosopher Jean-Jacques Rousseau's answer to this problem was the general will, the one thing that could reconcile duty and desire. Rav Kook had a similar notion of the will, but he assimilated it into holiness. One cannot expect a moral nation, but only a holy one, to be so transformed in holiness that its very self-love is beneficent.[29] Holiness, for Kook, entails the transformation of one's self and soul into an entity wholly good, beyond the neurotic strivings of morality. By implication, only one nation can evade the moral traps of nationalism. In the Kabbalah, Israel—the land and the people—along with the creative Oral Torah and the divine presence, the Shekhinah, are expressions of the tenth, and lowest, Sefirah, the indispensable crossing point between divinity and humanity. Thus, for Rav Kook, Israel's national identity is itself a revelation to and for the world.

Israel knows that universal love must feature in a God-saturated world; in Rav Kook's words: "Love for all creatures must live in the heart and soul, love for every individual, and love for all the nations."[30] Indeed, the existence of nations is only a way station until the joining of all humanity into a single family.[31] Israel experiences the ups and downs of all the nations, absorbing them all into its collective consciousness and restoring them to God:

> The sacred community of Israel* is the distilled essence of all existence . . . And Israelite history is the idealized distillation of general history, and there is no movement in the world, in all the peoples, whose like is not to be found in Israel. And its faith is the sifted essence of all beliefs, and the source from which idealism and the good flow to all the beliefs, and thus necessarily the force that clarifies concepts of faith, to the point that they achieve pure speech so that *they all may call out in the Name of God* [Zephaniah 3:9] *and your redeemer, the Holy One of Israel, will be called Lord of all the Earth* [Isaiah 54:5].[32]

*The phrase used by Rav Kook, "Knesset Yisrael," is one of several traditional Kabbalistic synonyms for the tenth Sefirah.

Secular nationalism, by contrast, is a virtual celebration of the crabbed and pathetic need to cry "mine, mine, mine"—indeed, the evils of xenophobia and economic injustice derive from this same twisted root.[33]

Though in Rav Kook's more tidal moments he sees all nationalities dissolving, at others he feels a necessity to maintain national differences, at least "in our time, after the differentiation into nations, [since] nobody can receive his spiritual influences outside the garment of the specific channel of his nation."[34] It was precisely his appreciation for the spiritual diversity of nations that required him to maintain a belief in Israel's distinctiveness. Israel suffered physical and spiritual degradation in order to absorb the elements of divine light while Jews lived in other nations, exile paradoxically paving the way for Israel's Jewish subjectivity, which, in a final paradox, will bring enlightenment to the entire world, to each nation in its way. One of Israel's tasks is to seek the divine light hidden in every language, culture, and religion.

Again and again Rav Kook returns to this question of election and the universal, and never really resolves it. Israel's distinctiveness is such an article of faith that it cannot be dispensed with, even in the eschaton, the sublime resolution of history. At the same time, the eschaton itself will require powerful universalism, and the heralds of that dispensation are none other than the seething Tohu souls or souls very much like them, such as those he found among the Jewish revolutionaries of his time.

> Some tzaddikim are great and immense and cannot constrict themselves to Israel alone, and they always seek the good of the entire world. And yet they are tied in their innermost point precisely to the sacred community of Israel because it is the epitome of the best in all the world, and the love and good that will come to her will encompass all creation. These tzaddikim cannot be nationalist in the external sense of the word, for they cannot bear any hatred or injustice, any

constriction or shriveling of good and kindness, and they are
good to all, like the attributes of the Holy Blessed One . . .
And yet they are very great scouts for redemption, for they
know clearly . . . that Israel's redemption is God's.[35]

For Rav Kook there is only one nation in the truest sense, one
collective that fuses the physical and spiritual, and that is Israel, ontologically different from all the rest. Yet he writes in
the end: "No one can really grasp character itself, not even
his own, let alone that of another, whether of an individual
or, all the more so, another nation. We circle the center of
knowledge, deal with speculations and guesses, judge by external acts, themselves largely hidden from us, their complicated
causes in particular . . . We must conclude that our knowledge
of this *hangs on a nothingness* [Job 26:7], *for judgment, it is God's*
[Deuteronomy 1:17]."[36]

There is here a space for an ethics based on epistemological
humility—although people can achieve some level of certainty,
ultimately they will never truly know. Neither nationalism nor,
for that matter, religious piety should ever displace natural
morality, the basic and universal intuitions of justice and kindness. To allow that to happen is to misunderstand what morality is, which is a way of loving the world and aligning oneself
with the divine will that is the world.

Israel's is the nationalism that—in tandem with social justice movements—is meant to cure the great global alienation
of which crude nationalism is the most vivid, viral, and violent symptom. Ethics is and must be central to Israel's identity. And what is ethics? It is the human will rising to meet
the divine will—the revelation, enactment, and unfolding, of
God's will in human action. The goal of ethics is holiness, the
total transformation of the person and the world, the fusion
of body and soul. To that end, "ethics is the corridor, holiness,
the palace."[37] But the corridor is indispensable. It builds on the

natural world and on natural moral intuitions. Rav Kook points out the necessity of keeping holiness grounded in ethics: "Fear of God must not displace man's natural morality, for such piety is impure. The sign of pure God-fearingness is when natural morality, implanted in man's intrinsically just nature, goes and ascends at piety's direction to greater heights than it would otherwise attain."[38]

Morality and ethics are how God's heavenly light manifests in human action. But ethics without the corresponding knowledge that God's all-encompassing light is that from which all flows, meaning that ethical demands are rooted in the very order of being and that all people are God's creatures, will inevitably decay into lassitude or, worse, anger. Rav Kook is explicit about the danger of anger: "We must despise anger with all the depth of our being . . . When we see any sect or party always expressing itself in anger, it is a sign for us that it has no understanding, no content with which to fill its emptiness, that in truth it's angry with itself, but that egoism comes and forces it to deposit the venom of its anger on others. The higher sages, who have reached the height of justice and kindness, are full of will, and kindness and truth garland them all the day."[39]

What sort of politics emerges from all of this? In some ways, not much of one, if politics is considered the art of the possible and the virtues of muddling through, what Max Weber called "the ethics of responsibility," prosaic cousin to "the ethics of aspiration." Rav Kook did not write much about the state, but when he did, it was of

> the state that is fundamentally idealistic, and that has had graven into its being the highest ideal, which in truth is the greater fulfillment of the individual. That state truly is the higher rung on the ladder of fulfillment, and this is our state, the state of Israel, the foundation of God's throne in the

world, whose entire desire is that *God be one and His name one* [Zechariah 14:9], which truly is the highest bliss.[40]

This is a heady, rare invocation of Hegel's apotheosized state, and he seems to sense the problem, since he adds in this sentence immediately afterward: "True, this highest bliss requires lengthy explication in order to raise its light in the days of darkness. But that does not mean it will cease being the greater bliss."

Rav Kook did not have much to offer democratic politics (indeed, he thought that democracy needed to be modified by the valorization of world-historical figures), but he thought powerfully about how to live in a pluralized society.

The third notebook in this series begins with an arresting analysis of contemporary Jewish life. Three forces, he writes, wrestle within all people: "The holy, the nation, humanity."[41] Modernity has whirled these three central dimensions of Jewish identity away from one another, each becoming the property of a party—nationalism, liberalism, and Orthodoxy, respectively —and they stubbornly refuse to be rejoined, because each fixates on the negative dimensions of the others. Yet all three dimensions are necessary, and each should appreciate the seemingly bad sides of the others, as well as their good sides. Ideally, liberals will grasp that the narrowness of nationalism comes from real love of one's community, and the zealousness of the Orthodox is rooted in a flaming desire for God. Liberals and the Orthodox will see that nationalists' placing solidarity above broader aspirations for universal ethics or transcendence arises from powerful, loving attachments to people and fellow feeling. Nationalists and the Orthodox in turn will see that liberals' preference for humanity over nationalism or religion is rooted in an ultimately divine perspective. The sacred, then, is the energy that synthesizes all three elements—religious com-

mitment, national identity, and ethical universalism—and a relationship to the All that lies beyond, before, and within them.

For Rav Kook, Orthodoxy has the inside track to holiness,
yet liberalism and nationalism are its ontological equals on
that journey. And he urged people to live a complex gesture, to
be actively tolerant while taking a genuine stand on behalf of
the ideals in which they truly believe, fighting for them in the
here and now. His political credo was something along these
lines: I should always recognize not only that my opponent is
human, but also that he has a piece of the truth that is unavail-
able to me. Secure in the rightness of my calling and in the
inevitable partiality of my vision, I proceed with faith in the
struggle itself and in its ultimate, harmonious resolution. These
ideas were not the fruit of theory, but the harvest of his very
real struggles with others and with himself.

Different lifeworlds course through Rav Kook's journals:
fidelity, rebellion, scholasticism, folk piety, romantic nationalism, ethical universalism, mystical experience, halakhic discipline, surging antinomianism, the exertions of intellect, and
the passionate religion of the heart. These he saw as his own
defining contradictions and those of his people, of all people
and times, manifestations of the immanent divine light hidden
in all the varied, jagged dimensions of existence, struggling to
join with the light of transcendence and be revealed:

> All the thoughts and ideas, the great desires, the awesome
> trials, that every tzaddik endures in his private self, the na-
> tion as a whole endures as well, and more broadly man in
> general, and more broadly the world, and all the worlds. . . .
> To the extent that he stands fast . . . becomes equal to the
> spirit of all worlds, and from his interiority takes in all, and
> the light comes to him from his darknesses so that he can
> truly survey the world from one end to the other, each one
> at his level, then he will see the greatness of God in strength

and joy, *and the path of the tzaddikim is like radiant light, ever brightening to the day* [Proverbs 4:18].[42]

The all-encompassing vision with which he tried to find the light in everything and, in so doing, to square a seemingly endless number of circles regularly left him on a knife-edge between despair and exhilaration, quickened by introspection into his own inadequacies. His critique and rewriting of traditional religious categories, especially repentance, extended to this inner work as well.

> One who grieves constantly for his sins and the sins of the world must constantly forgive and absolve himself and the whole world; and in so doing draw forgiveness and a light of loving-kindness onto all of being, and bring joy to God and to His creatures. He must first forgive himself, and afterward cast a broad forgiveness over all, the nearest to him first, on the branches of the roots of the soul, and on his family, his loved ones, his generation, and his world, and all worlds . . . And thus is revealed all the good that is hidden away in everything, and he attains the blessing of Abraham, since there is no generation in which his likeness does not emerge.[43]

His grief for his sins, as part of a world of sins, offers a paradoxical point of entry into the only thing that can offer relief—forgiveness. Not an abstract forgiveness, but acceptance of oneself, one's family and friends, world, time, and all times. He is, in this passage, undergoing a theurgic process, of human influence on the divine, and by mimesis in reverse, a human simulacrum of God's forgiveness, a great exhalation of forgiveness down below that brings about forgiveness from above—because it is itself the revelation of God's forgiveness, the grace of seeing God's light in all things. Sinfulness, then, is that which blocks the soul's natural ascent. Sin is an opacity thrust into a shaft of light.[44]

As the notebooks progress, and especially in late 1913 and early 1914, his view of the world and himself becomes increasingly expansive, straining against his and his world's limits while searching out the deep authenticity of each.

> *And I am in the midst of exile* [Ezekiel 1:1]. My inner, sub-jective I, whether of the individual or the public, cannot be revealed in its interiority other than in proportion to its ho-liness and purity, the supreme courage, soaked in the pure light of heavenly splendor that flames within it. We sinned, with our ancestors. Adam sinned, became alienated from his selfhood . . . He could not answer *where are you?* [Genesis 3:9] because he did not know himself, because his true "I" was lost to him by his sinful prostration to a foreign god. Israel sinned, *played the harlot to foreign gods* [Deuteronomy 31:16] . . . The earth sinned . . . followed goals and purposes, did not direct all its hidden strength to making the bark and the fruit taste the same . . . Learned educators . . . slake the thirsty with vinegar, stuff minds and hearts with everything that is external to them, and the "I" goes forgotten, and since there is no "I," there is no "I," and certainly no "You."[45]

Indeed, all morality, and even all the mitzvot, are an exercise in liberating the "I" and expressing the soul.[46] Yet the full expression of the soul is much more than morality and mitzvot can contain.

The third notebook of this series contains a series of extraordinary outbursts:

> Bolts of lightning will flash one after another in my soul, and my soul will ignite in flame after flame. The world will watch and wonder, contemplate and be astounded, rouse as if from sleep to the wonder of my light. And a new light will shine on Zion. People will come from afar and say "true!" *From Zion, the zenith of beauty, God will shine* [Psalms 50:2].[47]

He feels himself, in these throes of illumination, to be the microcosm of Israel and the voice of its collective, healing soul:

Our soul is very great, powerful, and majestic. It breaks iron walls, shatters mountains and hills. Infinitely wide it is, and must expand; it cannot contract. All our twelve million Israelite souls, at all ranks, in all their ascents and descents, all the mounts they have ascended and the valleys into which they have plunged, in all the city heights where they stand with head held high, in all the holes where they have hidden in *harsh degradation and humiliation, oppression and sorrow* [Psalms 107:39], our soul will spread in them all, embrace them all, revive and support them all, restore each one to the place of our house of life, *who are these flying like a cloud, like doves returning to their cotes* [Isaiah 60:8].[48]

And characteristically, this volcanic train of expression is, even if not quite checked, at least modified in midflight as this tidal expansion is channeled into the form of morality that through the Torah will shape the will: "We are full of moral feeling. We long to live life, a life of purity . . . And all those desires go unfulfilled without our inner and outer dedication to the light of God, the divine morality, revealed in the Torah, tradition, intellect, and righteousness."[49]

Maintaining the balance between structure and antistructure, the particular and the universal, the discipline of the law and the soaring of the spirit, the finite world and the infinitude of God, made for a constant struggle—perhaps his deepest one. At times, his exquisitely calibrated dialectic collapses into despair:

Who knows the depth of my sorrow, and who can imagine it? I am jailed in many straits, different boundaries, and my spirit longs for lofty spaces. *My soul thirsts for God* [Psalms 42:3] . . . All that is bounded is mundane compared to the supernal holy that I seek. *I am sick with love* [Song of Songs 2:5]. How hard it is for me to study, to adjust myself to details . . . *Unveil my eyes that I may look upon the wonders of your Torah* [Psalms 119:18].[50]

And in the paragraph immediately following, the veil indeed is lifted from his eyes:

> I see it with my eyes, the light of the life of Elijah rising . . .
> The holy in nature bursts its bounds and heads by itself to
> become one with the holy above nature, with the holy that is
> at war with nature . . . The Judaism of the past, from Egypt
> until now, was a long war with nature, with the nature of the
> world, with human nature, even the nature of the nation,
> and of every individual. We fought nature to defeat it, to
> discipline it in its own house. It has given in to us . . . Now
> we are drawing nearer to nature, and it is drawing near to us.
> It is conquered before us; its claims grow stronger with our
> noble* claims. The new generation, claiming its land, lan-
> guage, freedom, dignity, literature, strength, rightful posses-
> sion, and feelings, is borne along on a great flood of nature,
> whose inwardness is full of holy fire.[51]

The third notebook teems with gyrations as he tries to live
with this mounting vision of the unity of all things. So all-
encompassing are his visions that in them the blaze of the
holy fire coexists miraculously with the coolness and fecun-
dity of water: "Great rivers splash in my heart. Great and wide
fountains are opening before me."[52] At one point he seems
nearly to burst: "I am full of joy, full of greatness, full of lowliness, full of bitterness, full of grace, full of pleasure, full of love,
full of zealotry, full of anger, full of kindness, full of love for
all."[53]

He immediately reflects on this superhuman moment, and
seems almost shaken. His sense of greatness, he says, is but a
reflection of the godliness in his soul. The lowliness he feels is
his own, and is what he shares with all of humanity.

---

*The word that Rav Kook uses for *nobility*, *atzilut*, is also the Kabbalistic
word for *emanation*, the highest reality out of which the Sefirot emerge and
descend into finitude from the source of holiness.

My grandeur is of God. I take pride in the eternal God . . .
My lowliness sinks to the ground; poor am I and a cripple
of the spirit. I suffer within the pains of the world and its
afflictions, the poverty of its downtrodden poor, prisoners
of want, despairing of all hope, full of bitter venom in the
depths of their wounded hearts. A friend am I to the bitter
souls; I grieve with their grief. They are to be saved eter-
nally. The light of God will appear to them, and in His name
they will be exalted [after Psalms 89:18].[54]

In a closing reflection, aware of the sheer inexpressibility
and disorder of all that he is trying to say, he takes the measure
of his own inability to communicate.

Why can't I write the depth of my thoughts straightforwardly, without confusion, without overcomplication, but
words as they are, embodied in the order of their creation—
that is a hidden, deep mystery. The paths of life go round-
about, and the Holy Blessed One has made circuitous the
paths of the Torah . . . Yet we must fight the obstacles. . . .
*Look, I come with the scroll of the book written for me. To do what
pleases you, my God, I desire, and your Torah is in my guts. I proclaimed justice in a great assembly, Look I will not seal my lips, O
Lord, that you knew* [Psalms 40:8–10].[55]

The deeper he plumbed his own depths, the higher he vaulted
toward God, and the further and further he went from that
without which one cannot formulate law, theology, or even a
simple sentence, namely, structure:

Spaces, spaces, God-spaces, seeks my soul. Don't close me
in any cage, physical or spiritual. My soul sails in heavenly
spaces; walls of heart cannot contain her, nor walls of action, morals, logic, or manners. Above them all she sails and
flies, above anything that can be named, above every pleasure,
every grace and beauty, above every thing exalted and sublime, *I am sick with love* [Song of Songs 2:5].[56]

Rav Kook is tragically aware that this very exaltation, this very ascent, is what makes him and his furthest-reaching ideas ultimately inaccessible.

There is, of course, one kind of vision that is both the highest sort one can imagine and yet communicable in its very essence, both personal and collective, and that is prophecy. Rav Kook sought to revive it, sensing it in the air—though as the semiprophecy traditionally called *Ruach Ha-Kodesh*, the holy spirit, hovering in the ether of consciousness between the human and the divine. And at times, it seems, he felt that he and his time were close to it, a realization that scared and electrified him in equal measure. Sometime in early 1914, he wrote: "And I listen and hear from the depths of my soul, from the feelings of my heart: the voice of God is calling. And I am gripped with terrible fear. Have I stooped so low as to be a false prophet, *to say 'God has sent me'* [Isaiah 48:16] *and the word of God has not been revealed to me?* [after I Samuel 3:7]. And I hear the voice of my soul astir, stubbles of prophecies are sprouting, and the sons of prophets awake."[57] It is perhaps prophecy that will sidestep tradition's inability to deal with these unprecedented modern times. The raw, revivifying encounter with nature will find its verbal correlative in the rough-hewn idiom of the Bible and restore revelation: "To the fount of prophecy we are being called. Parched and thirsty we are, *but a garden fount, source of living waters* [after Song of Songs 4:15], lies before us . . . Winds are flowing and blowing from the wind of the messiah, and they are headed for us."[58]

Rav Kook knew that in his notebooks lay the fullest expression of his ideas, if such a thing were possible, and in 1914 he decided to publish one of them, as is. Since coming to Jaffa, he regularly had asked others, often his son, Zvi Yehudah, to edit his writings before publication. Zvi Yehudah was in Germany, at Binyamin Menashe Levin's suggestion, teaching in Halberstadt and studying philosophy. On May 25, 1914, Rav Kook wrote to his son: "I've been overpowered by a desire to publish some of my notes as is, and have begun to do so . . . under the title *'Arpilei Tohar* [The Mists of Purity]. . . . I hope that they as they are, with no prettifying or reworking, will also be for a blessing. Maybe they will be even better precisely for the absence of reworking, *warm bread, freshly taken away* [I Samuel 21:7]."[59]

"Mists of purity," taken from the Rosh Hashanah liturgy, is a reference to the fog into which Moses entered in order to encounter God and receive His Torah (Exodus 19:18). Rav Kook knew that his writing would appear foggy to the reader, and perhaps even to himself. But the fog of his writing is the meeting place for the new revelation. Zvi Yehudah wrote to his father that perhaps this was not the best idea, but Rav Kook proceeded anyway. In the end, the publisher had managed to typeset only the first eighty or so pages by midsummer 1914.

One staggering feature of Rav Kook's journals is that he wrote and recorded these far-reaching ideas and stunning religious experiences while fully engaged in a very busy public life as both communal leader and rabbinic authority. He wrote these revelations on days when his official duties included rendering halakhic opinions, allocating charitable funds, teaching, negotiating with the communal heads of Jaffa, meeting an endless stream of visitors. The crush of his responsibilities came to a head in the summer of 1914, when he was accused by the town council of organizing a slate of candidates to run against them in upcoming elections. He wrote to Zvi Yehudah, in a letter dated June 8, 1914, of his sheer exasperation with the endless petty clamor he sensed all around him, in which he strained to hear the voice of revelation: "I flee momentarily from the suffocating vapor of the picayune matters that push and stress people . . . And yet are they so small? Is there a way to measure the spirit and all these different standpoints, the cries from the depths of the heart with which each declaims his justice—don't we see in this base rumbling a sacred discourse? . . . Is there not radiant light in this darkness?"[60]

In that same letter he discusses an invitation to a conference in Frankfurt organized by Agudat Yisrael. Founded in 1912 by German Orthodox activists and intellectuals, the Agudah was an attempt by non- and anti-Zionist Orthodoxy to use modern techniques of organization and influence in its running battle with the excesses of modernity. Even this moderate form of organizational sophistication was for some too great a concession to the spirit of the times, and a number of ultra-Orthodox groups, Hasidim in particular, denounced Agudat Yisrael as a particularly insidious form of acculturation. Rav Kook was reluctant to leave the Land of Israel, where he had lived uninterruptedly for ten years. Yet he hoped that he could bring to the Agudah some of what he had learned in that decade, no matter how petty and irritating he found so many of his tasks from day to day. Further, his wife was not well, and her doctors urged them both to get away.

On June 28, he wrote Zvi Yehudah that they had decided to go to Frankfurt, with a stop first in Karlsbad. Rav Kook and Rivka set sail for Europe in the last week of July 1914.

4

The Gruesome Rites of Spring: St. Gallen, London, and the Great War

In a vision, every energy is rising . . . Whatever is
in every atom, even the smallest, in the least quiver,
and all the more so in every organism, every sprout
and every living thing, all go and flow, everything
is rising . . . Every inner explorer, every faithful
poet, each listener with the Holy Spirit meets
all of existence in its ascents, all the more
man, all the more nations and their souls,
all the more whole worlds, and utterly all
the more so, all the worlds and beings.
—Avraham Yitzhak Kook, *Shemonah Kevatzim* and
Orot Ha-Kodesh

THE KOOKS ARRIVED IN GERMANY exhausted from their
journey. In Berlin, physicians suggested that Rivka stay for
some medical treatment and that her husband take the waters

at Willingen before proceeding to the Agudat Yisrael conference in Frankfurt. Upon learning of the outbreak of World War I while in Willingen, he returned to Berlin.

They were among many stranded by the war. On a tram in Berlin, the Kooks met and befriended a younger, and very impressive, Talmudist from Lithuania, Yechiel Ya'akov Weinberg. On hearing of the younger man's difficult financial straits, Rav Kook turned to his wife, who held their wallet, and asked her to give most of their money away, over the young man's protests. People knew the Kooks and would take care of them, the rabbi assured the young scholar, but he too would be famous one day, but was yet unknown and should not go hungry.*

Easy return to Palestine was out of the question, and the Kooks faced internment as Russian nationals. They set out for neutral Switzerland, via Kissingen, where a local rabbi's intervention prevented their internment, and by the fall they were in Zurich. Zvi Yehudah had met his parents in Berlin, but it took him several months to leave Germany and rejoin them.

Meanwhile, there was no written communication with anyone they had left behind in Palestine. They made contact with others stuck in Europe and trying to make their way back, all to no avail. The Kooks turned to the Turkish consul in Bern, who replied that he had no intention of facilitating travel by nationals of the Russian enemy. Rav Kook busied himself in Zurich by teaching a daily Talmud class to the locals.

The Kooks eventually found refuge in St. Gallen, a textile center near Lake Constance in northeastern Switzerland. Its small Jewish community, one thousand residents out of a total population of fifty thousand to seventy thousand, was composed of established Western bourgeois and more recently arrived Eastern Europeans. One was Abraham Kimche, a successful businessman who had visited Jaffa and been deeply moved

*He was right. Yechiel Ya'akov Weinberg is now universally recognized as one of the greatest and most creative halakhists of the twentieth century.

by Rav Kook. He undertook to support the Kooks and found them an apartment on St. Leonhard Street, with a view of the Appenzell Alps.

As autumn turned to winter, it became clear that Rav Kook, his wife, and son were in Europe for the war's duration. The news all around was dire—the war itself, and the violence and starvation it was inflicting on Jewish communities from Poland to Jaffa and Jerusalem. He wrote letter after letter to anyone in Europe or America whom he thought could transmit financial assistance to Jaffa, with little success. He was in many ways an outsider where the relief and political organizations were concerned. For their part, Orthodox businessmen he met in Switzerland told him that what they had heard of the heresies and impieties abounding in Jaffa left them with little desire to send monies and run the risk of contravening Swiss neutrality.

In a cruel irony, Rav Kook's forcible wartime separation from home and most of his family gave him at last the time for the kind of study and contemplation that he had so often longed for in Jaffa. He kept up his correspondence, addressing missives to anyone he could think of who might be able to direct financial assistance to his community in Jaffa, where people were hungry and institutions were crumbling. And he wrote furiously in his notebooks, still trying to work through large questions of metaphysics and theology, the meaning of the times through which he was living, and the relations among them.

August 1, the day that Germany declared war on Russia and that France had begun to mobilize, was also the ninth day of the month of Av, a central date in the Jewish calendar. The Ninth of Av is a fast day commemorating the destruction of the Temples, the Crusades, expulsion from Spain, and the history of Jewish suffering overall—and, in rabbinic tradition, the birth date of the Messiah.

Many were caught up in the exhilaration of the early stages of the war, which unleashed energies all around. In late September 1914, Martin Buber, then a celebrant of pure experience, *erlebnis*, wrote a friend that ideally as a result of the war, "might and spirit would become one."[1] A few weeks later he wrote to another friend, a pacifist, that war with its horrors is "a fearful grace, the grace of a new birth." Hermann Cohen, the leading Jewish philosophical rationalist, likewise saw the war as a chance for the victory of Germanism, the idea of Germany, which for him was the apotheosis of moral autonomy and ethical universalism, and thus Judaism's twin.

Buber and Cohen each drank deep from the well of fin de siècle German thought: for Cohen, humanistic neo-Kantianism; for Buber, *lebensphilosophie*, the celebration of vitality and experience as the very glue of life and the portal to meaning. Rav Kook, in his way, drank deep too; early in the war, amid his own desperate circumstances and while trying to make sense of the colossal events all around, he thought, or hoped, that he was witnessing the stirrings of a new and better world.

> When there is a great war in the world, the energy of the Messiah wakes. *The time of zamir has come* [Song of Songs 2:12],* *the pruning of tyrants* [Zohar 1:1a, based on Isaiah 25:5]. The wicked are being swept from the world, the world is becoming fragrant, *and the voice of the turtledove is heard in our land* [Song of Songs 2:12]. The individuals unjustly swept away in the revolutionary churning of the flow of war bear an element of *the atoning death of the righteous* [Jerusalem Talmud Yoma 1:1] . . . and the greater the war, in quantity and quality, the greater the anticipation of the messianic steps it bears.[2]

And the war, calamitous as it was, would deepen the Jewish people's responsibility for the world.

Zamir is translatable as "pruning" or "nightingale."

The world structure currently in the midst of collapse, amid
the dreadful storms of the bloody sword, requires the building of the Jewish nation, which is one with the revelation of
its spirit, and one with the disintegrating world structure,
which is awaiting a force full of unity and a higher spirit . . .
World culture totters, the human spirit is weakened, darkness covers all the peoples, *night covers the earth, and mists,
the nations* [Isaiah 60:2]. And the hour has come . . . All the
world's cultures will be renewed by the renewal of our spirit
. . . Abraham's blessing to all the peoples of the world will
begin its work, and on that foundation there will begin anew
our building in Eretz Yisrael. The current destruction will
prepare a new rebirth, deep and transforming.[3]

Rav Kook was in St. Gallen for almost a year and a half,
and in that time he wrote in his notebooks almost as much as
he had written in the previous four years. Themes central to his
Jaffa years—the tzaddik, the souls of chaos, sacred heresy, the
transformation of nature—receded for much of the war, and
others came to the fore.

The conflict between the legist and mystic, the jurist and
the poet, had been with him for years. Once freed of all communal responsibilities (aside from his Talmud class in Zurich
and answering written queries), his longing for something beyond the law could be given freer, but not yet full, rein. The
pull of antinomianism, which had always been at work on him,
most obviously in his embrace of the secular radicals and revolutionaries, was checked not only by his own rabbinic identity
but also by his coming to see the root of contemporary evil, of
the war convulsing the world, precisely in the great antinomian
dispensation, Christianity. During this period, Rav Kook wrote
on Christianity more—and more harshly—than ever before or
after. He took greater pains to distinguish gentile culture and
religion from that of Israel. The Jews he loved so fiercely were
suffering terribly in Eastern Europe and Palestine, while his

own more radical ideas skirted the edges of the antinomianism on which he blamed the war.

He came to see the war as the most vivid enactment imaginable of God's alienation from this fallen world. The exile of the divine presence spoken of in rabbinic literature and the Kabbalah is no delicate metaphor, but a horror. Once the horror was past, the "natural faith" that Israel shares with the rest of humanity would assert itself. Indeed, Israel was the only nation able to grasp universal religious truth as a nation, and to actualize that vision in its terrestrial, collective life.

At times, Rav Kook's writing about the war is deeply disturbing—in his seeing a redemptive end in the terrible suffering of the war, a sentiment that would not have been much comfort to the dead and maimed in the trenches. His relentless valorization of the Jewish people is hard to take, as is his laying so much more of the blame on the church rather than on nationalism. He was perhaps saved from his own excesses precisely by his contradictions, by the universalism that presses against his particularism, by his being driven against his own mystic ecstasy again and again back to ethics and the law.

At times he saw his own exile, just on the cusp of redemption, as part of the drama of the times. His alienation from the matter-spirit apotheosis that is the Land of Israel retrospectively sharpened his understanding of how transformative his encounter with the land had been. It also led him to see this current detour as the painful, penultimate clarification of the land's charisma.

In early 1915, he received a letter from a despondent Ya'akov Moshe Charlap, who did not even have Rav Kook's address. (The letter came to him via the Red Cross.) "What can I say, what can I speak, since his light has departed, his majestic splendor gone afar, the whole world is covered in mist, *and I, where am I to go?* [Genesis 3:30]."[4] To Charlap's mind, while Rav Kook's departure had not caused the current global catastrophe, it certainly had made it possible. "When the exalted tzaddik, master of understanding and insight, reaches the Land of Israel, the entire world grasps a different form, and especially the Land of Israel." The tzaddik embodies and teaches the divine light irradiating the world. Because he teaches, correlates with, and catalyzes the fusion of body and spirit that is the Land of Israel, his presence energizes all around him and transforms all who choose to hear him. But when events conspire to take the tzaddik abroad and alienate him from the land, "the great visions are all stopped up, great confusions descend upon the world, *and people devour one another* [Mishnah Avot 3:2]."

Rav Kook answered him on February 3. His distancing from the Holy Land, he said, was, like everything, from God, "until He will reveal and show us His redemption . . . I am for now, *a prisoner of hope* [Zechariah 9:12] thirsting for deliverance, *a yearning soul in a land waste and parched* [after Psalms 63:2]."[5] He continued, in a passage bristling with Kabbalistic allusions, that he found himself contending with the metaphysical alienation operating in the dimension of space, which encases all that is outside the Land of Israel. That is the dark potency, the wedge of alienation that makes nations arrogant and seduces them into their own destruction. The deep humility embodied in the Land of Israel is precisely the cure for humanity's alienation from God, and for human beings' alienation from one another. All he could make out at the moment were dim shadows, he said, but he could discern the outlines.

In the enforced leisure of Switzerland, he could give his most radical ideas free rein. He meditated on spiritualized law, a nomian spirituality based in the Talmudic distinction between halakha—Jewish law—and Aggadah—nonlegal tales, interpretations, visions—which he saw as a matter not merely of genre and curriculum, but also of divergent, complementary religious sensibilities. "Halakha and Aggadah must be unified with each other, be studied together, and spiritually be unified," he wrote.[6] Of course, by Aggadah he meant not merely the nonlegal portions of Talmud but also the spiritual, literary, affective, and ideational dimensions of religion not captured by the idea of law: "The idea of bringing far-flung worlds closer together is the cornerstone on which the spiritual world is built, and bettered,"[7] whereas the alienation of law and Aggadah "yields a sick disjunction."[8] The creativity and fluidity of one must be joined to the order and structure of the other.

The dialectic of Halakha and Aggadah, of nomos and pneuma, of structure and antistructure, is not necessarily peculiar to Israel, but felt by all humanity. In a strikingly subversive bit of exegesis, he writes, the sin of the biblical Korah and his band was not their rebellion against Moses, but their attempt to transfigure the law before their time; "who in the future, will rise, as will all who fell from a surfeit of desire, a longing for ascent before its time."[9]

It was, he came to conclude, a latter day version of Korah's rebellion that was most responsible for the current, cruel war.

Christianity had, in different ways, been on his mind for some time. In his writings of the 1890s, he offered mild criticisms, not much different from others voiced by moderate Jewish thinkers of the time—for instance, that Christianity errs in thinking that right beliefs unaccompanied by right action can suffice for salvation. Shortly before leaving Boisk, in 1904, he had written an extraordinary reflection seemingly referring to Jesus as a potentially messianic figure who was disastrously misunderstood by the jurists of his time.[10] Two years later, he penned an article in which he wrote that Jesus was a great, tragically undisciplined soul overcome by his own spiritual élan vital.[11] That same year, he wrote in his book *Eder Ha-Yakar*, echoing Nietzsche, that the problem with Christianity was precisely a crippling absence of spiritual élan vital. In other words, Jesus—and this was a compliment—was no Christian. In a letter to his young disciple Moshe Zeidel in 1904, he had straightforwardly accepted the view of the thirteenth-century Provencal authority Menachem Ha-Meiri that fundamentally civilized and God-fearing societies are not to be considered idolatrous, including, he added, contemporary gentiles. Yet he immediately offered a barbed comment on what to his mind was a failed attempt by Christian ethics to inculcate high spiritual teachings among "masses who are unfit to receive them": "Under the veil of 'love thy neighbor,' pyres were erected to burn men who were of blameless morality."[12]

A decade later, trying to make sense of the calamity of global war, he focused less on issues of statecraft or the balance of power, which scarcely ever interested him, and more on what he thought were the underlying spiritual forces at work. While a conventional Orthodox rabbi would have blamed the secular revolutionary spirit of the age, the chief culprit that came into view for him was Christianity, against whom he waged, in his notebooks and in his mind, a furious, Nietzschean assault for its morbid despair of the world. He fixated in particular on two facets of Christian doctrine as he understood them: antinomianism, the principled rejection of the law in favor of love, most famously expressed by St. Paul; and the call to "render unto Caesar" (Matthew 22:21), which implicitly divorced the world of power from divine writ and moral responsibility. Both doctrines, to him, were rooted in the refusal to believe that the material world could be redeemed on its own terms. And that refusal lay at the root of the world's, and God's, current sufferings.*
Christianity's refusal to believe that holiness is to be found in this

*Interestingly, the pope at the time might have agreed in part. In the first encyclical of his papacy, *Ad Beatissimi Apostolorum*, issued on November 1, 1914, Benedict XV referred to the war, even at that early stage, as "the suicide of civilized Europe." He blamed the war on the absence of love and compassion, on the proliferation of materialism, on growing class and nationalist divisions, and on disregard for authority, which were, to his mind, related to the divorce of political from ecclesiastical authority. He urged a return to Thomism and doctrines of natural law.

world, its handing the world over unto Caesar—those ideas had
made possible, and perhaps even encouraged, the world war that
was plunging the divine presence into the very depths.

Early in the war, he called Christianity, "a halfway despair
over evil itself and evil and its own self-control, handing over
the material and the social world . . . to save with this despair
the interiority of life, the good side. This is the Christian longing."[13] (Halfway, in contrast to what he saw as Buddhism's
braver, though still misguided, thoroughgoing renunciation of
this world.) As the violence progressed, and his own rage with
it, he saw the Christian abandonment of the world as downright demonic, and the gravest heresy of all.

> *Minut* [the Talmudic term for Christianity] abandoned the
> law, planted itself in the imagined attribute of mercy and
> kindness, which destabilizes the world and destroys it . . .
> and thus is founded hatred among nations, the deep evil of
> the bloodshed that defiles, without even relieving the yoke
> on mankind's neck.[14]

The fatal weakness of Christianity had spread through all of
so-called civilization, and the mounting slaughter was the aw-
ful payment for the "machines of culture" and "their glorying
in ringing lies":

> *The sin stains deep* [Jeremiah 2:22], the blood-spilling nations,
> wanton earthly kings *make the earth shudder* [Isaiah 14:16], *the
> land cannot be cleansed of the bloodshed within it, but by the blood
> of him that shed it* [Numbers 35:33] and the atonement must
> come, a general undoing of all the cultured nations of today,
> with all their lies and deceit, all their evil contamination and
> serpentine poison . . . The spiritual and practical fabric that
> in its contemporary form could not stop, with all its beauti-
> ful wisdom, the great, great bloodshed and the destruction
> of the world in this dreadful way has shown itself to be putrid
> at the root . . . And so all the contemporary cultures will ut-
> terly be destroyed, and on their embers will be established

a universal edifice in truth and the knowledge of God. *The mount of God's house will stand firm above the mountains and tower over the hills* [Isaiah 2:2].[15]

He increasingly wrote of a universal alternative to Christianity, which he called "natural faith," a substrate of spiritual yearning shared by people of goodwill everywhere—not a delicate aesthetic, but a powerful lust for life.

> It is natural religiosity that we seek . . . This thirst does not leave us, nor the entire human race, nor any living thing or creature . . . In its first natural, essential form it rocks the world . . . It summons terror, destruction, war, revolution, illness, rot . . . And natural repentance comes from knocking at the door, the world returns to its root . . . Arrogant hearts are subdued, the evil abandon their evil, *they have surrendered, and I shall destroy them not* [2 Chronicles 12:7]. In natural religiosity is a great mixture of good and evil, light and shadows. We are called to take the natural root from the depth of its foundation, elevate and raise it as an offering to God.[16]

When he seems to attain that universal revelation, coming after the unimaginably complex dialectics of sacred history and his own internal gyrations, his prose exudes a stunning simplicity:

> The foundation of happiness is the love of truth in the mind, the love of righteousness in life, the love of beauty in sentiment, the love of good in action. And every man builds himself truth, righteousness, beauty, and goodness by himself by his own measure. And all of them, all these virtues of every single person, come together in one great treasure in which all the truth, righteousness, beauty, and good are ordered. With this, one attains both the free knowledge of God, full of holiness, and lucid piety.[17]

The war was a great and terrible purgation—and the very embodiment of *Galut Ha-Shekhinah*, as the Talmud called the exile of God's presence from the world, which was, for the

Kabbalah, His cleavage within Himself. For Rav Kook, such a terrible catharsis was accompanied by agony: "Those sparks of holiness still sunk in the deep fathoms of evil compel the scream felt in the body . . . So long as one must raise his sparks from the depths, screaming befits man. And there are tzaddikim who scream to God for the sorrow of the world . . . the sorrow of the Shekhinah as a whole, screaming in its pangs, like a gazelle as it gives birth."[18]

He saw, at times, a future union of Jew and gentile at a cosmic level, gentiles embodying, in Kabbalistic terminology, the surrounding light, and Israel, the inner light of the world: "In the elevation of the world, the two lights will be joined, and all the surrounding light will enter into the inner light, that is, all that transcends boundaries will be acquired by the immanent selfhood *to be drawn into the body of the King* [Zohar 1:217b], the foundation of all desires."[19] And at times he seemed to feel that unity in himself:

> We love all, and a double love for every pure soul in any place, in every nation and tongue, every corner and faith . . . We have mercy on all the creatures. We see all the souls yearning for the good, truth, and purity, yearning in their very depths, but their feet are caught in the net, and they await redemption. Every good will strongly beating in all, every true God seeker, every *Tzadik Yesod Olam*,* wherever he is found, revealed or hidden, is a constant redeemer of the souls of all creatures, he is the Messiah of the God of Jacob.[20]

The Messiah is the revelation of the ultimate unity of the spiritual search of all humanity, Jew and Gentile alike.

The climate—physical and spiritual—of Switzerland could not have been more different than that of Jaffa, but there were

---

*The *Tzadik Yesod Olam*, it bears remembering, is the "foundational tzaddik of the world," identified in Kabbalah with the ninth Sefirah, and thus the channel of spiritual energies into the world.

David Cohen Ha-Nazir, university student in Basel, 1916. Photo
courtesy of the Nezer David Foundation, Jerusalem.

searchers there too. One of them came to play a large role in
his life and afterward.

David Cohen (Kagan) was born in 1886 near Vilna. A Talmudic prodigy and restless soul, he left home early and wan-
dered from yeshiva to yeshiva. At Radin (in White Russia),
he studied with the legendary scholar and saint Israel Meir

Kagan, known as the Chafetz Chaim, perhaps the purest exemplar of Lithuanian Mitnagdic piety. At Volozhin, Cohen began the philosophical reading that subsequently led to his expulsion from the Mussar stronghold of Slabodka. He was twice detained by the police as a suspected revolutionary.

After attending a St. Petersburg institution for academic Jewish studies, he headed, in 1913, to the University of Freiburg to study philosophy. During wartime, the Jews of Frankfurt arranged for Cohen and a number of other foreign intellectuals (including Nahum Goldmann and Yechezkel Kaufmann) to be interned together in a pension in Bad Nauheim. Cohen forged a deep tie with another internee, a Hasidic mystic named Menachem Mendel Neu of Sandomir, and he took upon himself the practices of a Nazirite, growing his hair and abstaining from wine. After friends secured his release, Cohen made his way to Basel, where he taught in a Jewish school, resumed his philosophical studies at the university, and founded an association of religious students.

Cohen had been reading Rav Kook over the years, and while his own training and predilections leaned to the neo-Kantianism of Hermann Cohen, his internment sealed his Zionist, mystic, and messianic longings. When friends with business interests in St. Gallen offered to arrange a meeting between him and Rav Kook, he jumped at the chance. In late June 1915, on the traditional fast of the Seventeenth of Tammuz, he wrote to Kook, asking to meet "as a submissant and student . . . and though the vessels be unready to receive God's blessing, I come to purify myself."[21]

Rav Kook was unnerved by the sheer intensity of Cohen's request. A month later, Zvi Yehudah wrote to Cohen that he was welcome, though his father was uncertain about what exactly it was that Cohen hoped to study or what he could teach him. Zvi Yehudah added that, for his part, obstacles and delays themselves strengthen spiritual longings and help burst the bonds of convention. Rav Kook added in his own hand: "Though I'm unsure whether I might sate [your] spiritual thirst at all, it would nonetheless be a pleasure for me" if they were to meet.[22]

Cohen made his way to Basel in the second week of August 1915, hoping, it seems, that his years of spiritual wandering might finally be coming to an end. He performed a ritual immersion in the waters of the Rhine and, a treatise of Lurianic Kabbalah in hand, went to St. Gallen. From Cohen's journal, it seems that on his arrival, Rav Kook wanted to talk with the intriguingly bohemian yeshiva *bochur* about his university studies —but for that, Cohen had his professors. Hoping for something more, he lay restless until morning, when he heard Rav Kook praying, and then Cohen found what he had been looking for: "In bed, my heart knew no rest. My life's fate hung in the balance. And then it was early in the morning and I heard steps to and fro, in the morning blessings . . . in a supreme song and melody . . . and I listened, and I was turned upside down and became a different man. After the prayer I hurried to convey by letter that I had found more than I had hoped, I had found a master and rabbi."[23]

Cohen returned to Basel and wrote Rav Kook a week later. Thanks to their meeting, he wrote, he finally had grasped that humility was the cardinal virtue, not only in morals but also in theology, "since only that which has nothing in his own world, can attain the higher existence."[24] Rav Kook answered that, yes, he had indeed grasped that humility is the necessary condition of all true creativity, since all creativity emerges from what preceded it, which ultimately, of course, is God: "Thus man comes to see himself as one spark continuously flashing from the vigorous light of the sun, and all of life is sparks, sparks flashing from this light."[25]

Cohen maintained a correspondence with Rav Kook and Zvi Yehudah. Back at the University of Freiburg, he threw himself into the students' association, organizing and delivering lectures. During the day, he attended classes on natural science and studied the history of music and philosophy. At night, he plowed in singsong through *Etz Chaim*, the foundational text of Lurianic Kabbalah.

Living in exile intensified Rav Kook's longing for the Land of Israel and made clear in retrospect just what living there had meant to him and what it had taught him. The very words *Eretz Yisrael* became more talismanic for him than ever before, the very name, the cry of a shipwrecked lover.

> The heart longs for the comprehension of Eretz Yisrael, the faith of Eretz Yisrael, the sanctity of Eretz Yisrael. Where do we find the joy of Eretz Yisrael, the inner tranquility of Eretz Yisrael, the *unio mystica* of Eretz Yisrael, the truth of Eretz Yisrael, the vigor and courage of Eretz Yisrael, the security of Eretz Yisrael? O God, take pity, mercy, merciful and gracious God, have compassion, and make me worthy to return to You in perfect repentance, and return me to Your beloved land, make me worthy, let me share in the joy of Your people, to rejoice in Your people, Your legacy, Your legacy people. Have mercy, mercy, merciful father, please have pity, O redeem, redeemer God.[26]

As the end of his stay in Switzerland drew near, the formulations in his notebooks began to come together. Finally, the metaphysical status of the Land of Israel became crystal clear to him: "Eretz Yisrael is no extraneous thing, an extrinsic property of the nation, some means toward general unity and the maintenance of its physical or even spiritual existence. Eretz Yisrael is a thing in itself, bound in a living tie with the nation, embracing its very existence by its unique internal grace. And so one cannot grasp the substance of the unique sanctity of Eretz Yisrael, nor actualize its depth of affection—only by the divine spirit that is upon the nation as a whole, in the natural spiritual impress that is in the soul of Israel."[27]

What is the unique quality of the Land of Israel? It is "the sanctification of every mundane thing in the world." In Kabbalistic terms, the Land of Israel is identified with the divine presence, the Shekhinah, as well as with the Oral Torah, and is thus the very meeting point of God and the world, and is itself the stuff of revelation. Joined to all these synonyms for the Land in the richly suggestive language of the Kabbalah is Knesset Yisrael, the sacred community of Israel. In this densely allusive network of ideas, the concept of exile takes on new meaning. Israel's exile from the Land was part of the alienation of the eternal, unchanging written law from the vibrant, responsive oral law. These alienations—of People, Land, and Torah—all in turn reflect the divine presence's fundamental homelessness in the world—a metaphysical catastrophe whose horrific result was the slaughter of the trenches.

> Knesset Yisrael screams in its bonds: Woe am I, my soul is weary . . . The wise of heart arise at midnight, hands on their loins like women in labor: for the sorrow of the world, of Israel, of the Shekhinah, of Torah, they weep and wail. And they know the depth of the sorrow in its fount and origin, that all the sorrows and darkness, all the rivers and streams of spilled blood . . . are nothing but a faint result of the echo of the higher sorrow, of heaven, of the Shekhinah.[28]

Knesset Yisrael's universal counterpart is natural faith, the antidote to the destructive dimensions of nationalism. By contrast, gentile nationalism and collectivity is premised on alienation, among and within nations, and inescapably leads to violence. The rare individuals draw their sustenance not from their individual nationalities, but from the soul of humanity as a whole.[29]

At times, Rav Kook glimpsed a vision of universal harmony in which the orders of being—from individual to Israel to humanity to the cosmos and beyond—nestled in concentric circles.

> There is one who sings the song of his soul, and in his own soul finds all . . . And there is one who sings the song of the nation, who cleaves with gentle love to Knesset Yisrael as a whole, and sings her song with her, grieves for her sorrows and delights in her hopes . . . And there is one whose soul expands farther beyond the bound of Israel, to sing the song of man . . . And there is one whose spirit expands and ascends even higher, to the point of unity with all creation, with all creatures and all worlds, and sings with them all . . . And there is one who ascends above all these songs in a single union, and all sound their voices . . . The song of the self, of the nation, of man, of the world—all come together within him at every time, in every hour. And this perfection in all its fullness ascends and becomes a sacred song, God's song, Israel's song . . . Yisrael, shir-El, Godsong, a simple song, doubled, tripled, quadrupled, *the Song of Songs of Shlomo* [Song of Songs 1:1], *The King to Whom Peace, Shalom, belongs* [Shir Ha-Shirim Rabbah, 3:1(6), Vilna ed.].[30]

In early November 1915, Rav Kook received an invitation to serve as rabbi of the Machzikei Hadath congregation in London, home to traditional Orthodox immigrants from eastern Europe. The synagogue was apart from, but not athwart, organized Anglo Jewry and its chief rabbi, Joseph Hertz, a man of wide Jewish and secular learning and magnanimous disposition. Rav Kook was glad to receive the invitation. He was uneasy in St. Gallen, living on Abraham Kimche's unstinting generosity and peripheral to the great events all around him, and he wanted to get off the sidelines.

That same month, he entered into an intense correspondence with Shlomo Zalman Pines, a rabbi and scholar in Zurich, on the question whether there is an affirmative halakhic obligation to put one's own life at risk for the public good. Pines thought yes, but Rav Kook demurred, citing the long-settled halakhic presumption, a wary result of centuries of powerlessness, against endangering oneself, even for the sake of another or the community. Pines then asked Rav Kook a novel question, stimulated by modern politics: whether, to his mind, "the Jewish people" formed, in matters of politics and policy, a corporate body and legal category in its own right, perhaps thereby ringing its own changes on settled halakhic rules. Answering at length, Rav Kook suggested that collective self-help could fall under the Talmudic category of "the king's law"—extra-halakhic actions undertaken by the authorities for the sake of public order and justice, the prerogative for which lay with the nation. In the end, he concluded, if the survival of the collective Jewish people were at stake, one would be permitted not only to be killed but also, however provisionally, and as a matter of discretion but not of law, to kill.

Pines, who earlier in their correspondence had argued the permissibility of individual self-sacrifice, replied that it was inconceivable for divine providence to shape history so as to make Jewish collective survival dependent on violence. Rav Kook responded with great erudition, courtesy, and unmistakable vehemence: "The Jewish people . . . are the foundation of the entire Torah,"[31] and if they could survive only by doing that which otherwise was forbidden—just as a surgeon can save a patient only by inflicting violence of his own—then that necessity and the actions taken in response would themselves be the workings of Providence, whose seeming contradictions only God can understand. He then related traditional monarchy to modern notions of sovereignty. "It seems," he wrote, "that when there is no king, inasmuch as the king's laws also pertain to the general state of the nation, those legal rights revert to the nation as a whole."[32] Elected leaders agreed upon by the consent of the nation as a whole, ruling in the land and bearing the approval of the rabbinical court, could assume the right and responsibility of sovereignty, including the use of force.

Pines and Rav Kook exchanged further animated but friendly letters on the subject. Their correspondence closed in late January 1916, a few days before Rav Kook's departure for London. He wrote in conclusion: "We trust in God that He will so protect His people and His pious that we never come to this pass and never, God forbid, have need of these [violent] means."[33] At the outset of their exchange, Rav Kook had articulated a classic rabbinic quietism by which nothing was more important than preserving human life in the instant. Yet in the course of their argument, something shifted: as Rav Kook recognized the need to make room in the law for self-sacrifice when necessary for the commonweal, there unfolded before him a new view of the commons, the Jewish public sphere. There the people, with appropriate safeguards and even in the absence of the Temple and in conditions of modern life, could themselves bestow sovereignty and give a commoner, their designated representative, the authority of a king.

The Kooks arrived in London on January 28, 1916, and moved into lodgings provided by Mendel Chaikin, a Chabad Hasid and vintner. Rav Kook's synagogue, Machzikei Hadath, was on Brick Lane in the East End. He wasted no time in plunging into the work of the communal rabbinate once again, teaching classes, visiting the sick, and answering halakhic queries. (The congregation raised his modest salary when they learned of his habit of reimbursing housewives whenever he ruled that one of their chickens was unkosher.)

On arrival, he became the leading rabbinic figure of England's eastern European Orthodox community. A stranger to established Anglo Jewry, he found himself bumping up against settled ways. After signing one rabbinic ordination after another to save young men from conscription, he was called in for questioning by Scotland Yard; police investigators had noticed that many of his "rabbis" were in fact not religiously observant. He was let off with a stern warning but kept on, unimpressed by invocations of the moral significance of the British war effort. So long as people go on eating meat, he told a British Jew who chose not to avail himself of the military exemptions available to his sons, there is no hope for the human animal—until the Messiah comes.[34]

Late in the day on Saturdays, Rav Kook would hold *seudah shlishit*—the third meal of the Sabbath—in the Hasidic style, with singing and evocative homilies. The meals brought him an eclectic group of followers: Hasidim and intellectuals, East End Jewish radicals, workingmen, pious Jews from Leeds and Manchester as well as from all over London. On the Shavuot holiday nights, as he had in Jaffa, he would stand all night at a lectern, lecturing on Maimonides' *Book of the Commandments* and the roots of jurisprudence. During zeppelin bombings, he would stand by the door of the communal bomb shelter in Chaikin's basement, the better to see anyone wandering in the street and call them in. When all were safely inside, he would, in a mix of prayer and pastoral becalming, sit and recite, over and over, the six verses of Psalm 43: *Grant me justice, O God, and wage my struggle with a faithless nation, from a man of deceit and injustice save me . . .*

It was an exhausting life, but he was happier than in St. Gallen. In the late summer of 1917, he wrote Zvi Yehudah of how, on his return to London from a brief stay at a medicinal spa in Harrogate, he was "engulfed by the cares of our dear brethren besieged with worry from the seething violence of the time."[35] Yet he was strengthened by the call "to work with the community to revive their spirits and lessen their sorrow and pain." He concluded that "these are the very things closest to the sacred, in and through which God's light can be glimpsed."

London gave Avraham Yitzhak Kook his first real taste of life in a great metropolis. He was tutored in English by a young student, practiced it on an abridged translation of the Talmud, and eventually was able to read some of Charles Dickens and other English classics. His personal secretary, Shimon Glitzenstein, was a young Chabad Hasid from Palestine who had been stranded by the war. Together they strolled in the city's great parks, often pausing to leaf through their pocket editions of the Bible and the canonical eleventh-century Talmud digest made by Isaac Al-Fasi, which Rav Kook always carried with him. They visited the city's cultural sites. Years later, Rav Kook recalled:

> When I lived in London, I would visit the National Gallery, and my favorite pictures were those of Rembrandt. I really think that Rembrandt was a tzaddik. Do you know that when I first saw Rembrandt's works, they reminded me of the legend about the creation of light? We are told that when God created light, it was so strong and pellucid that one could see from one end of the world to the other, but God was afraid that the wicked might abuse it. What did He do? He reserved that light for the righteous men when the Messiah should come. But now and then there are great men who are blessed and privileged to see it. I think that Rembrandt was one of them, and the light in his pictures is the very light that was originally created by God Almighty.[36]

Zvi Yehudah had remained in Switzerland, for reasons likely financial (he survived there by teaching and by accepting stipends from Kimche, preferring that what little extra money his parents had be sent to his sisters in Palestine) and legal (the difficulty of border crossings in wartime). He steadily corresponded with his father on matters big and small as Rav Kook peppered him with questions about his life and his studies. Zvi Yehudah regularly sent along Talmudic discourses, with which his father, though answering affectionately, was never quite satisfied. In the summer of 1916, perhaps sensing that a rabbinic career was not entirely in the offing, he suggested that Zvi Yehudah learn the crafts of circumcision and kosher slaughter, reminding him that while vegetarianism was an ideal, kosher meat eating was a necessary step along the way. Zvi Yehudah complied with his father's wishes, learned to slaughter, and at the turn of 1917 became a vegetarian. His father did not hide his disapproval. The war, it seems, had darkened his view of what had come to seem naive humanitarianism, and he wrote Zvi Yehudah that while many vegetarians were great and holy people, most were subtly but unmistakably misanthropic. He also argued for the spiritual value of mindful meat eating in the messianic process. Eating meat in accordance with kashrut is a step toward the spiritual transformation of matter, which forms the basis of ethics and, ultimately, redemption. That, he wrote, "would do far more" to redeem the world than "any spirit-choked compassion could give, with her weakness and anger."[37]

In early 1917, Rav Kook published a slim volume entitled *Rosh Milin* (*The Beginning of Words*), a series of mystical reflections on the Hebrew alphabet, reportedly written in just three days.* In 1915, Chaim Nachman Bialik had published a monumental essay, "Revealing and Concealment in Language," which explored, in nearly mystical terms, the reciprocal, tensile relations between disclosure and occultation in every spoken or written word. Those same problematics had long been on Rav Kook's mind.

Letter mysticism was one stream of the Kabbalah, most

---

*The title was and is pronounced "Reish Milin," owing to Rav Kook's Lithuanian accent. On December 18, 1916, he wrote Zvi Yehudah that he hadn't planned to tell him of the publication in advance, since he assumed that the latter would disapprove of its being published unedited, but his mother, Rivka, had already spilled the beans.

famously employed in the mystical-prophetic techniques of the Zohar's contemporary, Abraham Abulafia, and in Lithuanian Kabbalah. In the Jaffa notebooks, Rav Kook regularly referred to "the revelation of the letters." In Switzerland, he wrote that "the soul is full of letters,"[38] that they "float in thought like delicate birds on the delicate spiritual canopies in the great skies of thought . . . The practical and contemplative mind absorbs them, the imagination sculpts them, feeling awakes and song rouses and beats out waves."[39] Letters are the vehicles translating inchoate thought into words and thus ideas, and the very shapes of the letters reflect the undulations of the mind. The unfolding in the mind of Hebrew letters, vowel points, cantillation markings, and scribal ornamentations is the unfolding of human consciousness, and thus of revelation.

Thoughts precede letters—they are "unrepresented representations."[40] The curving stroke of the first Hebrew letter, aleph, points to the asymptotic nature of all language, and the words themselves are "delicate partitions" behind which "the representation remains in obscurity, in the depth of silence." It is by pushing, playing, and sculpting that boundary that letters and consciousness do their work of revelation. And onward the book proceeds through the Hebrew alphabet, its combinations of strokes, points, circles, and empty spaces, each a different figuration of consciousness, pendant between articulation and nothingness.

The volume closes with a series of brief observations that perhaps explain this profoundly esoteric response to the war. In ordinary times, he wrote, noble ideals may be derived from contemplating human society and its mores: "Not so when life falls into pits full of evil darkness and chaos. Then the visible world reels . . . There comes the burning thirst for the hidden substance, the inner perspectives that rise above the open field of life."[41] Rav Kook, it seems, like so many others, despaired of finding any obvious rationality in the organized madness of wartime. Rational thoughts are epiphenomenal and episodic, he continued, "but the selfhood of life . . . in the depths of the soul never stops," and all of people's study is meant to attune them to their souls. All translation, including translation into thought, is ultimately sleep, a twilight of consciousness that is prelude to wakefulness, "the preparation and education that leads to the primal, future scene of *then I will make the peoples pure of speech so that they all call out in the name of God* [Zephaniah 3:9]."

The Balfour Declaration, issued on November 2, 1917, hit Rav Kook like a thunderbolt. Some thirteen years earlier, Herzl's sudden, premature death had seemed to confirm an esoteric messianic reading of the time. Now, with the Great Powers declaring support for a Jewish homeland in Palestine, there could be no doubt. On November 12, he wrote to Zvi Yehudah that God has pierced the darkness, and "the soul flows with light."[42] He added that the new developments were rousing in him "old-new thoughts of spiritual and practical work."[43] He renewed his long-neglected halakhic projects. His first literary response was an ecstatic siddur commentary that Zvi Yehudah supplemented with other manuscripts and eventually published as *Olat Reiyah*. And despite his earlier reservations about the use of force, he became an enthusiastic supporter of the Jewish Legion, which he hoped would play a role in the capture of Palestine.

Aside from an open letter in which he had excoriated established Anglo-Jewish leaders who opposed Jewish nationalism in general and the declaration in particular, he had been largely uninvolved in the frenzied debates and diplomacy that led up to it. He was, despite the great esteem in which he was held, simply too marginal a figure in Anglo Jewry, too removed from the quotidian realities of politics and diplomacy, and too independent. His idiosyncratic understanding of Zionism was too esoteric, idealistic, and complex for him to be a conventional political actor of consequence. In March 1917, Rav Kook had met with Nahum Sokolov, a leading Zionist intellectual, journalist, and activist as well as right-hand man to Chaim Weizmann, the British Zionist leader whose monumental diplomatic efforts eventually secured the declaration.* Weizmann had urged the meeting, yet it turned out they had little to discuss aside from Sokolov's attempts to find warrant in the Zohar for the ideas of Spinoza, which Rav Kook found unconvincing.[44] Sokolov reported to Weizmann:

> As much as I would like to induce him to some Zionist propaganda work amongst our orthodox brethren I realize the great difficulty in the way of doing it. Rabbi Kuk [*sic*] has ideas of his own concerning Zionist politics, ideas which may be somewhat interesting and are undoubtedly well meant but are full of *sancta simplicitas* and impracticable. I would classify him as an individual Zionist who is not induced to cooperate in an Organization like ours.[45]

The Hebrew writer and combat veteran Avigdor Ha-Meiri titled his memoirs of World War I *The Great Madness* and *Hell on Earth*.† The massive, hitherto unimaginable horror of the war forced many to rethink their beliefs. While Hermann Cohen believed in the ethical ideals of the higher Germanism to the end, he knew that the concrete Germany had not lived up to them. Buber, for his part, shifted course in mid-1916 and, while still a Zionist, became an opponent of both the war and

*Sokolov had secured his own place in history in 1902 with his translation of Herzl's utopian novel *Altneulnd*, which he titled *Tel Aviv*, providing the name of the first Hebrew city, founded seven years later.

†On being marched as a prisoner of war through Agnon's hometown of Buczacz, Ha-Meiri broke ranks to ask a threadbare Jew on the street whether he could point out to him the great writer's house. His interlocutor, Ha-Meiri wrote, looked at him as though he were a lunatic and cried, "Something to worry about! Agnon! I wish I knew where I lived!"

of uncritical nationalism. "The way to Zion," he wrote in August 1917, "cannot lead through the highway of this madness."[46]

Among Christian theologians, it was Karl Barth who formulated the most vigorous and lasting response to the slaughter. Like Rav Kook (of whom he certainly never had heard, and vice versa), he believed that the war showed the pathetic weakness of liberal Protestantism in the face of evil—indeed, showed that all civilization was shot through with evil. Barth's answer to the crisis was a new dialectical theology: God, the "Wholly Other," on the one side and all else on the other shore, with nothing in between.

For Rav Kook, even if God's infinitude was Wholly Other, there streamed between Him and creation endless rivers of light, finally breaking through the clouds. The slaughter of World War I was redeemed by the Balfour Declaration. The redemption of Israel would make for the redemption of the human race, and the union of spirit and matter was essential to that vision. Israel's return to Zion would make for the possibility, at long last, of the emergence of an ethic that can sustain the world precisely because it does not despair of it but rather seeks to have the natural world realize its own participation in the divine.

His ability to think that way, and see providence at work in the agonizing carnage of the war, was certainly astonishing. "Death is a mirage," he wrote not long after arriving in London, "its defilement is its lie. What men call 'death' is but the strengthening of life in its essence."[47] His faith in the ultimate reality and goodness of the living God was perhaps what made such a statement even utterable, at least by him. And the time and energy he spent tending to the needs of the sick, the bereaved, and the poor bespeak deep compassion for human suffering. Perhaps the historic magnitude of Jewish suffering and longing made this providential reading of the war plausible. Perhaps it was the vindication of his instinct, from the first days of the war, that so great a conflict would have to yield an equally great deliverance. Perhaps, but his theodicy of the war remains a mystery.

He was not the only rabbinic thinker to be electrified by the Balfour Declaration: on hearing of it, the Chafetz Chaim interpreted it in Kabbalistic terms as *ke-'eyn it'aruta di-le-tataah*, "akin to the arousal of divine potencies from below."[48] Yosef Chaim Zonnenfeld reportedly said, "Let's say there was no rain for two thousand years, and then all of a sudden a slight cloud appeared in the sky. Wouldn't everyone be shaken and say, anxiously, 'And maybe in spite of it all?' And isn't this declaration at least a slight cloud like that?"[49] But Rav Kook was the one ready with a sacred historiosophy, fashioned from elements old and new, with which to interpret it.

He had written in St. Gallen that if the war demonstrated the reality of conventional politics, then the Jews wanted none of it.

> We left world politics under a duress that had an inner will, until that fortunate time when it will be possible to run a polity without evil or barbarity, the time for which we hope . . . And now the time has come, very near. . . . We received [in biblical times] but the necessary foundation for a people, and once the sprout was weaned, we were deposed from sovereignty, diffused among the gentiles, sown deep in the earth, *until the nightingale time and the voice of the dove will be heard in our land* [Song of Songs 2:12].[50]

In other words, Israel's exile and return enacted a dialectical progression from power to powerlessness to moralized, redemptive power.

If, at any rate, Israel was to return to politics, it could not, he thought, be of the conventional kind, which he saw as the alienation to be overcome by the fusion of body and soul that is the Land of Israel. There are, he wrote in St. Gallen, two

fundamental, deeply antagonistic worldviews: that which unifies, and that which divides, or in Kabbalistic language, *yichuda*
and *peiruda:* "Statesmen, societal leaders, are rooted deep in
the perspective of division . . . and the world is yet unfit for
leadership deriving from the unifying vision."[51] The two will,
he wrote, be synthesized in the messianic end-time, but not
before: "The very light of Messiah, God's seat in the world . . .
is built on the perspective of actual unity . . . whose occultation
is a necessity," since it is precisely the elusiveness of unity that
keeps pushing humanity and the world upward. The Land of
Israel is a fermenting agent illuminating the soul to grasp at the
possibility of unity.

By this line of thought, he deflected the inescapably political nature of Zionism, arguing that the Land was ultimately beyond politics. One senses here as well, for all his messianism, a
deeply ingrained exilic perspective, a wariness of power and the
seductions of enthusiasm in a still-unredeemed world. Those
final scruples were washed away by Balfour. Soon he tried to
overcome this dichotomy by a transpolitical move of his own.

On December 20, 1917, Sokolov wrote Rav Kook, "The
sacred work is not ours to do, [we] vessels of the mundane . . .
The duty and mitzvah of sanctifying the renaissance movement
is up to you."[52] The next day Rav Kook wrote to Zvi Yehudah:
"Truly great things for our future are being done here . . . Our
obligation now is to illuminate things, raise and exalt them."[53]
Two days later he wrote that his mind was racing, with no time
to order his thoughts. "It's very hard these days to write in clear
lines about the broad things happening before our eyes," he
wrote two weeks later. "The acts are so wondrous, to the point
where the eye dims from looking and the ears from all the
hearing and listening."[54]

A few days later he issued a proclamation, in Hebrew and
Yiddish, entitled *Degel Yerushalayim (The Banner of Jerusalem).*

Throughout Jewish history, he wrote, *Zion* has signified political sovereignty, indispensable and sacred in its own way, while *Jerusalem* has signified the sacred in and of itself, the highest goal of Israel and humanity. Our goal, he wrote, is for Jerusalem to walk peacefully with Zion under *degel Yerushalayim*. There is no doubt that God's power is being revealed through world events; the Jewish message of redemption must emerge from hiding and become the active force in Jewish national life and on the world stage. Jews must convey to the whole world that the recent wondrous world events, so obviously targeted at their redemption, will usher in the redemption of the human race.

A few days later he wrote his Boisk disciple Moshe Zeidel, then living in America, who had asked whether Rav Kook really and truly thought that the messianic advent was underway. Yes, he answered, without a doubt. But Zionism as presently constituted was not the way. It embraced the modernity that had just discredited itself in the war. And as a movement, it fundamentally did not grasp the nation's soul. Accomplishing that would take activists of an entirely different kind, and they, paradoxically, would emerge from the ranks of the Orthodox, who had, until then, opposed Zionism—and the Degel Yerushalayim movement would be their vehicle.

There was, of course, a religious wing within the Zionist movement, the Mizrachi, founded in 1902. Rav Kook never hid his ambivalence about the Mizrachi, premised as it was on tamping down religious fervor and willingly accepting secondary status within the Zionist movement.

In this episode as elsewhere, his intuition regarding the deeper philosophical and spiritual issues at work at the tectonic level of politics was uncoupled from a concrete understanding of the everyday realities out of which those politics were made. He grasped the moral rot in conventional politics and nationalism that had been revealed by World War I. Like the cultural Zionists inspired by Ahad Ha-Am, he saw that in the absence of a vital connection to Jewish history, culture, and ethics, political Zionism would be unable to sustain even its strictly political agendas and the struggles and sacrifices they would entail. He also grasped, as did many Zionists, that the traditional masses of Eastern European Jewry, who provided Zionism's moral suasion and would produce its future demographic heft, needed somehow to be brought into the ranks of the national revival. Yet he deeply miscalculated the reactions of the groups and players he sought to sway, and overestimated as well as his own very limited organizational capabilities.

The official program of Degel Yerushalayim unintentionally illustrated the confusions at the heart of his effort.[55] He declared that he did not mean to compete with, let alone supplant, the Zionist movement in the political or diplomatic sphere. Yet he was willing to engage in agitation to convince world public opinion, on religious grounds, of the justice of the Jewish claim to Palestine. He discussed clearly ideological and literary efforts to complement Zionist institutions, such as yeshivot and publications, but also talked about a network of rabbinic courts as well as the movement engaging in its own land purchases. He wrote, with utter sincerity, that Zionism and the national movement as a whole would come to see themselves together as a branch of Degel Yerushalayim.

Thus, he seems genuinely to have been taken aback when the Mizrachi began to accuse him of trying to usurp their movement. In a letter to an unnamed correspondent, dated August 21, 1918, he wrote that he had affection and respect for the Mizrachi, whom he nonetheless referred to as "the last of the Mohicans," obsequiously eager to impress their cultured betters with their own relative degree of civilization.[56] His analysis was not without merit, but utterly failed to reckon with the concrete realities of the time. In the end, Degel Yerushalayim did not amount to much: a few supporters and chapters in England, Switzerland, Poland, and Jerusalem; a number of articles and meetings; and a scattering of educational projects. The movement roused little interest and, once the Mizrachi realized its limited prospects, little opposition. The ideas behind it, though, shaped his efforts in the coming years.

On March 10, 1919, he wrote Zalman Pines, "I am not a politician and relish not at all divergences of opinion. I see only the good side of phenomena," and that, he added, was precisely was why his movement was needed, to bring out to all the good sides of Zionism.[57] And that refusal to make distinctions was, aside from his own organizational inabilities, the movement's crucial flaw. As in his tenure at Jaffa, his all-encompassing dialectical perspective offered a way of thinking about and seeing unity in roiling times by insistently repressing serious disagreements among political actors. He correctly understood that the lifeblood of political actors was debate, disagreement, and maneuver, yet his reluctance to join in the contentious, aggressive fray doomed him to ineffectiveness in an arena he sought to transform.

Back in Palestine, the Yishuv, Old and New, had suffered greatly during the war from mass deportations, conscriptions, forced labor, social disintegration, and hunger. By war's end, the Ashkenazi Old Yishuv in particular was on the ropes, not least because Zionist representatives were firmly in charge of the disbursal of relief funds from abroad. The Old Yishuv was able to improve its position in part by making common cause with secular groups unloved by the Zionists, in particular the people and institutions identified with the Francophile humanitarian group Alliance Israelite Universelle. At the same time, the Zionists realized they needed the support of religious Jewry more than ever before. They were less wary of the literal price they would have to pay than the figurative one, in the form of some sort of formal recognition of rabbinic authority, and an official status for religious education, in the institutions of their emergent national homeland.

No single commanding rabbi had emerged in Jerusalem since the venerable Salant's death in 1909, though clusters of leaders were emerging. The most conservative elements were still led by Yitzhak Yerucham Diskin and the much more vigorous Yosef Chaim Zonnenfeld. Stepping into the leadership vacuum among the comparatively moderate Orthodox were two of Zonnenfeld's juniors—Charlap and a brilliant young rabbinical judge, Zvi Pesach Franck, who had developed ties to Rav Kook while taking respite in Jaffa from the perennial furies of Jerusalem.

In April 1918, Chaim Weizmann, by then the preeminent Zionist leader, arrived in Palestine and spent weeks in fruitless talks with the Jerusalem rabbis over instituting educational and rabbinic judicial reforms in exchange for funding. The failed, exhausting negotiations did succeed in effectively dissolving whatever unity the Ashkenazi rabbis of Jerusalem had maintained during the war, yielding three distinct camps: the avowedly pro-Zionist and unmistakably outnumbered circle around Charlap; Franck's group, which sought neutral accommodation; and the zealots led by Diskin and Zonnenfeld, who made no effort to hide their ideological animosity.

Only one man, it seemed could offer secular political Zionists the religious legitimation their movement needed in the eyes of Jewish and gentile public opinion. Only one man could give Religious Zionists the self-confidence to assert themselves within the Zionist movement, and endow moderate rabbis with the halakhic and spiritual authority without which the hard-liners would devour them. And that man was waiting in London.

On August 9, 1918, while on an annual pilgrimage to the Tomb of the Patriarchs in Hebron to mark the first of the penitential Hebrew month of Elul, the moderate Orthodox rabbis of Jerusalem decided to issue a formal invitation to Avraham Yitzhak Kook to be the Ashkenazi chief rabbi of Jerusalem. Franck had begun working on that possibility the previous December, just before the British general Edmund Allenby's triumphal entry into the city. Through the first half of 1918, Rav Kook had been parrying as best he could queries from Jaffa about when he would return, while he waited to see what would happen.

A formal invitation to join the Jerusalem rabbinate arrived, but he did not accept it at first, wanting, as he had before coming to Jaffa, to garner as much local legitimacy as he could. He asked for broad support from the range of Ashkenazi institutions, the Sephardim, and relevant non-Jerusalemites. He likewise sought to secure the approval of the Eastern European figures who still were the undoubted leaders of Orthodoxy. They, for their part, were too busy rebuilding their war-ravaged communities, and too mindful of the Jerusalemites' well-earned reputation for endless ideological combat, to want to get involved.

After months of maneuver by his supporters and foes, in the first week of May 1919 a conclave of forty-five rabbis from throughout the country, convened by Ben Zion Uziel and declaring themselves "the rabbinic assembly of the Land of Israel," unanimously asked Rav Kook to return. He decided, finally, to go home.

Toward the end of his time in London, his earlier energies came back to him as he sensed the stirrings of return to Eretz Yisrael. He was, he hoped, recovering his best self: "When we forget our own souls, get distracted from looking into our own inner lives, all is confused and uncertain. The first repentance, which immediately lights up the darknesses, is to return to oneself, the root of one's soul, and immediately one returns to God, the soul of all souls . . . and this is true for a lone individual, a whole people, all of humanity, or the *tikkun* all of

being, whose ruination always comes from forgetting itself."
Repentance without returning to oneself, he continues, is a
fraud, "and that is the secret of the light of the Messiah."[58]

The Kooks sailed from Liverpool to Port Said in mid-
August 1919 and from there made their way by train. At the
Rafah crossing point from Sinai, he threw himself on the
ground, kissed the earth, and prayed. On arriving at Lydda
(Lod), he was met by Ben Zion Uziel and other dignitaries
from Jaffa. A delegation from Jerusalem offered him a letter
of appointment, which he said he was refusing. According to
some accounts, he had, on the train, been handed a letter warning him not to accept the invitation without first receiving permission from Diskin and Zonnenfeld and signing on to their
ban against secular education in Jerusalem. Addressing the assembly in Hebrew (during his time abroad, he had had to do
almost all his public speaking in Yiddish), he spoke of how the
rabbinate as an institution was in need of fundamental change,
though he left unclear exactly how. He was traveling on to Jerusalem, he said, not as a rabbi, but as a private citizen. The
Jerusalemites roared their approval, while Uziel and the other
Jaffans asked him to reconsider. He told the crowd that during
a zeppelin bombardment he and his wife had sworn that if they
ever were to return to Palestine, they would go embrace the
Wailing Wall. Nonetheless, he said that they did want to go to
Jaffa first, and there they spent the night.

He arrived in Jerusalem the next day, the third day of Elul,
Friday, August 28, 1919. (The day before, Jerusalem zealots had
printed and begun to distribute a booklet against him, whose
distribution was halted on orders from Diskin and Zonnenfeld,
out of common courtesy and prudence.) Thronged by crowds
of well-wishers, Rav Kook visited the Wailing Wall, walked
through the Old City, and then went, with Charlap, to Zonnenfeld's home in the Jewish Quarter. Zonnenfeld did not hide
his reservations about Rav Kook becoming rabbi of Jerusalem,

though he tried to be polite. "I wish for you that you become the High Priest once the Messiah rebuilds our Temple,"[59] he told him. Rav Kook replied that he would gladly serve as a run-of-the-mill priest if he could. Zonnenfeld, that day and afterward, never referred to him as anything but *Yafer Rov*, the Jaffa rabbi: the mysteriously compelling, staggeringly learned, obviously brilliant, undoubtedly saintly, probably misguided—and not a little threatening—rabbi of the New Yishuv, returning, electrified, from Europe, to build the New Jerusalem.

5

Dear, Wounded Brothers: Jerusalem

What do I want, what do I long for? . . . To shine
the light of faith, of holiness, in the Land of Israel,
the Hebrew Land of Israel, the Land of Israel that is
steadily being redeemed, that Land of Israel that is
ridding itself of the dustiness of exile, degrading and
depressing . . . We must redeem the Shekhinah that
is within us from its exile . . . That is my goal, but
oh how heavy is this burden on my soul. How much
salvation from on high do I need to lift and carry
this! *Please, God, save us. Please, God, make us flourish*
[Psalms 118:25].
—Avraham Yitzhak Kook, *Pinkesei Ha-Reiyah*

The patient city gathers in people with the strangest
ideas, philosophers, freaks, madmen, all of whom
add to her a measure of themselves and disappear.

Sometimes she seems to be built as much out of
obsessions as of stone.
—Shulamit Hareven, *City of Many Days*

THE KOOKS RETURNED to a Palestine different from the one
they had left. The Turks were gone, replaced by the British—
a colonial power pledged, at least in theory, to Jewish aspirations. And in Jewish Palestine, the Zionists were now firmly in
charge.

Two large structural changes, one internal the other external, were fundamentally reshaping the nature of the Yishuv
and more. Internally, the energies of the Yishuv were turning
from ideology to nation building. The prewar decade of emigration to Palestine, the Second Aliyah, emerged in retrospect
as the heroic period of spiritual and philosophical Zionist debate. The chief task after the war was to forge viable political,
economic, and social structures, and the move from ideology
to institution building shifted the meaning of both conviction
and compromise.

Externally, the aim and shape of nationalism fatefully
changed. Before the war, nationalism, as a political movement
and, no less crucially, a moral argument, was directed upward
against large, autocratic, often despotic empires—the Austro-
Hungarian, Russian, Ottoman, and others. With those gone,
national groups pressed their claims horizontally against one
another. Through the Second Aliyah, the Arabs of Palestine
and the Jews of the Yishuv had been Ottoman subjects, maneu-
vering as best they could. Now they were rival claimants in a
contest no longer constrained by the policies of the Ottoman
Empire. To be sure, soldiers of a new empire, the British, had
arrived. Their task, however, was not to plant the Union Jack
once and for all, but to sort out, or at least manage, the contradictory promises made to both groups in the press of wartime.

This development—nation building by competing nationalisms—in Palestine as elsewhere, set the template for so much of what has defined the modern Middle East: groups of people who would rather not live with one another—Arab and Jew, Old Yishuv and New—being forced to find some modus vivendi in a space whose borders were drawn by someone else.

The war left Europe in a deep cultural crisis from which it has in some ways never recovered. The war had thoroughly discredited *lebensphilosophie* (at least for a while), and intellectuals turned either to irony (bordering on nihilism) or to increasingly desperate attempts to create a rational, liberal order, such as the Weimar Republic and the League of Nations. Zionists emerged from the war with no such crisis, most obviously because of the Balfour Declaration and because the wartime ravaging of Eastern European Jewry seemed to bear out Zionist analyses of the Jewish predicament. There was much work to be done, and much pressure on the Yishuv to do it. The Zionist movement emerged from the war victorious, with a renewed sense of its own historical mission. The Jews' dreams of restoration seemed closer to fulfillment than ever before.

In this new situation, the very thing that made Rav Kook the indispensable man—his seeming ability to unite in his person the contending currents of the Yishuv—made him not quite fully able to swim in any one of them. Because he was working his way toward some new synthesis of old and new, Orthodoxy and heresy, engagement and spirituality, he had no real social, political, or cultural base of his own. And a sacred *lebensphilosophie* was still his key to reading the times and their increasingly obvious messianic direction.

He had thought hard about how to take one's place in a diverse and contentious society. Back in Boisk, he had written in his Aggadah commentary on the Talmudic dictum that "sages multiply peace in the world" (BT Berakhot 64a), playing on the root—*shalem*—of shalom, peace: "There are those who erroneously think that world peace will only come from a common character of opinions and qualities. But no—true peace will come to the world precisely by a multiplicity [of] all the opinions and perspectives . . . Peace [is] the unification of all opposites. But there must be opposites, so that there will be those who labor and that which will be unified . . . Hence, peace is the name of God, who is the master of all the forces, *all-capable and gathering them all* [from the High Holy Days liturgy]."[1]

In his Jaffa journal, Rav Kook had written about how the sacred was the thread running through the warring camps of the day—the religious, universalist, and nationalist—and how one had to try and see the good working through even the bad sides of each, without surrendering one's own commitments. In a letter to Moshe Zeidel in February 1918, he was even more forceful: "Tolerance is the fount of life . . . but when it comes from faintheartedness, and weakness of spirit, it is poisonous and destructive, bringing in the end jealousy, bitter and hard as death, whose proponents will precisely be those who speak in the name of tolerance. The kind of tolerance that seeks to block the lively vigor that would stand up to whatever would ravage the nation's soul . . . is like that of someone who sees his home being vandalized and says nothing."[2]

He had in earlier controversies displayed equanimity, self-confidence, and courage. Now he was sailing into the teeth of controversies bitterer—within Orthodoxy, within the Yishuv, and among the Yishuv, the British, and the Arabs—than he could have imagined. Precisely because the time to build had come, all the contradictions in his life and personality emerged in full force. He tried to stay above the political fray while taking an inescapably public and inevitably political role. He wanted to make everybody happy, and just could not.

His most steadfast and regularly vicious antagonists were the fabled Jerusalem zealots. They held the advantage because, like all zealots, they knew what they wanted. The appreciation of complexity that makes moderates like Rav Kook so attractive turned into a stumbling block when he was faced with such determined religious foes—and determined secular ideologues, left and right. On top of all that, he was trying to achieve a complicated, very personal synthesis of a life of public action with the constant meditative state in which he lived. (For decades, he wore tefillin all day, a small pair given to him by Aderet. At night, he regularly held midnight vigils of prayer and meditation at the Wailing Wall.)

In the fall of 1919, the Jews of Palestine announced elections for a national assembly that would govern the Yishuv. Would women vote and stand for office? The ultra-Orthodox announced that if so, they would boycott the elections and the assembly. The Religious Zionist Mizrachi party asked Rav Kook his opinion, assuming he would support female suffrage, thereby enabling them to participate at full strength with rabbinic sanction. They were mistaken. At a gathering on September 23, he announced his opposition. In a letter to the Mizrachi, he subsequently explained that as a matter of halakha, men, and not women, were charged with communal responsibility and that commingling of the sexes was certainly inappropriate in burgeoning national institutions. He framed his opposition also as reflecting his understanding of Christian Zionism. (This was gleaned in part from what the new high commissioner of Palestine, Herbert Samuel, shared with him of the views of British prime minister Lloyd George, whose pro-Zionism was explicitly biblical.) The Balfour Declaration and the sentiments behind it were predicated on a vision of the Jews, Rav Kook wrote, not as modernizers, but as the people of the Bible. He suggested, instead, as had the ultra-Orthodox Agudat Yisrael, that there be two parallel assemblies, one for the secular public, in which women could vote and stand for office, and another for the Orthodox.

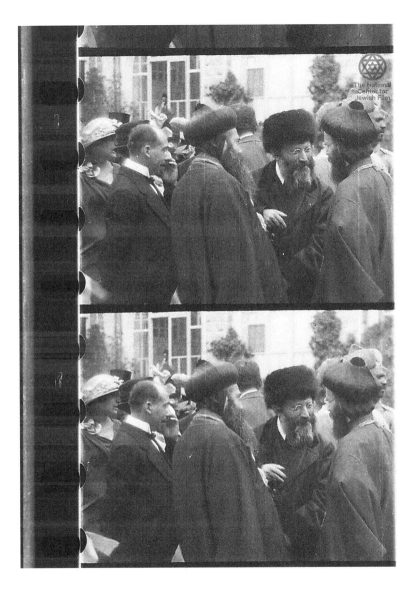

Rav Kook conversing with Coptic and Syriac bishops at a reception for the first British high commissioner for Palestine, Herbert Samuel, Jerusalem, 1920. Still from the documentary film *Dreamers and Builders.* Courtesy of the Steven Spielberg Film Archives of the Hebrew University of Jerusalem and the World Zionist Organization, and the National Center for Jewish Film (www.jewishfilm.org).

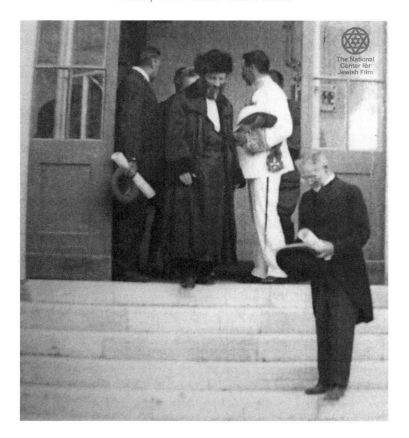

Rav Kook and Eliezer ben-Yehudah (in foreground) at a reception for the high commissioner Herbert Samuel, in white uniform, standing in doorway, Jerusalem, 1920. Still from the documentary film *Dreamers and Builders*. Courtesy of the Israel Film Archive – Jerusalem Cinematheque and the National Center for Jewish Film (www.jewishfilm.org).

This left all parties in a quandary. The Zionists needed a broad-based assembly to deal effectively with the British, whose enthusiasm for Balfour was already starting to fade. Chaim Weizmann decided to defer elections until May 1920.

In ruling as he did on women's suffrage, at the time a contentious question in Western democracies, Rav Kook was in step with much, even if not all, rabbinic opinion of the time. Interestingly, his arguments were not formally legal; rather, he expressed what he took to be the inarguable spirit of the laws.

Rav Kook's writings are largely devoid of the misogyny that can be found in rabbinic and Kabbalistic texts. Throughout he depicts women not only as the guardian spirits of the private sphere, but also, and more interestingly, as the avatars of passion, intuition, and imagination. That characterization is clichéd—yet in Rav Kook's thought-world, passion, intuition, and imagination are dynamic, divine principles, and the keys to prophecy—and at times, superior to the mind. In the grip of mystical vision, he sometimes imagined a world in which distinctions between genders would be erased, along with those between Jew and gentile. Yet gender distinction itself was not problematic for him, unlike the distinction between Jew and gentile, which regularly tugged at him. Still, no matter the possibilities of the far messianic future, in the here and now, and precisely in an era of national renaissance, the distinction between gender roles, he thought, had firmly to be maintained.

The Mizrachi did not try to hide their disappointment. Among the most critical was Rabbi Yehudah Leib (Fishman) Maimon, the head of the movement and editor of its newspaper. Ten years Rav Kook's junior and richly learned in his own right, Maimon regularly said that Kook's early essays had inspired him and others in the founding of the Mizrachi in 1902. He was, though, a disciple of the Mizrachi's founder, Yitzhak Ya'akov Reines, who chose to work within the Zionist movement, keeping his messianic hopes to himself. Differences between Maimon and Rav Kook had surfaced at their first meeting, in 1908. Now they were out in the open. Maimon wrote that the Mizrachi recognized the value of women's participation in the national renaissance, on principle.

Maimon was not the only one upset with Rav Kook. Rebbe Binyomin, who had suggested turning to Kook in the first place, wrote that his stance was no less than "a desecration of God's name," and thus a cardinal sin. How could you, he wrote him, stand shoulder-to-shoulder with the rabbis who reject the national enterprise and turn your back on the Mizrachi, "who dwell among their people? This is not the way."

The secular newspapers were even harsher. On the left, the *Young Worker* editorialized: "If the sainted Avraham Yitzhak Ha-Cohen Kook . . . wishes in all humility to be the leader and light of the community . . . who's stopping him? . . . For our part, he can also deal with philosophy, prayer, and will always find a bunch of jokers who lick their fingers from his wisdom and depth. But don't bring his wisdom and depth into our lives, to our detriment and that of the Yishuv, and please don't come during the current time of crisis and give aid to our enemies."[3]

And on the right, Ze'ev Jabotinsky, cofounder of the Jewish Legion and leader of Zionism's more militant wing, was unsparing: "We've given in to clericalism of the most Negroid kind. We've given in to clericalism at war with the equality of woman . . . We've given in to the prohibition of geniuses whom nobody in the world outside of Meah Shearim knows who or what they are, or of the scientific work of R' Kook, the typical literary production of some auditor-student, half-educated and undigested."[4] As for Rav Kook's ultra-Orthodox foes in Jerusalem, his having taken their side on this matter impressed them not at all.

It took him a while formally to accept his Jerusalem rabbinic appointment, in part because of personal tragedy. Shortly after Sukkot, in late October 1919, the Kooks' daughter, Esther Yael, fell from the roof of the house in which they were living on Jerusalem's Prophets' Street, and died shortly thereafter.

Twelve years old, she was perhaps her father's favorite. In a wartime letter to Chaim Perlman,* who had studied in his Jaffa yeshiva, he referred to her, then turning eight, as "wise and sharp-witted beyond her years."[5] Six months later, he wrote to Zalman Pines, "The wound stays deep, deep in our souls."[6]

On March 19, 1920, in his official capacity as rabbi of Jerusalem (he had formally accepted the appointment in December), Rav Kook reiterated his opposition to women's suffrage, calling for a rabbinic council. It convened, eighty-five strong, on April 14 and declared against it. The next day, Maimon announced to the central committee of the Mizrachi that "on purely religious matters we will ask the rabbis, and on public affairs, the rabbis can ask us."[7] Religious Zionist women would vote.

Elections were held on April 19 throughout Palestine, but postponed in Jerusalem. There, during Passover in the first week of April, Arab rioters had attacked Jews, killing six (including a child), wounding several dozen, and raping two women. Jabotinsky and nineteen others who organized self-defense were arrested by the British, and the Yishuv was deeply rattled. Notwithstanding his harsh criticisms during the suffrage controversy Rav Kook sent Jabotinsky a message of support, for which the latter expressed his gratitude. Then, on April 25, the major Allied powers and Japan, meeting in San Remo, Italy, redrew the map of the Middle East, ratifying Britain's civil authority in Palestine, as part of the process set in motion by the Balfour Declaration.

Taken together, the violence of the riots and the diplomatic progress at San Remo drove home the necessity of national unity. And so when elections finally took place in Jerusalem on May 3, with two sets of polling stations—men-only and mixed— Rav Kook openly took part, voting at one of the former (where each vote counted twice, on the assumption that wives would

*Perlman, a restless prodigy, eventually became the legendary, mysterious teacher of Elie Wiesel and Emanuel Levinas known as Monsieur Chouchani.

have voted like their husbands). Out of 314 seats in the National Assembly, the majority went to leftist parties; the non-Mizrachi Orthodox garnered among them several dozen; and the Mizrachi, nine.*

In the late spring of 1920, Rav Kook published *Orot* (*Lights*), a seventy-page selection from his journals, culled and edited by Zvi Yehudah. His son adroitly wove brief essays out of the vast sprawl of his father's notebooks, clarifying abstruse formulations, sharpening the nationalist, messianic, and Land of Israel themes while blunting the most theologically subversive passages and modifying the more biting criticisms of conventional Orthodoxy. But that could not diminish the sheer radicalism of his father's ideas, and the Jerusalemites' darkest suspicions of him were confirmed at a stroke.

Charlap inadvertently added fuel to the fire. Yitzhak Ben-Tovim, a supporter of Rav Kook's, wrote Charlap, asking him to clarify some of the volume's more unconventional passages, especially chapter 34 of the second section, in which Kook wrote: "The exercises with which young Jews in the Land of Israel strengthen their bodies so that they may be vigorous sons of the nation betters the spiritual strength of the heavenly tzaddikim . . . This sacred service [of exercise] elevates the divine spirit higher and higher, like its elevation by the songs and hymns of David the king of Israel in the book of Psalms."[8]

While the passage could have been read as referring to the calisthenics of the burgeoning Jewish self-defense organizations, this was far from clear—and even if so, it would hardly have diminished the sheer shock of his pronouncement. Charlap answered with a discourse on the ethics of epistemology. Good and evil are not external categories, but products of the

---

*The controversy left some very hard feelings; in a letter to her family in 1922, Henrietta Szold, the founder of Hadassah, wrote that Rav Kook "has not an iota of grace or even humanness."

visions of goodness and evil people carry in their minds and enact with their wills. If we would purify our minds and wills, evil would cease to exist. Thus, as Jews come to recognize the good that lies deep within the ostensible sinners of Israel and to act on that recognition, the latter's sin will be transformed into goodness: "Revealing the interior to heal the exterior, that is the goal of chapter 34 . . . to learn how to look with a piercing eye into the interiority of everything and whip it upward."[9]

Ben-Tovim speedily published their correspondence in a pamphlet, *Tovim Meorot* (*The Lights Are Good*), allowing all to see what Charlap had learned from his master. The rabbi of one of Jerusalem's most pious neighborhoods, as learned a Talmudist and Kabbalist and as devout an ascetic as the Old Yishuv could have hoped to produce, adopted an esoteric angle of vision in which conventional religious categories of sin and righteousness were dissolved in messianic expectation.

There quickly followed a pamphlet banning *Orot*, which included frontal attacks on Rav Kook and Charlap, and a declaration signed by Zonnenfeld, Diskin, and others: "We were astonished to see and hear gross things, foreign to the entire Torah, and we see that which we feared before his coming here, that he will introduce new forms of deviance that our rabbis and ancestors could not have imagined . . . He turns light to darkness, and darkness to light . . . It is to be deemed a sorcerer's book, and let it be known that it is forbidden to study [let alone] rely on all his nonsense and dreams."[10] The activists behind the pamphlet, led by Akiva Porush, the descendant of a venerable Lithuanian clan, were even more explicit. In closing, they added: "We are at war with Rabbi A. Y. Kook, and Rabbi Y. M. Charlap, who trails alongside him."[11] To make the point, they burned the volume in public.

Rav Kook had published unconventional opinions before. But this was the reading public's first exposure to the full gusts of his journals, the seething mind of the man who was no longer rabbi of Jaffa but the religious custodian and authority of Jerusalem. Discerning readers began to get a sense of the magnitude of whom they were dealing with and what he was trying to do. Rebbe Binyomin noted the book's relentless attempt "to unify that which will not be unified, to express the inexpressible," perceptively noting that "this sheaf of leaves is to be thought of as confessional literature . . . a sort of confession of the soul."[12] But what a literary sensibility could savor, rabbinic authority could not.

It was well-established British colonial practice to rule as indirectly as possible, through indigenous groups' communal and religious leaders, and the *milliyet* system of the Ottomans— granting religious authorities jurisdiction over charities, marriage, divorce, and inheritance—had left just such an arrangement waiting for them in Palestine. Under the Ottomans, the chief Jewish—invariably Sephardic—religious authority was the *hakham bashi*—literally, in a mix of Hebrew and Turkish, "head sage." The current holdover was a nonentity, and though many in the Yishuv were glad to dispense with the office altogether, the British decided to continue the institution that had served their colonial systems and the Ottomans' so long and so well. It was clear to all concerned that there would have to be an Ashkenazi chief rabbi along with a Sephardi, and that it would have to be Rav Kook.

He had, for his part, begun to formulate plans for a chief rabbinate almost immediately upon his formal acceptance of the Jerusalem rabbinate. Unsurprisingly, his Jerusalem opponents issued declarations that his Jerusalem appointment was null and void, since he had not won the approval of the entire community, still had commitments in Jaffa, and was a dreadful administrator; besides, he utterly lacked learning and piety and was, worst of all, a modernist. The publication of *Orot* did nothing to blunt those attacks.

While some liberals and women's organizations opposed creating a chief rabbinate, the Zionist leadership envisioned an institution that would deliver religious services, smooth religious-secular relations, and respectably represent the religious side of the Yishuv when appropriate, all while staying firmly under their control. Rav Kook had bigger plans. The rabbinate he hoped to create would parallel the Zionist movement and its institutions: alongside the Zionist Executive, the Yishuv's government in waiting under the Palestine Mandate, would be the Rabbinate Council; alongside the judiciary, the rabbinical courts; alongside the nascent Hebrew University, a Central World Yeshiva. The new rabbinate, he wrote in an essay, would rise above parties and take upon itself the spiritual dimension of the national renaissance as a whole.[13]

The Old Yishuv could live with the creation of the office of chief rabbi as they had with the official rabbis once appointed by the tsar, who generally lacked authority and were easily ignored. But the body envisioned here, the Chief Rabbinate Council, was to be voted on—and staffed—by religious and secular Jews alike. It seemed designed to introduce reforms into the halakha, and was to be headed by their archenemy, a scholarly, charismatic heretic who refused to be drawn into the open for a good fight.

The British, who wanted to see the rabbinate established for reasons of their own, announced the creation of an assembly that would vote it into existence on February 22, 1921. The vote occurred on February 24, and Rav Kook was unanimously voted in as chief rabbi for the Ashkenazim. His Sephardic counterpart was Ya'akov Meir, an urbane scholar and native Jerusalemite who had served as wartime rabbi in Salonika. The British managed to bring the body into being by promising the secular jurists on the council real responsibilities (which they were never given) and promising Zonnenfeld and Diskin that the rabbinate would have no jurisdiction over them (which, indeed, it never did). Rav Kook's two closest allies on the council, Zvi Pesach Franck and Yerucham Fischel Bernstein (known as Fischel Dayyan), an esteemed rabbinic judge, served as his institutional tie to the Old Yishuv and the religious legitimacy it still embodied, its fanaticism and fury notwithstanding. The leaders of the Ashkenazi Old Yishuv, who had not the slightest intention of recognizing the new body's authority, organized a council of their own, headed by Zonnenfeld, as astute as Rav Kook was idealistic.

As mentioned previously, Rav Kook had written, at the time of the First Zionist Congress in 1897, an essay calling for a renewed Sanhedrin, the ancient court of Temple times. With the establishment of the Rabbinate Council, he published it. Designed along the lines of the Great Court outlined by Maimonides, this constitutional court would be in Jerusalem, near the Temple. He had written then that even necessary halakhic change could not be brought about in conditions of exile. Finally, a quarter of a century later, amid the national revival, the time for change, he hoped, had finally come.

At the founding assembly, Kook laid out the Maimonidean framework for an integrated judiciary. During the sesame oil controversy, he had advocated strong independence for local rabbinical courts. Now he envisioned something different, an organized and more centralized system. And he addressed the liberals who were wary of the rabbinate's very establishment: "Judaism is the ideal of the entire nation. I have never thought or conceived of imposing the rabbinate's rule over our secular sectors. My intention is directed to the ideal of Judaism—whose bearers are the rabbis—such that it may influence all our lives. I think and believe that in the greatest Jewish heresy there is more faith than in the houses of worship of other peoples."[14]

Had his secular listeners read his journals, they might have known that he ultimately had in mind a transformation of Judaism that dissolved the categories of religious and secular, body and soul. But he was not about to say that then—precisely because he believed that that transformation needed to result from a dialectical process in which the secularists, qua secularists, had a key role to play. His tolerance of secularism was thus provisional, but at the same time his conception of religion was provisional too, even if it needed to assert itself then and there.

Although the British largely left the chief rabbis to their own devices, they were not unaware of them. Ronald Storrs, the military governor of Jerusalem from 1917 to 1921 and then civil governor of Judea and Jerusalem until 1926, recorded his impressions of Zonnenfeld, Kook, and Meir in his memoirs:

> The Orthodox Rabbis, remote from politics and administrations, moved in a world of their own, their sunless, sedentary lives, their furry *streimels*, their venerable faded velvets, combined to produce an *ensemble* so repellent to most visitors that they would commiserate with me on having to govern such apparitions. On the contrary, the extreme Orthodox such as Rabbi Sonnenfeld and the followers of *Agudath Yisroel* never occasioned either to me or to the police the faintest trouble whatever. From the Administrator's point of view they were ideal subjects, for all they desired was to be left in peace and the practice of their religion. . . .
>
> [As for the] two official Chief Rabbis . . . Rabbi Kuk, a dignified figure with the folds of his rich black silk robe carelessly disguising his cruciform Order of the British Empire,* and his ample beaver hat, spoke always at formidable length, and with a confidence (hardly rivaled by the Latin Patriarch himself) that his words must be accepted as *ex cathedra*. His colleague, Rabbi Meyer, late of Salonika, with his command of French and his air of a man of the world who would not be disturbing

*Whether Storrs saw this as colonial's insolence or as a mark of Kook's sartorial style is unclear, though Rav Kook seems to have been trying to show respect for His Majesty's Government without wearing a cross around his neck. In posed photographs, he took care to half cover the cross with his lapel.

the Governor but in this particular protest had to associate himself with a more rigorous partner, was as pure Levant as his Egyptian turban of blue satin wound tightly round a soft red fez, and his galaxy of those Balkan decorations which used to reward diplomacy in the Ottoman Empire.[15]

In April 1921, Avraham Mordechai Alter, rebbe (grand rabbi) of the Gerer Hasidic dynasty and a leading figure in Agudat Yisrael, came from Poland to see firsthand the religious and communal infrastructures awaiting the growing numbers of Polish Hasidim immigrating to Palestine. While Hasidic groups had at first opposed the creation of Agudat Yisrael in 1912, seeing in the very attempt at creating an organized sociopolitical movement a devilish concession to the logic of modernity, many eventually came to regard it as a necessary and even valuable vehicle. Agudat Yisrael became the patron of the Orthodox community of Jerusalem, and through the interwar years the Agudah's leadership coalition of Polish Hasidim, Lithuanian Talmudists, and German bourgeois intellectuals managed the group's increasingly fraught relations with the volatile ultra-Orthodox partisans of Jerusalem. Zonnenfeld and Diskin, for their part, along with Agudat Yisrael's secretary in Jerusalem, Moshe Blau, needed to stoke the coals of the fervent while keeping the flames from getting too high.

The rebbe visited Rav Kook, and the two had a respectful, friendly conversation. Almost immediately, the rebbe was denounced in the time-honored Jerusalem medium of *pashkevilim*, wall posters distinguished by their creative use of textual allusion set at a fever pitch of rhetorical violence. In response, he refused at first to meet with Diskin and Zonnenfeld's representatives and relented only after being placated appropriately.

During his return voyage to Europe, the rebbe wrote a letter to his disciples, which became a canonical ultra-Orthodox pronouncement on Rav Kook. Contrary to how he has been depicted, the rebbe wrote, Rav Kook was a man of real nobility, learned in all aspects of the Torah, and his admirable loathing of money was unmistakable: "Yet his love for Zion is boundless . . . and thence derive the strange things in his writings. I argued with him at length that while he means well, his actions etc.,* and he extends his hand to sinners who persist in rebellion and in desecrating all that is holy. And when he says that he is trying to follow in God's ways, as is written *You extend Your hand to sinners* etc. [Yom Kippur liturgy], I say for that we confess *for the hand that struck at Your temple.*"[16]

The verbal playfulness accompanying this deadly serious exchange is unmistakable. Not surprisingly, Rav Kook explained himself to the rebbe in terms of the classic Hasidic doctrine of *ha'alat nitzotzot*—"the raising of the sparks"—which he had taken to greater sociohistorical dimensions than ever before. The rebbe did not buy it: "Even his theory of *ha'alat nitzotzot* is a dangerous path; so long as they don't repent of their sins, their sparks have nothing to them . . . And this is why the rabbis instructed us *O Sages, take care with your words* [Avot 1:31]."[17] The rebbe continued that he had secured from Rav Kook a letter recanting the more far-reaching pronouncements in his works, in exchange for which the rabbis Diskin and Zonnenfeld revoked their ban on them, which they said had been published without their consent. Had they all been able to talk this over in private, they assured the rebbe, it all could have been avoided. That will never be known. Certainly, in recognition of their growing demographic, political, and economic dependence on Agudat Yisrael, Diskin and Zonnenfeld wanted to calm things down.

Partisans on either side were unsatisfied. The rebbe of Munkacz (Mukachevo, Ukraine), a leading halakhic authority

---

*The rebbe is using a well-known formulation from the opening chapter of Yehudah Ha-Levi's twelfth-century philosophic classic *Sefer Ha-Kuzari:* "You mean well, but your actions are wanting."

and an original thinker whose passionately Kabbalistic, anti-modernist, and anti-Zionist doctrines were the photographic negative of Rav Kook's (whose ideas influenced the arch anti-Zionist Yoel Teitelbaum, who later achieved fame as the Satmar rebbe), attacked the Gerer rebbe for "prettifying the name of Rav Kook, who through his defiled writings instigates and seduces."[18]Among Kook's supporters, Chaim Hirschensohn, a brilliant Talmudist who had emigrated from Palestine to Hoboken, New Jersey, where he authored volume after volume seeking to synthesize Halakha with modern democracy, wrote Rav Kook that he had conceded too much. Rav Kook answered that he had admitted only to regretting the style, not the substance of his writings—and that he had publicized his apology on the understanding that Zonnenfeld's group would do likewise (which, in the end, it did not). He was sure they meant well and urged Hirschensohn and others to put it all behind them.

This was a pattern that recurred again and again in his relations with the ultra-Orthodox. He urged his supporters to impute noble motives to their opponents and turn the other cheek, to be conciliatory and give the benefit of the doubt to those who never dreamed of doing the same toward him.

In the first week of May 1921, the Arabs of Jaffa rioted, murdering forty-seven Jews, among them the writer Yosef Chaim Brenner. There is no record of Rav Kook's immediate response to Brenner's murder, but he spoke about him several years later with Hillel Zeitlin, who was close to both men. Born in 1871 into the same offshoot of Chabad as Rav Kook's maternal grandfather, Zeitlin left Hasidism in his late teens after his father's death, threw himself into literature, philosophy, and, for a while, Zionism, befriending Brenner and other writers. In 1907, he moved to Warsaw, where he stood at the center of Hebrew and Yiddish literary and intellectual life. Indeed, part of Rav Kook's general learning had come from Zeitlin's essays, published in Ahad Ha-Am's journal *Ha-Shiloach* and elsewhere, on philosophy, mysticism, and comparative religion. In time he returned to traditional Judaism, bringing with him discoveries from his explorations. In voluminous writings on Kabbalah, Hasidism, mysticism, and philosophy, he tried to summon what he called "a new religious current" that would save the Jewish people, who, he was eerily convinced, were headed not for redemption but apocalypse.

On Brenner's death, Zeitlin wrote that for all his frank heresy, open rebellion, and merciless criticism of Jewish society, he was a saint who asked nothing for himself and sought the good of his people and humanity. Brenner, "the most ethical individual," had lived, wrote, thundered, and bled like one of the biblical prophets: "There wasn't anyone among the Hebrew writers—and not only the writers—anyone who longed, as he did, for the *Divine Presence.*"[19]

In 1925, Zeitlin visited Palestine and talked with Rav Kook. He later recounted their conversation:

> "I told him [Rav Kook] that I didn't see in 'depth' the wonders that he, the rabbi, sees; the relationship of the pioneers and freethinkers to religion is humiliating and dreadful, and I don't understand why he goes on at length praising those builders."
>
> "I read what you wrote after the death of Brenner," Rav Kook answered.
>
> "And that answers my question?"
>
> "Yes. I read everything you wrote about Brenner, and Brenner wrote many things that grieved the heart of every Jew who cares for his religion. . . . And among the young people in Eyn Charod and those like them, there are many Brenners, big and small. . . ."*

*Zeitlin may not have known this, but Eyn Charod was perhaps the most antireligious kibbutz in Palestine.

"But," Zeitlin continued, "*what use have I for these secrets of the Merciful One?* [Berakhot 10a]."

"No," Rav Kook answered, "not so. Precisely *the secrets of the Merciful One* . . . These years are not like all the previous ones. . . . We are not just living in a time of the footsteps of the Messiah, but we are seeing before us the very beginning of the messianic time itself. Now we must take in and look at men's souls, and not judge them by what meets the eye, but by the longing for redemption and the deeds that they do for the sake of redemption."[20]

After they covered this same ground a few more times, Rav Kook pulled off the shelf a volume of the Tikkunei Zohar and read Zeitlin the passage that he had cited to Ridvaz years earlier, that the generation of the Messiah will be ugly from without, and good within.

On that same trip, Zeitlin paid a visit to Zonnenfeld. They discussed the secular pioneers and their rabbinic defender. "We are at war with them," Zonnenfeld said, "and there is no room for compromise. I can't speak peaceably with them; they are my enemies. The rabbi of Jaffa tries to draw them near in all sorts of ways, but not me. I suspect them of every sin."[21]

Zeitlin gamely tried to explain that one could not judge the youngsters solely on the basis of their attitudes toward religion. They had to be good inside, he said—look at how they sacrifice themselves for the redemption and settlement of the land. Zonnenfeld replied: "Yes, the rabbi of Jaffa talks that way too, but I don't think that is the right path. What do I have to do with their inner lives? *God will see to the heart* [I Samuel 16:7], but we humans, all we have to go on is what we see and to rule according to the law and the halakha . . . and if God has hidden secrets—let Him do as He will." Zonnenfeld, unequivocal as he was, paid the freethinkers the compliment of seeing them as they saw themselves. They wanted no part of traditional Judaism, and he wanted no part of them.

In 1922, Rav Kook began to move forward with another key element of his vision: a yeshiva that would create a new kind of rabbi, one as committed to national rebirth as to tradition. He would be versed not only in the Talmud and the codes but also in the Bible, philosophy, Kabbalah, and belles lettres; trained in rhetoric and composition; and engaged with modern society. In a lecture on December 21, 1920, he laid out his vision, published under the auspices of a new body, Mercaz Ha-Rav (the Rabbi's Center) billed as "the seed and foundation" of the yeshiva to come. The departure from tradition was evident in his opening words: "I call upon you to create. That is the supreme point toward which we must strive. The waves of the national renaissance storm . . . They affect us, and we them."[22] He laid out a detailed program of educational, scholarly, and literary work, including systematizing the vast halakhic corpus as a first step toward making it fit for use in the national revival.

In a way, he was rearticulating the program he had sketched in his abortive journal *Ittur Sofrim* in the late 1880s. Back then, however, his program had only the vaguest connection to the social and political tenor of the times. Four decades later in Palestine, it was part of the institution building going on all around him, and was linked to his larger religious vision and philosophy of history.

He arranged for David Cohen, the university student from Basel, to come to Jerusalem to work on the yeshiva. Cohen became a recognizable Jerusalem figure, known simply as Ha-Nazir, "the Nazarite," for his long locks, vows of silence, and increasingly ascetic ways. At Rav Kook's request, he drafted a curriculum. Its stated educational objective was no less than "the rebirth of the prophetic spirit in the Jewish people and the Land of Israel through the unique effluence of our master the Rabbi."[23] He proposed an astoundingly ambitious and wildly eclectic six-year curriculum featuring numerous (and extraordinary) departures from traditional yeshiva curricula, such as the Bible, Semitic languages, biblical criticism, history, exhaustive study of Jewish philosophy and Kabbalah from all periods, and fields Cohen sought to invent (such as "Hebrew logic"). In keeping with Cohen's university training, even the traditional subjects of the Talmud and halakha were to be taught systematically.

Rav Kook approved nearly all of it—but it took awhile for the yeshiva to get off the ground, since no political or religious institutions wanted to fund it. The culture wars raging around Rav Kook in Jerusalem did not help. Mercaz Ha-Rav opened unexpectedly when two students arrived from Poland and said that they wanted to study in Rav Kook's yeshiva.

As chief rabbi, Rav Kook was thrust into a more crushing press of work than any he had known before. In addition to writing halakhic opinions, adjudicating disputes, and comforting people in distress, he tried to oversee a growing national religious apparatus. He wrote thousands of charity appeals, letters of recommendation, and approvals for immigration certificates. He attended receptions with the colonial secretary, Winston Churchill, birthday celebrations for King George V, and garden parties at the high commissioner's residence. He churned out correspondence at a grueling pace, including exchanges with distinguished rabbis from Eastern Europe, a number of whom, as much as they disagreed with his ideology, respected his learning and piety. They knew also that they needed his help for their own projects, which he gave, knowing he would receive little public support in return.

As an active halakhist, Rav Kook issued detailed answers to a broad range of legal questions, including novel issues pertaining to the Land of Israel, and further developed his method of integrating philosophical and policy concerns into rabbinic adjudication.

Rav Kook and behind him Yosef Chaim Zonnenfeld (with white sash) at a
reception for Colonial Secretary Winston Churchill, Jerusalem, 1921. Churchill is visible in profile in doorway. To Churchill's right, on the stairs, is the
Emir Abdullah of Transjordan. Still from the documentary film *Dreamers
and Builders*. Courtesy of the Israel Film Archive – Jerusalem Cinematheque and the National Center for Jewish Film (www.jewishfilm.org).

He invested much time and effort in other projects too.
One was his supercommentary on the Gaon of Vilna's terse
glosses to Yoseph Karo's sixteenth-century authoritative code,
Shulchan Arukh; he painstakingly reconstructed the Gaon's sourc-
ing of the code's rulings to ancient texts, thereby effectively
slicing through centuries of rabbinic argumentation. A second
project, begun just after the Balfour Declaration was issued,
was the annotation of the entire Talmud with the concrete
legal rulings of Maimonides and the *Shulchan Arukh*, alongside
a systematic method of tracing the evolution of the law. Taken
together, the projects were meant to streamline Talmudic and
halakhic study and refit them for nation building.

Ha-Nazir began another, deeply consequential project in 1922. One day, in the third-person formality of rabbinic etiquette (used down to today), he asked Rav Kook:

"Our master bears holiness, the spirit, and a distinctive, unique effluence. But does the rabbi also have a distinctive body of teaching? A method?"
"Yes, of course."[24]

Rav Kook handed Ha-Nazir the eight notebooks containing the bulk of his journals from 1910 to 1919. Ha-Nazir spent years reading and rereading the thousands of entries, trying to fashion from them a systematic metaphysics, theology, and moral doctrine, whose cardinal principles were, as he came to see it, the holy, universal life, the all-encompassing unity, the encompassing good, and the elevation of the world.

He edited differently from Zvi Yehudah, in both style and substance.* While Zvi Yehudah wove together passages from the notebooks' immense associativeness to create smooth-running, self-contained essays, Ha-Nazir presented individual entries as they had been written, one or, at most, two to a page. Rather than sculpt them into essays, he set them into a latticework of headings, categories and subcategories of his devising. Whereas Zvi Yehudah tended to emphasize the more obviously nationalistic dimensions of his father's teachings, Ha-Nazir, while certainly an apostle of Israel's unique vocation, presented Rav Kook's teachings as a universal philosophy and phenomenology of religion, metaphysics, and ethics. This was a magnum opus, and he called it *Orot Ha-Kodesh* (*Lights of the Holy*).

---

*Aside from *Orot*, Zvi Yehudah edited another major collection of Rav Kook's essays in his lifetime. *Orot Ha-Teshuvah* (1925) gathers Kook's teachings interpreting repentance as a force of love and freedom coursing through the universe. Zvi Yehudah edited many other posthumous volumes after his father's death.

Zvi Yehudah Kook, 1920s. Photo courtesy of the Nezer David
Foundation, Jerusalem.

Rav Kook played little role in the editing. He asked Ha-
Nazir once, slightly puzzled, why he was devoting so much time
and energy to the project. He said that he had three reasons:
First, the rabbi had brought him under the wings of the Shekhinah, and so he had to do something for him in return. Second,

the rabbi's ideas and thoughts were close to his own. Third, love has no reason.[25]

In the spring of 1924, Chaim Nachman Bialik left Europe for good to settle in Tel Aviv. Though he and Rav Kook had missed each other in Volozhin, they had kept abreast of each other through the years. Their meeting during Bialik's first visit to Palestine in the spring of 1909 reportedly left deep impressions on both.

Some years later, in 1917, Bialik published a major essay, "Halakhah ve-Aggadah" (which can be roughly, though misleadingly translated as "law and legend"), many of whose ideas bore a striking familiarity to Kook's own reflections. The two genres, legal and nonlegal, which together comprise the classic rabbinic corpus, Bialik wrote, represent essential aspects of Jewish life, and each without the other leads to vapidity and cultural death. Of course, the two men's ideas were not identical. Rav Kook remained faithful to traditional halakhic practice; Bialik was faithful to the *idea* of halakha, the notion that commitments had to be put into practice if they were to mean anything at all. But he insisted on his break with tradition: "If you take me to be saying say let's return to the *Shulchan Arukh*, you've understood nothing at all."[26] That way of thinking may indeed have been at the further end of some of Rav Kook's visions, but was never articulated with the same sort of finality or rebellion.

Once in Palestine, Bialik threw himself into public activity in the thriving cultural center of Tel Aviv. On Bialik's trips to Jerusalem, Rebbe Binyomin would accompany him on visits to Rav Kook. Rebbe Binyomin later recounted: "The poet who just on the way there had been a gushing fountain sat in modest humility before the master, taking it all in."[27]

Literature mattered greatly to Rav Kook as the vessel and vehicle of subjectivity, self-expression, beauty, creativity, the prelude to the holy spirit, and thence, perhaps, prophecy. Yet while he had his literary admirers, such as Bialik and Agnon, with deep roots in the tradition, he never won the recognition among the literary classes that he hoped for. He confided to a young disciple that he was disappointed at the poor reception that the literati accorded his essays, which he had tried to write in a poetic style. What's the point, he asked in despair, of writings on current affairs that find no echo? Better to write words of Torah, which will always find readers in the *beit midrash*.[28]

There was a genuine problem with his writing in these years. His essays and open letters were often hortatory, disappointing, and flat, displaying none of the inner conflict or dialectical tension that makes his journals so riveting. They made him seem much more serene than he actually was. For there is often a dark, brooding tone in his journals of the early 1920s, reflecting the situation in which he found himself (at times he expresses a seeming terror of gloom and guilt, perhaps, not unrelated to the loss of his daughter). He tried to fight off fear again and again by unmasking alienation as an illusion:

> The darknesses of being are inlaid with groundless fear . . . The penitent fears that his sins have done away with him and his hope is no more—and he doesn't grasp that [precisely] in his fear lie hidden the lights of his salvation. The earth, too, was scared and so didn't bring forth the tree to perfection, [so that] its [bark] would taste like the fruit . . . The moon was scared . . . Humanity is scared of the values of freedom. This world fears the appearance of the world to come.[29]

He was impatient and anxious, and even *spiritual* seems too pale a word for his deepest aspirations.

> Is it in vain, this sorrow, that I may not utter aloud the Divine Name? Isn't it a sacred fire, scorching and burning in the soul?[30]

As much as the zealots hated him, had they read his notebooks they would have hated him even more:

> In every process in life, the secular-mundane awakes first, and then the sacred must necessarily follow, to complete the rebirth of the mundane . . . Woe unto the secular . . . that says *there is none beside me* [Isaiah 47:8], and woe unto the sacred that goes to war with the secular . . . whose deep inside derives from the supreme holiness, sucking from the holy of holies.[31]

On March 18, 1924, Rav Kook landed in New York, accompanied by two distinguished Lithuanian Talmudists, on a fund-raising trip for the Central Relief Committee, an Orthodox body created to help Jewish communities devastated in the war. They were taken to city hall for a reception with Mayor John Hylan, who was pleasantly surprised when Rav Kook spoke in English. The rabbis were based in lodgings on West 76th Street provided by the philanthropist Henry Schiff. They visited Montreal, Pittsburgh, Cleveland, Detroit, Chicago, Philadelphia, Boston, and Baltimore. Almost everywhere they were greeted by mayors and dignitaries and feted at charitable dinners. Rav Kook was the outstanding member of the group, his charisma, according to journalists, felt even by hotel clerks.

On April 15, he met at the White House with Calvin Coolidge, to whom he presented a hymn he had written for the occasion, in Hebrew. A rabbi of the relief committee read it in English, with Rav Kook answering "amen" to every stanza. Coolidge politely expressed his support for a Jewish national home, effectively the only time in his presidency that he endorsed the Balfour Declaration. Afterward Kook was received at the British embassy, where, according to a press account, "the Ambassador invited Rabbi Kook to lunch and the Rabbi

Rav Kook in Washington, D.C., on the day of his White House visit,
April 15, 1924.

accepted the invitation, but partook only of fruit,"[32] diplomatic
hospitality not extending as far as providing kosher food.

The group had planned a three-month visit, but the fund-
raising went so poorly that they extended their stay. Throughout their excursions, Rav Kook was reluctant to collect money
for his own projects and institutions. On November 12, the
rabbis were wished off by thousands of New Yorkers at the pier.

The United States seems to have left almost no impression on him. He hardly wrote or spoke about it, aside from
unsuccessful attempts to forge an educational partnership with
the fledgling Yeshiva College. While there, he wrote Zvi Yehudah that the United States was "exile, albeit festooned with
guilders."[33] Nevertheless, he was impressed by the growing
political influence of American Jewry, which he credited with
arranging the official receptions he was accorded, and through

which, along with much of the ceremonial tributes that he had to sit through, he seems genuinely to have suffered.

At least one encounter, though, left a deep impression. Five years later, in 1929, Yosef Yitzhak Schneerson, the sixth Lubavitcher rebbe, pilgrimaged to Palestine en route to the United States. He met with Rav Kook and, among other things, asked for suggestions of people who might aid his efforts to save Russian Jewry from the Soviets. Kook named two, the philanthropist Harry Fischel and Louis Brandeis. Of the latter, Rav Kook said: "I spoke with him at length, in German. I saw he's a very great man who can't bear injustice being done to anyone, anywhere . . . His soul is hewn of the purest marble."[34]

The Hebrew University of Jerusalem was inaugurated on April 1, 1925. This was a jewel in the crown of the Jewish national revival. Among the many dignitaries in attendance was Lord Balfour himself, who, beside his stature as statesman, was an accomplished philosopher. After being invited to participate, Rav Kook decided, after much hesitation, to attend.* Asked to deliver the first oration, he spoke at even greater length than usual, to the visible irritation of Weizmann, Judah Magnes (the American Reform rabbi, leader, and intellectual who served as the university's first chancellor), and the other notables present.

His remarks were shot through with ambivalence about the university. He began with verses from Isaiah's sublime prophecies of restoration: *Lift your eyes and look about, they all have gathered and come to you . . . and you will see, you will glow, your heart will fear, and expand* [60:4–5]. Whence the fear? The

---

*Rav Kook reported that Weizmann secured his participation by promising that no biblical criticism would be taught at the university, an issue which he and others followed closely for years after, to disappointing results.

Jewish spirit, he said, proceeds along two channels—one immanent, unique to Israel, entirely holy; another expansive, in dialogue with other nations and cultures and necessarily accompanied by fear of contamination.[35] How to allay it? By ensuring that the expansive, outward motion, embodied by the new university, goes hand in hand with the yeshiva, and that its professors be pious Jews whose faith will fuel and shape their scientific and intellectual exploration. Then, truly, will be fulfilled the prophet's vision that all nations will come to learn the Torah in Zion and the word of God at Jerusalem.

Once again, everyone was upset with him. The academics were understandably offended by his patronizing tone and his legitimizing their work by the degree of their subservience to tradition. The ultra-Orthodox, for their part, were inflamed by his participation in the groundbreaking for the institution that threatened them where it mattered most: the life of the spirit and the mind.

As for Rav Kook, he was, once again, speaking out of an unconventional, largely hidden skein of ideas all his own. Not long before, he had written at length to an American correspondent who had asked for his views on general culture.[36] The Torah, he answered, is the soul and fermenting agent of culture. Humanity, he continued, is composed of four dimensions of the spirit—divine, moral, social, and religious—synthesized by a human faculty, aesthetics. The divine spirit is manifest in sacred form as prophecy, and in secular form as poetry and philosophy. The moral spirit is manifest in law, compassion, and justice; the social spirit, in politics, statecraft, nationhood, and the family; the religious spirit (not to be confused with the divine), in the various religions. All these, Jewish and non-Jewish, constitute culture, a genuine dimension of revelation and the necessary foundation of the sacred. This was a theology of culture that might have moved his listeners had he expressed it outright, and not in a hortatory homiletic intended to give no offense to the ultra-Orthodox. They attacked him anyway, with renewed abandon.

In 1923, thanks to the American benefactor Harry Fischel, the Kook family moved into a home of their own, on a side street near the city center and just off the main thoroughfare of Jaffa Road. Fittingly, it lay across the street from the printing press founded by Yoel Moshe Salomon, who had first brought him to Jaffa. When Rav Kook would write through the night, Salomon's grandson, Shlomo Zalman, now managing the press, would often come and pick up the manuscript first thing in the morning and set it directly into type, with no editing or rewriting.

Their neighbors were Albert and Anna Ticho, he a physician, she a painter (known in particular for her watercolors of the Judean hills), whose home was frequented by the literary, cultural, and intellectual elite of Jerusalem. Rav Kook began to attract their notice. Samuel Hugo Bergmann, a philosopher and the guiding spirit of the Prague circle of Jewish intellectuals that included Max Brod and Franz Kafka, became fascinated with him. Bergmann, the founding librarian of Hebrew University, lent the rabbi rare volumes to study. Bergmann's colleague at Hebrew University (and in the Brit Shalom binationalist movement), Gershom Scholem, then laying the foundations for his monumental historical studies of the Kabbalah, also made Rav Kook's acquaintance, through Agnon and others. Rav Kook was deeply impressed by Scholem's vast erudition; Scholem, for his part, was deeply impressed with the rabbi's unmistakable mystical gravitas, but wary of his messianism.*

*Scholem also made the acquaintance of Ha-Nazir, who left a deep impression on him, saying, "I had thought there were no more Kabbalists, and here in Jerusalem there walked a living Kabbalist, creating Kabbalah in our times." Yet, Scholem added, "All my efforts to get to the bottom of his thinking came to naught." It was a pity, he said, that Hillel Zeitlin hadn't occupied a similar place at Rav Kook's side.

Another visitor brought by Agnon was Marc Chagall, during his visit to Palestine in 1931. The painter was very taken with Rav Kook and wanted to draw his portrait. Rav Kook demurred, saying, "What good would it do the Jewish people?" After they left, Chagall asked Agnon, "Where do you get a holy face like that?"[37]

Rav Kook restored and deepened ties with prewar disciples. Aryeh Levine was born in 1885 to an impoverished family in Belarus; after years of wandering among yeshivot in a life of grinding poverty, he made his way at age twenty to Jerusalem. Zvi Pesach Franck, the rabbinical jurist, introduced him to his sister-in-law, Zipporah Shapiro, a daughter and granddaughter of distinguished Lithuanian rabbis, and they married. In 1916, he was made *mashgiach*, "spiritual tutor," of Yeshivat Etz Chaim, a citadel of the Old Yishuv, headed by Yechiel Tikochinski, a post Levine held for the rest of his life. But his real calling was beyond the walls of the institution. From early on, Reb Aryeh, as he was known, devoted his days and nights to visiting the sick, arranging anonymous donations to the poor, and counseling the distressed. He was not a major Talmudist, but a genius of human kindness.

On Rav Kook's move to Jerusalem, Reb Aryeh became one of his closest disciples. Largely removed from politics and ideology, and beloved among Zionists and anti-Zionists alike, he and Rav Kook shared a tie that ran along deep currents of the sheer empathy and asceticism that they shared.

As the mandate wore on, Arab-Jewish tensions rose. Zionist aspirations fell increasingly out of favor with the British, and arrests of Jewish activists became more common, leading the British authorities to ask Rav Kook to recommend a Jewish chaplain for the Jerusalem jail. He unhesitatingly suggested Reb Aryeh. When asked why, Rav Kook said, "There is in Reb Aryeh something of his being compassionate in his very body—that is the secret of his soul and the *tikkun* it works in the world."[38] It is perhaps not too far-fetched that in the translucent kindness of Reb Aryeh, this diminutive, poverty-stricken saint, he glimpsed what he had written about in his notebooks, the transfiguration of the body in radiant goodness. Another time, when asked why he loved Reb Aryeh so much, he said "I've never heard him say anything good about me, or bad about anyone else."[39] "If only we had in our time three Jews like him," he said, "the Messiah would come."

Once, when one of the zealots verbally assaulted him for his closeness to Rav Kook, Reb Aryeh said nothing. An ultra-Orthodox onlooker, seeing Reb Aryeh's distress, offered to walk him home.

"Do you know what you did to deserve that?" he asked him.

"Perhaps I sinned before God," Reb Aryeh said.

"No, it's because you're close with that rabbi."

"Do you think I did right by my restraint?"

"Of course, it is a sign of your virtue. As the Talmud says, 'the humiliated who do not humiliate in return, who bear abuse and do not respond in kind, of them it is said, *And the enlightened will shine like the splendor of the sky* [BT Shabbat 88, after Daniel 12:3].'"

"Then you should know that that is what I have learned from 'that rabbi.'"[40]

Rav Kook was never a partisan man, and his relations with the multifarious parties and factions of the Yishuv and the Zionist movement were always distant and complicated. On the Left, his genuine enthusiasm for the pioneers of the Second Aliyah did not easily translate to the new world of the mandate when they shifted from being an ideological vanguard to the heads of institutions, as he had done. (Fundamentally supportive of the workers, he ruled that strikes and labor actions were permitted under Jewish law.) Jabotinsky's secular Zionist Right did not speak to him, distanced as it was from both Jewish tradition and the moral pathos of the Left. Throughout, Rav Kook engaged in lengthy and futile battles against Sabbath desecration in public, but those efforts neither made the workers change their religious mores nor convinced the ultra-Orthodox that he was anything other than a delirious supporter of the Left, and the Left of him.

The straits in which he found himself are well illustrated by the recollections of a student in his yeshiva, Azriel Carlebach. On Passover Eve in 1925, he and his classmates accompanied Rav Kook to a militantly secular kibbutz near Jerusalem to offer them matzot.[41] The workers chased them away. Two days later, on the first day of Passover, Kook was attacked by young ultra-Orthodox zealots on his way to prayers at the Wailing Wall. On their way back from the kibbutz incident, Carlebach recalled, Rav Kook—in whose writings the idea of reincarnation scarcely appears—had confided to his students that he thought he bore within him a reincarnated spark of the soul of the biblical Joshua, Moses's embattled disciple (in rabbinic tradition, Moses is the sun, and Joshua, the moon).*

There was one exception to his nonpartisanship. A religious Left workers' party, Ha-Po'el Ha-Mizrachi, was formed in 1922. Unlike the original Mizrachi, their religious roots were less in Lithuanian Talmudism and more in strains of Polish Hasidism that emphasized personal authenticity while rejecting religious and social conventions. Their leader, Shmuel Chaim Landau (known by his acronym, "Shachal"—"young lion"), urged "the sacred rebellion," a fusion of religious practice with the spiritual rejuvenation through labor preached in the Second Aliyah by Aharon David Gordon. They were joined in the

---

*Carlebach eventually returned to Germany, obtained a doctorate in law, and turned to journalism. On his return to Palestine, in 1937, he founded the mass-circulation daily *Yediot Acharonot*, and later another daily newspaper, *Ma'ariv*.

late 1920s by new religious kibbutzim founded by young Religious Zionists from Germany, latter-day disciples of Samson Raphael Hirsch and inheritors of his ethical pathos and passion for institution building. The German Religious Zionists joined the neo-Hasidim in Ha-Po'el Ha-Mizrachi to create an alternative to what they saw as the too respectable and spiritually and ethically compromised Mizrachi of Yehudah Leib Maimon and Meir Berlin.

This small group of young people was the one political movement that Rav Kook ever loved. He became their patron, obtained funds for them as best he could, and made them feel welcome in his home. "I truly am not a party man, and cannot be," he wrote to one of their activists, "but I see in Ha-Po'el Ha-Mizrachi the perfect fulfillment of pious Judaism."[42]

It was long Rav Kook's custom on Shavuot to lecture all night on the jurisprudential introduction to Maimonides' code. On Shavuot night in 1927, a young man, newly arrived to Jerusalem, came to listen. He asked one question, then a second, and after the third, Rav Kook asked him to come by after the holiday. Saul Lieberman was a Talmudic prodigy and autodidact from Belarus studying Talmudic philology and Greek at the fledgling Hebrew University. Rav Kook took him under his wing. Even while trying to build his yeshiva, he did not give up the idea of fostering some synthesis of academic Jewish studies with traditional learning, and perhaps even with soul. His disciples Binyamin Menashe Levin, Moshe Zeidel, and others were trying to work that seam, and he hoped that Lieberman would too.

In 1928, the Yishuv finally settled on a structure for Jewish self-government, the Constitution of the Communities. In the new arrangement, a Zionist body called Knesset Yisrael would represent the entire Yishuv, across the ideological spectrum.

Those who did not want to be a part could opt out, which, unsurprisingly, the ultra-Orthodox did. But so did many moderate Orthodox—including Rav Kook's two most important colleagues on the Chief Rabbinate Council (as it was called), Franck and Bernstein—and for good measure, Ya'akov Meir, his Sephardi counterpart, did too.

Rav Kook had been noncommittal throughout the lengthy negotiations on the constitution. He was ideologically committed to the program of national inclusion, yet under the new constitution, the rabbinate was just another administrative entity firmly under the jurisdiction of the Jewish National Council. Franck and Bernstein had put him in an impossible situation. He needed their support on his right flank, but it was simply inconceivable that members of the Chief Rabbinate Council of the organized Yishuv would refuse to be members of Yishuv institutions as a whole. Caught between his allies, his constituents, and his ideology, Rav Kook bobbed and weaved and frustrated everybody. His unwillingness to give offense to anyone neutralized his friends and fueled his enemies, and fruitless negotiations on restructuring the rabbinate went on for years.

Paradoxically, the ecumenism of Rav Kook's approach to the rabbinate paralyzed it. Without partisan political backing, the institution went nowhere during his lifetime. Chronically underfunded, it worked out of a basement. Rav Kook never drew a salary from the rabbinate, his meager living provided by his position as president of the General Committee of Knesset Yisrael. Visitors to the Kooks' home were regularly struck by the sheer material want in which they lived.

Attached to the second floor of their home was a *beit midrash*, the site of the yeshiva, which slowly grew. A picture of the yeshiva emerges from the memoirs of Haim Cohn, who arrived from Germany in 1930, along with his brother. He decided to study there after seeing Rav Kook at the third Sabbath meal. "We heard him, but understood nothing," Cohn wrote. Yet "it was clear then and there that we would study here. I was enchanted by the rabbi's kind and shining eyes, and couldn't take mine off him. There was in his visage a kind of sanctity that had taken fleshly form. His delicate hand motions and soft beneficent speech were testament to the nobility of his soul."[43]

There were some eighty students, weekly lectures, but few fixed classes, Ha-Nazir's elaborate program notwithstanding. Rav Kook gave a weekly Talmud class, always in the evening, speaking quickly and softly in Ashkenazic Hebrew for hours on end. Charlap was officially the *rosh yeshiva*, overseeing the students and their studies and giving regular lectures. Unlike Rav Kook, Cohn noted, he spoke unhurriedly, encouraged the students to interrupt and ask questions, and made himself as available as he could. Ha-Nazir taught Maimonides' *Guide*, which he explained "in language as complicated and involved as Maimonides himself." Ha-Nazir could be a delightful and cultured conversationalist, but not on Shabbat, when he spoke sparingly and only on sacred matters. Zvi Yehudah gave a weekly Bible class, and there was a young spiritual tutor, Yitzhak Arieli. Politics, Cohn says, never came up in the yeshiva, other than regarding the ultra-Orthodox wars with Zionism. Zionism itself was rarely discussed, but assumed.*

The inclusion of Bible study and philosophy in the curriculum were genuine departures from traditional yeshivot, as

---

*Cohn eventually left the yeshiva to study law at university; while he says in his autobiography that it was with Rav Kook's blessing, his study partner Yechezkel Kutscher, who left with him, said that Rav Kook was furious. Charlap later told Kutscher, who remained religious and became an eminent philologist, "the rabbi saw with his *eyna pikcha* (literally in Aramaic, "open eye," a Kabbalistic term for divination) that one of you would come to a bad end, though he wasn't sure which one." Cohn became an agnostic, eminent jurist of Israel's Supreme Court, and the founding father of Israeli civil liberties. In later years, Zvi Yehudah, alluding to the most infamous heretic of the Talmud, referred to him as "the Elisha ben Avuyah of our time."

was the use of Hebrew as the language of instruction. The yeshiva was a sociological departure too. Jerusalemites began to notice a new kind of yeshiva boy: in modern dress, unmistakably pious, and unabashedly Zionist.

Rav Kook had not given much thought to the Arabs of Palestine; he bore them no enmity, had cordial relations with non-Jewish religious leaders, and spoke generally in terms of coexistence and cooperation. He did not, in the early mandate years, advocate any changes in the status quo of religious sites, for necessary modifications would come peacefully, he was sure, in the fullness of time.

The most contentious site of all was the Wailing Wall, known to Jews simply as Ha-Kotel, "the Wall," situated in an alleyway running in the Old City's Mughrabi Quarter. The Jews long resented but lived with the Ottoman policy that while they could congregate there and pray, synagogue accoutrements such as benches, and certainly Torah scrolls, were expressly forbidden. The British had no desire to upset the status quo, which, in addition to being sound colonial practice, was to be maintained as an official part of their charge under the terms of the mandate. The Muslims, for their part, were as alert as they were resistant to any change in the status quo, however trivial, that might favor the Jews. The *waqf* (Islamic religious endowment) officials who oversaw the Temple Mount and environs were no longer willing to look the other way when Jews brought benches to the Kotel. Nor was the Supreme Muslim Council, which had been created by the British in January 1922 and was headed by the mufti of Jerusalem, Haj-Amin al-Husseini.

The council, like the rabbinate, was intended to take the place of the institutions through which the Ottomans had managed their colonial subjects' religious affairs. Yet the two institutions and their occupants could not have been more different.

In the mid-nineteenth century, the Husseinis had managed to make the office of Mufti of Jerusalem, then a not terribly influential position, into their family business. When the incumbent died in 1921, Haj Amin, one of his younger brothers —in his midtwenties, a favorite of nationalists, but of no scholarly or spiritual distinction—lost the election but was appointed anyway by the high commissioner (who sought to maintain a balance between the Husseinis and the other leading Jerusalem Arab clan, the Nashishibis, one of whom the British had made mayor the year before). He then claimed to be the supreme mufti of all Palestine. The British had hoped that the Supreme Muslim Council would smooth the administration of Muslim religious affairs, satisfy some Arab nationalist aspirations, and forestall further agitation. They were wrong.

The mufti's overall strategy for confronting the Zionists was to convert the local contest in Palestine into a pan-Arab and pan-Muslim struggle. And so, from the beginning, the mufti and the council—as well as its internal opposition, the Nashishibi clan's Arab Executive Committee—took the position that the Jews had no rights to the Wall. The Zionist leadership, understanding the political hay that the mufti was seeking to make, tried to keep the status quo as best they could. So did Zonnenfeld, the formal rabbinic authority over the sextons of the Kotel, both because he felt the Jews needed to understand that they were still in exile, and because he had no desire to see authority over the Kotel pass to the Zionists. But harassment and attacks on Jewish worshippers at the Kotel became more frequent.

On Yom Kippur 1928, British constables forcefully removed a makeshift *mechitzah*—a partition separating men's and women's sections—in the middle of services, and a melee ensued. When Rav Kook called for public fasts on October 22, 1928, to protest the indignities at the Kotel, the ultra-Orthodox ignored him, as they studiously ignored every prayer meeting and fast day that he called.

A British white paper of November 1928 reaffirmed the status quo at the Kotel and forbade the Jews to make any changes. For months after, the mufti and the council issued one protest after another, groundlessly asserting that the Kotel's *mechitzah* was proof of a Zionist plot to take the Temple Mount and raze its mosques. Through the year, the mufti's own status had begun to waver among his constituents, and a violent uprising against the Jews, always a tempting thought, became more appealing than ever.

As tensions mounted, the Zionist Executive tried to keep the situation calm and discouraged Jewish demonstrations. To the Jabotinskyites, who in 1925 had launched their own party, the Revisionists, this was self-defeating, dishonest, and servile. On the fast of Tisha B'Av in 1929 (August 15), they staged a demonstration at the Kotel, in response to which Arabs attacked worshippers there two days later. Rav Kook met with the demonstrators and encouraged them after the fact, to the great irritation of the British authorities. In a newspaper interview he gave on the night of the fifteenth, published on the eighteenth, he said that the streets around the Kotel ought to be purchased and cleared, while stressing that the Temple Mount should be untouched and its ultimate disposition left to the hand of divine providence. His comments were taken as further proof of a Jewish plot to seize the Temple Mount and its mosques. A few days later, Muslims staged a march through the Mughrabi Quarter, further inflaming matters. Harry Luke, the acting high commissioner, made a feeble and futile effort to get Arab and Jewish leaders to announce a peaceful resumption of the status quo ante.

On August 23, riots broke out across the country. Among the Jews, 133 died and 339 were injured; among the Arabs, 116 died and 232 were injured. Most of the Jews killed were in Safed, Jerusalem, and Hebron. The attackers did not distinguish between Zionist and non-Zionist. Many were murdered horrifically, and their bodies mutilated. As it turned out, almost the entire formal leadership of the Yishuv was out of the country, returning home from the Sixteenth Zionist Congress, which had just concluded in Zurich. Rav Kook was one of the most senior Jewish leaders still in Palestine.

Yitzhak Ben-Zvi, a Labor member of the National Council, the Yishuv's internal self-governing body, rushed to Rav Kook's house, it being Shabbat, to bring him the news. They hurried to the nearest available telephone, at Hadassah Hospital on Mount Scopus. Rav Kook got on the line, and on hearing of the atrocities, fainted. When he came to, he tore his clothes, recited the traditional prayer on hearing of a death, and sat like a mourner on the ground. After regaining his composure, he called Luke and asked for British intervention. Luke said that he did not know what exactly he could do under the circumstances. When Rav Kook suggested he order the police to shoot, Luke replied that he had no such authority. He was as unmoved by the rabbi's declaration that he himself would assume full responsibility as by his appeals to "human conscience" and Luke's civic obligations.

Rav Kook hurried back home and issued a telegram calling on the outside world for help (although he did not have to sign it himself, he did, to make the point that saving lives overrides the Sabbath). His home filled up with Jews fleeing the riots in the southern part of town. He threw himself into organizing relief efforts and making contact with any authorities that he could. Aside from a few cups of tea with milk, he ate nothing for three days. "His activity," Ha-Nazir recalled, "like his pain and grief, had no limit."[44]

The anti-Jewish riots of 1929 were unprecedented in their scale and savagery, and the Yishuv was deeply shaken. In response to the riots, Rav Kook published an open letter, "Return to the Citadel"[45] (taken from Zechariah 9:12: "Return to the citadel, prisoners of hope"). In it he reaffirmed that the material and spiritual revival of the Yishuv, the World War, and the Balfour Declaration were all driven by the "hidden spark of the light of Messiah, the Redeemer revealed, then hidden, and then revealed once again." The latest setback should thus not cause despair, "for the greater the occlusion, the greater the light to be revealed."

Like rabbis before and since, he responded to persecution with a call for repentance. But that, for him, meant the rediscovery of spiritual self-consciousness and a process of national reconciliation. And so he called for mutual recognition between the Old Yishuv and the New, the root and the branch; one the repository of the spiritual heritage that was the ultimate root of the other's dynamic rebuilding of Israel's material—social, political, economic, and cultural—life.

He was, in characterizing the Old Yishuv and the New as root and branch of the same sacred élan vital, describing them in ways dramatically at odds with the self-perception of each. But once again, his seemingly willful naivete went hand in hand with a powerful intuition. Zionism's continuities with Jewish history, messianic longings, and—in its Hebrew revival—literary riches, and ultra-Orthodoxy's dependence on the New Yishuv, both for physical as well as even cultural survival, were deeper than either cared to admit. On a more prosaic level, if the mufti and his men ignored the distinction between religious and secular, the Jews would be well advised to do the same.

Another open letter by Rav Kook, this one addressed to the mufti, was published in the leading Zionist organ, *Ha-Olam*, on October 18, 1929, and subsequently reprinted in the *Times* (London) and Arab publications. He began by dismissing the mufti's denial of historical Jewish connections to the Wailing Wall and his claim that the Jewish "demonstration" of August 15—on the ancient fast of the Ninth of Av—was political. There was no way that the age-old Jewish mourning practices of that day could justify the murder, rape, and destruction that followed.

The mufti had argued that the riots' having been limited to Jerusalem, Hebron, and a few other locations pointed to their spontaneity. To the contrary, Rav Kook wrote, what it pointed to was the Arabs' recoil from violence as a whole and the mufti's hand in the murders that did take place:

> I know for certain that the Arab nation as a whole and the majority of the Arabs of the Land of Israel itself are full of sorrow and shame at the evil deeds of a minority, through the fault of their inciters. And we hope that the tradition of peace and mutuality, to build together with all the inhabitants of the Land of Israel this beloved and forsaken land . . . will vanquish all the lying and cheating plots, the impurity and malice, which warmongers and the bloody-minded seek to spread.[46]

He was perhaps being wishful, but he refused to demonize Arabs or Islam or to play the mufti's game of declaring holy war. (Not to mention that there were Arabs who, out of pragmatism, resentment of the Mufti, a less absolute view of nationalism, or local reasons of their own, continued to cooperate with the Zionists.) He eschewed as well Jabotinsky's call for an "iron wall" of force as the necessary guarantor of Zionist aspirations.

The following spring, he wrote in support of Zionist land purchases. "As we return to capture our land," he wrote, "we do so not by might or the sword but the path of peace, paying in full for every footstep of our land, even if our right to the earth of our holy land never lapsed," whether wrested from Israel by cash or by the sword. "We want to fulfill the mitzvah of *love thy neighbor* [Leviticus 19:18] not only toward individuals but also toward nations so that none of the gentile nations will bear any claim or resentment against us."[47] Thus Israel would lawfully acquire the land twofold, by dint of peaceful acquisition as well as its eternal covenant with God.

The Zionist leadership, though, started drawing darker conclusions and preparing for the worst. As for the ultra-Orthodox, the riots of 1929 ended once and for all any thoughts they had entertained of coming to a separate peace with the Arabs. The British may have thought them, as Storrs wrote, "ideal subjects," but at the moment of truth had done nothing to protect them. The ultra-Orthodox did not relax their ideological opposition to Zionism, but understood the need to cooperate with it in order to survive. In January 1930 at a League of Nations inquiry into the status of the Kotel, representatives of the chief rabbinate sat alongside colleagues from Agudat Yisrael.

But the vilification of Rav Kook never let up, especially among members of the Agudat Yisrael youth movement, who heckled him, attacked him in posters, and at times threw buckets of water in his face as he walked down the street.

On the eve of the Seventeenth Zionist Congress, set to convene in Basel on June 30, 1931, Rav Kook added his signature to a letter asking the congress to encourage public Sabbath observance, alongside an endorsement of the Zionist movement's fund-raising arm. The zealots were incensed, not least because one of the other signatories was Isser Zalman Meltzer, an outstanding Talmudist and famously gentle soul, who also sat on the Supreme Rabbinic Council of Agudat Yisrael. Meltzer, a former classmate of Kook's in Volozhin, had arrived to Palestine in 1925 to lead Jerusalem's Yeshivat Etz Chaim. A major scholar of impeccable ultra-Orthodox credentials, Meltzer resolutely defended Kook against attackers on the right. He was wont to say, "Let them, any of us, pray on Yom Kippur the way Rav Kook prays on an average weekday."

The zealots took to the billboards of Jerusalem (the *pash-*

kevilim mentioned earlier), skewering with a characteristic mix of malice and delight the figure they referred to as "that man" —the classic rabbinic euphemism for Jesus. Addressing themselves to the many rabbis who had enlisted Rav Kook's support in their quests for funds and other benefits, they sought to remind them:

> "That man" is an instigator and seducer, holding fast to the views of the freethinkers and to the funds of the Zionists . . . digging his defiled claws into all the walls of Judaism to topple them, seducing many innocents with his style, smooth tongue, movements, and demeanor, like so many lambs led to slaughter. Even if, when great sages come to him, he shows them his kosher claws, he is to our mind the greatest force for defilement and the very seat of the Other Side itself.[48]

The heads of Agudat Yisrael in Europe were upset. Much as they disagreed with Rav Kook's ideology, they greatly respected him. Moreover, their cohorts, now emigrating from Poland and Germany in great numbers, wanted and needed better relations with the Yishuv than the zealots were letting them have. They urged their clients in Jerusalem to rein them in, to no avail.

On March 23, 1932, the eve of the holiday of Purim, the Jerusalem chapter of the Agudah youth staged a mock trial in which Rav Kook was tried for heresy. Next, they mutilated him in effigy as the youngsters danced around and sang. A few days later, Yosef Chaim Zonnenfeld passed away at age eighty-three, and with him went the last possible restraint on the zealots. In the coming months, they stepped up their heckling at Rav Kook's public addresses and even eulogies. When, in January 1933, he sent a letter of greeting to the Maccabi sports association, wishing them luck and kindly asking them not to play on the Sabbath, the billboard rhetoric against him reached a new pitch. "That man, the *min* (that is, Christian), hypocritical, flattering, like a pig rummaging in trash and raising a stink, and his helpers, assistants, ass lickers." Zonnenfeld's successor, Yosef Zvi Dushinsky, newly arrived from Romania, was even less inclined than was his more distinguished predecessor to restrain the zealots. "I did not come to Eretz Yisrael," he said, "to be labeled a heretic at the end of my days."[49]

The zealots utterly misread Rav Kook's—and their own—situation. They imputed to him greater suasion, influence, and identification with secular Zionism than he ever had. Powerless to stem the Zionist tide and the mounting secularization all around them, they struck out at the nearest target, whose defense of the Zionist project was all the more infuriating for his looking, and largely living, just like them. Yet he not only never responded in kind, but instead did favors, wrote letters of recommendation and fund-raising appeals, and arranged favors and benefits, for even some of his bitterest foes.

One night a disciple of his came upon him while taking a walk. On reminding Rav Kook of the Talmudic adage that a *talmid chakham*, a rabbinic sage, ought not to walk about alone at night, lest he be set upon by demons, Rav Kook answered, "I have nothing to worry about; in this city the demons don't think I'm a *talmid chakham*." At other times the abuse was harder to take. His assistants would sometimes find him sobbing to himself in Yiddish, "What do they want from me?"

He tried, despite the crush of work and the many pressures on him, to call on his parents every day. His father passed away in 1929, his mother in 1931, and at her *shiva* he was inconsolable. One visitor tried to comfort him with the understandable suggestion that his mother must have been unimaginably proud to see her son designated chief rabbi of the Land of Israel. Yes, he said, that is true. But still, she was the only person in the world who would call me "my child," *mayn kindt*.[50]

By the early 1930s, he was not well, and the years and relentless strains were taking their toll. In his journals he turned to God more directly than ever, in the second-person singular, perhaps because the mists of purity, suffused with light, were lifting and revealing a darker reality in which the oceanic tide of being was replaced by lone dialogue with God.

> My soul thirsts for the higher light, the endless light, light of the true God, God of my life, living God, light of the universes, and the longing devours my strength, physical and spiritual . . . O sate my pleasure and sate me with your beautiful light, quench my thirst for your light, shine your countenance, and we will be redeemed.[51]

The public role that he had cast for himself—builder of new institutional structures—left him unable to express the oceanic overflow he felt within:

> Who is it that stops me, why can't I reveal in writing all my thoughts . . . who is stopping me . . . My spiritual forces within roar in grief. They feel . . . imprisoned without just cause. They are right; justice and righteousness are on their side . . . When will I speak and write all that rustles in my heart . . . Light, light, light, *God is my light and salvation, from whom will I fear* [Psalms 27:1] *[Sit though I may in darkness] God is my light* [Micah 7:8].[52]

Perhaps he felt such a crisis of inhibition because his visions were too subtle for words.

> The distinction between [one degree of] the sacred and [another] is deeper and more wondrous than that between sacred and mundane . . . Differences of degree . . . that the mouth cannot utter nor the heart understand.[53]

On the evening of June 16, 1933, Chaim Arlosoroff, a brilliant young intellectual and head of the political department of the Zionist Executive's successor body, the Jewish Agency, was shot and killed while walking with his wife along the beach in Tel Aviv. Three days later, Abba Achimeir and Avraham Stavsky, two members of Jabotinsky's Revisionist movement, were arrested and charged: Achimeir (born Gaisinovicz) was a thirty-five-year-old journalist and intellectual (his doctoral dissertation was on Spengler's *Decline of the West*). He admired European strongmen like Marshall Pilsudski of Poland and, for a while, Mussolini, and was cofounder of an anti-British movement called Brit Ha-Biryonim, "The Thugs' Covenant." Stavsky, the accused shooter, was an undistinguished twenty-seven-year-old card-carrying Revisionist, just arrived from Lithuania. A third Revisionist, Zvi Rosenblatt, age twenty-one, recently of Czernowitz (Ukraine), was arrested several days later.

The temperature of the Yishuv, never low, had in the months preceding the murder been more feverish than ever as Labor and the Revisionists fought for control over institutions and for public opinion with mounting intensity ("Yes, Break It!" was the title of Jabotinsky's manifesto against the Histadrut, the labor federation of Ben-Gurion's Workers' Party, known by its Hebrew acronym, Mapai). Hitler's rise to power in January 1933 had ratcheted up the fear and complexity suffusing an already complicated situation. The Revisionists advocated a total boycott of Germany, while the Zionist Left and Center sought legally to transfer as much Jewish property as possible to Palestine. In the early stages of the Nazi regime, emigration from Germany was still the official preferred solution to the "Jewish problem," and Arlosoroff had represented the Zionist Executive in negotiations with the Germans, which were coming to a head (and resulted in several agreements later that year).

The morning before the murder, nearly all of page 2 of the Revisionist newspaper, the *National Front*, was devoted to an attack on Arlosoroff by a friend of Achimeir's, Yochanan Pogrebinsky. Titled "The Stalin–Ben-Gurion–Hitler Pact," it accused "Mister Arlosoroff . . . the Red wonder child" (he was thirty-four with a doctorate in economics), of having "sold the Hebrew people's dignity, rights, security, and standing throughout the world for filthy lucre, to Hitler and the Nazis." "The red diplomat of Mapai," it continued, "crawled on all fours to Hitler and his chums"; the screed ominously concluded that "the Hebrew people" had always known how to deal with sellouts.

Ben-Gurion, who was in Europe at the time and had been physically assaulted by a Jabotinskyite in Warsaw, was convinced from the outset of the Revisionists' guilt. A telegram from him published in Berl Katznelson's *Davar* on June 18 mourned the death of Arlosoroff "at the hands of thugs, *biryonim*, who thirst for our blood." Katznelson, Histadrut leader and Mapai's intellectual conscience, was similarly convinced, if a little less explicit. At a memorial service held nearly a fortnight later in Jerusalem, he denounced an unnamed (but unmistakable) "sect . . . focused on the myth of one man." At the same gathering, Bialik thundered, choking with tears: "Defiled words have been cast into us, hitherto unknown . . . 'fist,' '*biryon*'—let there be no place for them. Let our camp be holy. 'Fire and blood' and all those expressions signifying nothing, but nothing, let them have no place among us."[54]

Jabotinsky, for his part, did not take all this lying down. On June 28, he declared, "The vast majority of our people are embittered by the pogrom and blood libel being waged by Jews against Jews. But I warn them that by their cowed silence . . . they are helping the enemies of the Jews and Zionism distort the investigation into the murder from the true sources of the crime, who are undoubtedly those whom we have to thank for the riots of 1929."[55] Urging his supporters to stand fast and proud, he doffed his hat to Arlosoroff, who, he said, had muttered as he lay dying that no Jew had killed him.

Over the coming months, the Yishuv tore itself apart. Class and ideological tensions between Labor and the Revisionists that had simmered throughout the previous decade finally exploded. In elections for the Eighteenth Zionist Congress, to be held later that summer in Prague, the Revisionist share of delegates dwindled to 14 percent (and stayed there for forty years).

For many, the Revisionists' guilt, collective and individual, was obvious, even overdetermined. The rhetoric of Achimeir and others was truly violent; their admiration for fascism and their vilification of Ben-Gurion and Arlosoroff were unmistakable; their antipathy to Labor Zionism and their open challenge to its ideology and authority were on constant display; and all their manifold anxieties had been raised to an unnerving pitch by the rise of the Nazis. To borrow a phrase from a political trial of another era, even if there were no smoking gun in the hands of a Revisionist, the room was full of smoke.

As the investigation stretched on, through the fall and winter and into spring, some—even Laborites—began to doubt the Revisionists' guilt. As early as mid-August 1933, Bialik confided to Ben-Zion Katz, a journalist working on a pamphlet arguing for the defendants' innocence, that notwithstanding his loathing for Jabotinsky, he was convinced that the killers were not Jews. In January 1934, Abdul Medjid, an Arab jailed on other charges, confessed to involvement in the killing. Then, under pressure from the Arab Executive, he recanted and said the Jews had tried to bribe him. The father of one of the officers who took Mejid's testimony sat on Ya'akov Meir's rabbinical court, and he and Rav Kook became privy to the details of the confession. The resignation of the ranking Jewish officer on the police investigation, Yehudah Tenenbaum (Arazi), also gave some observers pause.

Meanwhile Rav Kook kept his own counsel and refused to be drawn in. Associates and people he respected were to be found in both camps. When pressed, he said he wanted to let the justice system run its course.* At a meeting in Tel Aviv on March 13, 1934, with Meir Dizengoff (Tel Aviv's mayor), Bialik, and others, he and other rabbis asked for a cease-fire in the war of words, along with a temporary suspension of judgment regarding guilt or innocence.

Shortly afterward, Rav Kook was visited by a rabbinic colleague and passionate Zionist, Natan Milikovsky. His son Ben-Zion, a Revisionist journalist, saw Achimeir in Jerusalem the night of the murder, and Milikovsky had become utterly convinced of the defendants' innocence.† For hours, he went over the details of Katz's pamphlet, exercising the rhetorical skill with which he had turned thousands of Siberian and Polish Jews into Zionists, climaxing in the rhetorical question whether Rav Kook wanted to be responsible through his silence for a new crucifixion in Jerusalem.

Rav Kook began to tell close associates that he was convinced of the Revisionists' innocence. On April 24, 1934, a day after the trial began, he added his signature to a letter signed by a number of public figures, announcing a fund to pay for the defense of the defendants, "our three imprisoned brothers." On May 16, Achimeir was acquitted of murder, but was kept in jail for his sub-

*In addition, the Yishuv had known political murder before. On June 30, 1924, Jacob De Haan, an attorney, ultra-Orthodox intellectual, and scarcely closeted homosexual who, as de facto foreign minister of the ultra-Orthodox community, sought common cause with Arab nationalists in the battle against Zionism, was shot and killed in Jerusalem. It has long been believed that his death was ordered by high echelons of the Haganah, the prestate, mainstream Zionist military force, though recently it has been suggested that it was done by a tiny splinter group called Ha-Mif'al ("the enterprise"). Either way, De Haan was certainly murdered by Jews. At the time, Rav Kook was in the middle of his lengthy trip to the United States, and while he presumably heard about it, it is unclear how much of his attention it received.

†One can only speculate whether this spectacular trial had some role in fueling Ben-Zion's later career as an eminent historian of the Inquisition, which he pursued after Hebraizing his last name to Netanyahu.

versive activities. He went on a hunger strike, and at Milikovsky's request, Rav Kook wrote to ask him to desist, addressing him as *sofer yakar*, translatable as "dear writer" or "precious author." This was too much for the Left to bear. Mapai's the *Young Worker* editorialized that Rav Kook had placed on Achimeir's head "a frontlet [like that worn by the high priest in the Temple] engraved with the sign of Satan and the swastika."[56] Ha-Po'el Ha-Mizrachi did its best to defend him; the movement's paper editorialized that this was "a slip of the pen," but to no avail, and anyway Rav Kook himself said that it was not. Left-leaning publications and organizations denounced him up and down.

It is unclear whether Rav Kook was at all familiar with the writings of Achimeir, who had been up to then a marginal figure. Indeed, his students and family said Rav Kook had never even heard of Achimeir before. But as a result of the letter sent to Achimeir, Kook became seen as an ally of the Right, whether he had intended that result or not.

When, on June 8, the court exonerated Rosenblatt but sentenced Stavsky to death, Rav Kook threw himself and all his stature behind the latter's defense. While his first public letter had left open the question of guilt and had only solicited funds for defense, now he figured prominently in an open letter signed by 180 notables, arguing for Stavsky's innocence.

On June 19, Abdel Medjid repeated his confession to Mordechai Eliash, an attorney close to both Arlosoroff's widow, Sima, and Rav Kook. His resolve stiffened, Rav Kook rebuffed official British suggestions that he "reinterpret" his position. He signed one letter, proclamation, and telegram after another to Jewish communities, the archbishop of Canterbury, and anyone else he could think of to ask for support, rallies, and declarations. Jewish communities throughout Europe and North America organized in response, inadvertently leading many to think that the rabbis as a whole were aligned with the Right. Ben-Gurion accused Rav Kook in Mapai's central committee of naivete at the least and perhaps hatred for the workers; he put forward a resolution calling for abolishing the rabbinate, which was narrowly defeated.

Rebbe Binyomin, one of Kook's closest associates on the left, asked him to clarify his position. He answered: "I call heaven and earth to witness that I care greatly, with all my heart and soul, for all our people as individuals, and all their parties, because I believe with perfect faith that each one of them is a special limb in the measure of the [divine] body, sacred and wondrous, that is the ecclesia of Israel." "I am convinced," he continued, that Stavsky "is clean, in the right, entirely innocent of any guilt and suspicion of murder."[57]

On July 20, 1934, an appeals court unanimously dismissed the lower court's conviction for lack of corroboration; the Revisionists won. Jabotinsky, who had denounced Rav Kook as an untutored savage during the debate over women's suffrage fifteen years earlier, asked sincerely whether he could be installed as high priest.

Rav Kook had no desire to be a totem of the Right. In trying to rebuild his bridges to the Left, he offered to try to sway landowners to hire Jewish workers, long a pet cause of Labor. If he wants, Ben-Gurion replied, he can come to see me. Young Mapai activists left graffiti on his house and sometimes disrupted his prayers. Berl Katznelson tried to repair Mapai's ties to Kook, but it was an uphill fight. In fact, his relationship with the Left never recovered, and the two camps, Left and Right, grew further apart. The furies of the Arlosoroff affair, which in some ways never healed, set the tone in Zionist politics for decades to come.*

*Stavsky returned to Poland, where he organized immigration to Palestine. Refused reentry to Palestine by the British, he spent the war years in the United States, where he was part of the Bergson Group of activists (led by Rav Kook's nephew Hillel) and returned illegally in 1947. He was one of the organizers of the attempt to bring arms to the new state of Israel under the auspices of the Revisionist Irgun on the *Altalena*, which was shelled on Ben-Gurion's orders. He was killed in the ensuing battle with the Haganah forces

Rav Kook triumphed in Stavsky's acquittal and in his ability to mobilize a great public effort, but he also lost. He was not a man of the Right—Achimeir's violent rhetoric and Jabotinsky's volatile mix of secular liberalism and hawkishness were deeply foreign to him—but that is how people were coming to see him, removed as he was from the philosophical materialism and occasional Bolshevism of the Left. For once he had thrown pluralism to the winds and taken a stand. Yet once again, and even in seeming triumph, and surrounded by disciples and well-wishers, he was essentially left alone. The deepest truth of the matter for him was what he had told Rebbe Binyomin. He not only truly believed in Stavsky's innocence, but also saw in every Jew a sliver of God's revelation on earth. This was no abstract doctrine but a vision in whose light he had done his best to live—in fact, he had staked his life on it.

The Zionist enterprise that spurred Rav Kook's messianic visions had set in motion a range of furies and energies that he could not overcome or even contain. It all reached a fever pitch once the Jews became caught in a grimmer political vise than anyone could have imagined, and that horror strained the contradictory impulses of Jewish political and cultural life—in the Arlosoroff affair and after—to the breaking point.*

It was getting dark. On Rosh Hashanah 5694 (September 21, 1933), Rav Kook preached in the Old City's Churva syna-

---

under the command of Lieutenant Colonel Yitzhak Rabin on June 22, 1948, on the beach at Tel Aviv. The death sentence pronounced on Abdul Medjid and the other Arab participant, Issa Darwish, was eventually commuted to ten years' imprisonment. The latter subsequently disappeared somewhere in Syria; the former made his way to Jordan and lived to old age.

*The affair has left its mark on Israeli politics to the present day. The rhetorical bitterness of Israeli partisanship, the politics of *ressentiment* on the right, the Manicheanism of the Israeli hard Left, and the impossibility of rabbis' avoiding getting trammeled in politics can all be traced to, or at the least prefigured in, the still-unsettled murder of Chaim Arlosoroff.

gogue on the shofar of redemption. He discussed the three types of shofar discussed in halakhic literature—the preferred, the acceptable, and one obtained from a nonkosher animal, to be used only as a last resort. These, he said, corresponded to three types of movement toward redemption: from a healthy desire for rebirth and renewal; if not that, then from a prosaic desire for a dignified national life; and last and least, from the pressures of anti-Semitism, the shofar "that raises such a racket that it gives us no peace in exile": "The shofar of the defiled animal becomes the shofar of the Messiah. Amalek, Petliura, Hitler, etc. . . . we pray that God not bring us to hear the unfit, defiled shofar against our will."[58]

The following summer he published an essay, "The Cloud of Torah and the Cloud of Redemption," a meditation on the cloud imagery attending the biblical revelation at Sinai. Unlike natural light, divine light can be revealed only through occlusion because of the inadequacy and cowardice of the human mind and heart: "[The divine light's] being enwrapped and contracted and hidden is precisely its revelation."[59] The same is true for the light of the Messiah: "And in these our days there can be no doubt that once again the light of the Messiah, of redemption qua mystery, appears and gleams before us, and that from the great splendor largely inlaid in the thick of darkness, to the point of dreadful occlusion, it is proceeding and being drawn along . . . For from the utmost cloud that hides the divine light will emerge the light to appear over all souls, all Israel, and from thence to all peoples, for *behold I am coming to you in the utmost cloud* [Exodus 19:9]."

Rav Kook had been diagnosed with cancer, and was not getting better. He had continued working intermittently on the Aggadah commentary he had begun half a century before, in Zeimel. His very last comment there, written sometime in 1934, is a plea for simplicity: "After all the supreme attainments in wisdom and piety, *the simpler is better* [BT Rosh Hashanah

26b] . . . The root of everything is directing oneself toward simple wholeheartedness, *be whole with the Lord your God* [Deuteronomy 18:13] . . . Let your constant effort be founded not on the great innovations, but on perfect simplicity, which bestows health and life to body and soul."[60]

The Maimonides octocentennial was celebrated in 1935 with commemorations, conferences and publications in Europe, Palestine and North America. Rav Kook wrote two articles, both directed against another subtle but powerful challenge to his vision of unity. This was the suggestion put forth by a number of writers (including his old friend Zev Yavetz) that Maimonides' halakhic and philosophical enterprises were separate and distinct. Not so, he wrote—they were one and the same.

God's voice comes to us in many forms, he wrote, sounding in two fundamental registers, "the voice of the soul's own natural longing for closeness to God" and "the voice that purifies and refines that very longing."[61] Only a rare soul can sound both, the longing for union and the focus of restraint, and such was Maimonides. At moments in his journals, Rav Kook experienced the synthesis of focus and longing:

> All [holiness and *tikkun* are] founded on the point of truth within the soul. So long as it is strengthened and expands its writ over all the avenues of life, all the energies, feelings, thoughts, and motions, thus everything rises, all is sealed in *the seal of God, which is truth* [BT Shabbat 55a]. . . . All the exercises of the Torah are meant to expand the rush of truth, unhindered, with no antinomy or contradiction, as all the fountains flow together from different directions . . . to that place where there is no contradiction or separation. *Only absolute peace, that is the vessel that contains blessing for Israel* [after Mishnah Uktzin 3:12]. And what is the blessing inside that vessel? *You must love truth and peace* [Zechariah 8:19].[62]

Dialectical to the end—the search for the truth of one's own being yields the great dissolution into God:

> To the degree that someone sees himself as having no value, if he grasps his own nullity, or how he is even less than nothing, his utter disability, precisely thus he returns to renew his form, draws on the primal source, and stands in the place of absolute light.[63]

One constant frustration remained: he still had not truly expressed himself: "A great loss it is, not to write the good thoughts growing out of a ready spirit and gather them for oneself in times of spiritual drought and for others in different ways."[64]

He kept up his pace as best he could, despite his illness, even in his last year writing some four hundred letters pertaining to halakhic opinions, charitable causes, and public affairs. He spent an hour a day studying with Saul Lieberman, who became head of an institute organized in the spirit of Rav Kook's program to integrate academic methods with traditional textual study. Around the same time, Rav Kook told Ha-Nazir that in this dialectically structured world, every element of the sacred, inner, vital truth must have its secular, empirically visible, trace-like counterpart: philosophy was the secular trace of divinity, and biblical criticism, "the secular trace of the sacred itself."[65]

Rav Kook's illness worsened, and he moved on doctor's orders to the suburb of Kiryat Moshe. As he lay dying in the summer of 1935, visitors steadily came. One was a disciple of the Munkaczer rebbe, come to query his support of Zionism. Another was the son of the Gerer rebbe, who brought a note of good wishes from his father. Yet another, from Boston, was Joseph Soloveitchik, age thirty-two and already known for his Talmudic genius, which he had supplemented with a doctorate in philosophy. Back in Volozhin, Soloveitchik's illustrious grandfather Chaim had been leery of young Kook's unconventional piety. Now his grandson had taken his first steps on an unconventional path of his own.

When public calls were made to pray for his health, signed by leading rabbis, Rav Kook demurred. Why make a fuss over me, he said, claiming to be no different from any Jew lying in the hospital. As the cancer metastasized, it left him in terrible pain and bleeding profusely. He did his best to cheer his visitors and tried to see his agonies as what the Talmud calls "afflictions of love": "When the sorrow becomes inescapable, then are we purified to the utmost and run for help to the fount of life, to cleave to the light of life in total honesty with not a trace of deceit."[66] He confided to some that he feared he was being punished from on high for having revealed too much.

That summer, in response to violent clashes between left- and right-wing activists in Haifa, Rav Kook wrote one last open letter, the title taken from Jeremiah, "For the Shattering of My People" (Jeremiah 8:21):

> From my fount of tears, which I cannot stop, I call to you, my brothers, *each one a seal upon my heart* [after Song of Songs 8:6], no matter your party . . . I don't know who is to blame—better to say we are all to blame . . . What has become of us! And now, House of Israel! *My holy name defile no longer* [Ezekiel 20:39]. Lay aside anger, learn to look at each other, party to party, with the eyes of compassionate brothers cast together into great trouble, willing to unite for one sacred goal: the common good, its dignity and sacred service . . . *return, and live* [Ezekiel 18:32], dear, wounded brothers.[67]

He signed it: "Your faithful servant, broken and shattered, awaiting speedy redemption for the prisoners of hope." His vision of unity was, like his body, evanescent—and doomed.

In his very last days he reread the Bible, Mishnah, some Talmud, and Bahya ibn Pakuda's eleventh-century classic, *Du-*

ties of the Heart. One day he asked one of his two physicians, Bernhard Zondek, how long he had left to live. The physician, hesitated, Rav Kook insisted, and the doctor asked why he wanted to know. To plan my Mishnah study, he said. The doctor offered his opinion, and Rav Kook answered, "Then I can finish the Mishnah one last time."[68]

On the first day of Elul, the penitential month, Ha-Nazir brought him the elegantly designed title page of *Orot Ha-Kodesh.* Rav Kook wept and asked that on the title page he be referred to simply as "Rav" and nothing more.

The last day of his life was September 1, 1935, the third day of Elul, sixteen years to the day since his arrival in Jerusalem. He was surrounded by his rabbinic colleagues—Charlap, Franck, Isser Zalman Meltzer, Yechiel Mikhel Tyckoczinsky, Aryeh Levine. Ha-Nazir stood in the courtyard downstairs, his face buried in a tree. At the very end, Rav Kook's lips were moving. Charlap leaned over him, and heard him say, "Even now, my hope in God doesn't falter."[69]

Rav Avraham Yitzhak Ha-Cohen Kook turned his face to the wall as the attending physician rinsed the blood from his body, and then faced them all once again. They began to say the *Shema* together, and he joined them on the final word, "one."

Conclusion: Afterlight

He was fundamentally a lonely man. Rarely was he
properly understood by those around him.
　　　　　—Isaac Breuer, *Yitzhak Breuer*

How CAN WE UNDERSTAND and perhaps assess those great
religious thinkers who elide normal categories and reshape our
intellectual and spiritual worlds? By their lives, their writings,
and their teachings—and by the disciples and the institutions
they leave behind. But there the slippage begins. The disciples
are their own people, and time inevitably shifts the ground
under all our feet. Spiritual giants are made great by their complexity, their ineffable and deeply personal mix of audacity and
faithfulness. The translation of that nearly untranslatable synthesis into concrete realities is as essential as it is nearly impossible. The results can be exhilarating or tragic, or both.

Some fifteen thousand people, nearly a third of Jewish Jerusalem, followed Rav Kook's coffin along the streets as thousands more stood and watched from the sidewalks and rooftops. The city shut down for the afternoon as the procession made its way from his home and yeshiva to the Mount of Olives.

The Nineteenth Zionist Congress, meeting in Lucerne, held a memorial service just a few hours after news arrived of his passing. Menachem Ussishkin, the president of the Jewish National Fund and long Rav Kook's chief interlocutor in the Zionist leadership, recounted what became a famous conversation, in which Rav Kook analogized the present historical moment to the building of the Temple, when all shared in the labor together. Meir Berlin spoke next. Rav Kook, he said, "loved the Jewish people the way only a father can love his children. Nobody is left after him who will love his nation that fiercely . . . He understood his people, the situation of the generation, and its life conditions, and that is why he forgave them everything."[1] In the following weeks, memorial services were held all over Palestine and in Jewish communities around the world, and the Jewish National Council was flooded with telegrams of condolence.

Members of Agudat Yisrael attended the funeral and paid their respects. The zealots, though, hounded Kook until the end, and even afterward. They posted *pashkevilim* against him as he lay dying, interrupted memorial services after his death, and announced in a *pashkevil* that though he was no longer living, "Our doctrine regarding that man is clear, that is, we find him to be the greatest destroyer of our land and polluter of Orthodox Judaism, and [our] war against him has no limit."[*][1]

For its part, the Supreme Muslim Council expressed its

---

*To this day, the *pashkevilim* and graffiti in the Meah Shearim neighborhood of Jerusalem label ultra-Orthodox figures who seem willing to make concessions to Zionism and modernity as "= Kook."

condolences to the Jewish National Council after the Arabic newspaper affiliated with the mufti editorialized that it was looking forward to a bitter and divisive succession struggle over the rabbinate. They were in for a disappointment. In December, Isaac Herzog, a distinguished, worldly halakhist who had been the chief rabbi of Ireland for the previous two decades, was unanimously voted in to be Rav Kook's successor as Ashkenazi chief rabbi, defeating Charlap, who had stood for the office. Ben-Zion Uziel was voted in as Sephardic chief rabbi in the summer of 1939. Firmly allied with the Mizrachi, both set about the work of rationalization and system building that Rav Kook had projected but proved unable to do. They propounded a mix of traditionalism and humane values, less stirring than Rav Kook's complex visions, and less combustible.

Not long after the seven-day shiva, Agnon went to visit Rivka Kook, now a widow. As they were talking, she sighed and said, in Yiddish, "*azah heiliger guf*"—such a holy body.[2]

With Rav Kook's death, his writings began to emerge. Meir Berlin created a society to promote and oversee the publication of the many thousands of manuscript pages he left behind. In 1937, Yehudah Leib Maimon edited a massive three-volume memorial, including a first, lengthy biographical essay, and created a publishing house, Mossad ha-Rav Kook, "The Rav Kook Foundation." In the coming years, many posthumous volumes appeared: first, Rav Kook's halakhic writings and then the philosophical and theological works, nearly all of them, except for Ha-Nazir's *Orot Ha-Kodesh*, edited by Zvi Yehudah. In their distinctive white bindings, the volumes became known over time, with reverential wit, as *Ha-Shas Ha-Lavan*, the White Talmud.

People began to try to take the measure of his thought. In an important essay of 1939, Hillel Zeitlin noted Rav Kook's deep affinities not only with the philosophic Hasidism of Chabad, but also with the radical Hasidic teachings of Izbica and Breslov. Through the early 1940s, a self-described Rav Kook Circle met for sessions of textual study and lectures by, among others, Zvi Yehudah, Charlap, Ha-Nazir, Zeidel, Agnon, Zalman Shazar (Katznelson's successor at *Davar* and later Israel's third president), and others. The circle as a whole steered clear of reading the works in light of Western philosophy. To do so, Zvi Yehudah wrote in the preface to the group's proceedings, would be to contradict the works' true meaning and would be a kind of "spiritual miscegenation." (When in 1930 he had shown his father an essay by Scholem on Franz Rosenzweig, his father said that Rosenzweig, though undoubtedly great, failed to grasp that "Judaism is in no wise to be included with the ordinary spiritual frameworks of the world.")[3] From the outset, Zvi Yehudah presented his father's teachings as esoteric and entirely sacred, a corpus whose very study was itself part of the redemptive process. And while Ha-Nazir never tried to hide his own general education, the source notes he provided for the first two volumes of *Orot Ha-Kodesh* consist entirely of references from Jewish sources, even for those passages in which Rav Kook explicitly discusses non-Jewish philosophers.

Yet it was chiefly philosophers who studied the works in those first years after Rav Kook's passing, sensing him to be a thinker of broader horizons than his disciples imagined. (Indeed, it was only by appeal to academics that Ha-Nazir raised the funds to publish *Orot Ha-Kodesh*.) Hugo Bergmann suggested that Rav Kook be thought of not as a pantheist, for whom the world is identical to God, but as a panentheist, for whom the world lives within God. He eventually reached the striking conclusion that for Rav Kook, the astounding mission of the Jewish people was nothing less than the vanquishing of death. On his own deathbed, he penned a series of reflection on the triumph over mortality in Rav Kook and Friedrich Schelling.

In studies written in the 1940s, Natan Rotenstreich, a distinguished philosopher at Hebrew University, noted that for Rav Kook, the ascent to heaven was a means of looking down into one's own depths in an ongoing, revelatory, healing encounter with the world and oneself. This was, he observed, a religious world without dialogue, since even our inner lives are part of God's monologue with Himself. Yet, we might add, it is God's monologue with Himself about how He can grow through us.

Across the ocean, Jacob Agus, an American rabbi and philosopher, in pioneering studies of the 1940s, grasped the mystical experiences at the heart of the edited volumes starting to appear. Agus—in a characteristically American, democratizing, and (William) Jamesian touch—wrote that it is precisely the rootedness of Rav Kook's teachings in experience and intuition that endows them with universality. He also grasped the intensely literary character of the writings, noting that Rav Kook was perhaps "the first literary mystic," and he brilliantly observed that the chief theological problem for Kook was not the existence of God but rather the existence of the world.

Rav Kook's disciples went their various ways.

Binyamin Menashe Levin managed to publish two-thirds, some twelve volumes, of his own magnum opus, a vast collection of Talmud commentary by the Geonic sages of late antiquity, before his death in 1944.

Moshe Zeidel taught Bible and Semitics at Yeshiva College in New York and for two decades headed a teachers college in Jerusalem. Though he published several volumes, his richest contribution to Jewish literature was the passionate, fatherly correspondence he had elicited in his youth from his master.

Saul Lieberman eventually moved to New York's Jewish Theological Seminary, where he became the greatest academic Talmudist of the twentieth century. A cool, cerebral Litvak to the end, when recalling his studies with Rav Kook, he referred to him, as he referred to nobody else, as *ha-gaon ha-tzadik*, the genius and saint.*

Shai Agnon kept writing novels, stories, sketches, and, later, anthologies that preserved the text-soaked Jewish history whose passing in modernity he had chronicled so mordantly. In 1966 he won the Nobel Prize in Literature.

Aryeh Levine went on visiting the sick, attending to the poor, helping the forlorn, and ministering to the jailed until his death in 1969.

Ya'akov Moshe Charlap succeeded Rav Kook as head of the yeshiva, renamed Yeshivat Mercaz Ha-Rav Kook. In the late 1930s and into World War II, his thinking became acutely apocalyptic, pushing Rav Kook's esoteric reading of reality as far as it could go. The Land of Israel was, for him, no longer God's entrepôt to the world, but literally higher than the Garden of Eden. Charlap had never kindled to the universalistic elements in Kook's teachings, and the Holocaust drove him to a darkly dualistic view of non-Jews. Charlap saw around him a time of cosmic rebirth under the sign of Messiah ben Joseph, an era of purest darkness in which the ontologically vapid gentiles, facing spiritual evaporation, had to try to destroy Israel. The "souls of Tohu"—for Rav Kook, the pioneers of the Second Aliyah—were now, he said, the sainted martyrs of Europe, who could not bear the alienations of this world and so ascended to God in flames. After the war, he wrote that redemption was near, since Israel's goodness and the nations' evil had each come to their fullest expression. He died in 1952.

David Cohen remained a Nazirite, taught in Mercaz, and worked on *Orot Ha-Kodesh*. The first volume appeared in 1938;

---

*Gershom Scholem's personal copy of *Rosh Milin* contains a note in which he says that Lieberman told him that Rav Kook had told him that by now he didn't understand the book himself. As for Lieberman, he famously referred to Scholem's work by saying, "Nonsense is nonsense, but the history of nonsense is a very important science."

he published two more in his lifetime, and the fourth appeared in 1973, a year after he died. He never finished the projected fifth. Ha-Nazir wrote a number of volumes of Kabbalah and philosophy of his own, most of which remain in manuscript. The first (and thus far only published) volume of his theological magnum opus appeared in 1970, an erudite reading of the entirety of Jewish theology. The work is a great exercise in what he obscurely calls "aural logic," a synthesis of tradition and reason in which ideas unfold out of one another. He called it *Kol Ha-Nevuah* (*The Voice of Prophecy*). He thought he had heard that voice in his master's tones, and all his life he strained to hear and sound it himself.

Zvi Yehudah succeeded Charlap at the helm of the yeshiva and continued to edit and publish volume after volume of his father's works, following the pattern he had set with *Orot*, blunting the more radical theological leaps and harsher critiques of conventional religiosity, and subtly but unmistakably heightening the nationalist dimensions, in marked contrast to the more philosophical and universal editorial work of Ha-Nazir (though both kept the more personal visions under wraps). Zvi Yehudah was wont to say that while *Orot Ha-Kodesh* was the sanctum, *Orot* was the sancta sanctorum, the holy of holies.[4]

His father's death had left him to face the Holocaust alone.* Anti-Semitism did not interest Rav Kook, so he wrote little about it, nor had evil figured prominently in his thought. He had, perhaps, left some suggestions behind: the sermon of late 1933 on the evil shofar that would lead Israel out of exile, and his eschatological reading of World War I. As he reflected on

---

*Zvi Yehudah's wife, Chava, died in February 1944; he never remarried and never had children. For decades, Jerusalem's zealots confidently asserted that Zvi Yehudah's personal misfortune, as well as other illnesses among Rav Kook's descendants, along with the tragic death of Esther Yael in 1919 were the result of curses laid by Kabbalists in retaliation for Rav Kook's unforgivable sins.

the Holocaust, Zvi Yehudah came to see a massive divine hand at work. So enormous a horror could be explained only by the terrible necessities of redemption. As he put it: "The Jewish people were taken, excised from the depth of exile to the State of Israel . . . The entire people underwent divine surgery . . . From this cruel excision . . . is revealed the meaning of our lives, of the rebirth of the nation and the land, of the Torah and the sacred . . . One must see this . . . And seeing is more than understanding: seeing is encounter, encounter with God."[5] If so radical a surgery had been necessary to return the Jews to the land, then the land had to be more central than anyone had imagined.

Yeshivat Mercaz ha-Rav was for years a small, sleepy, and not terribly distinguished institution. Rav Kook's writings, though not part of the official yeshiva curriculum, were taught in homes, at off-hours, by Zvi Yehudah, Ha-Nazir and others, adding to their already esoteric aura. Zvi Yehudah was a respected but far from influential figure in Israeli cultural or religious life. That began to change in the 1960s as young Religious Zionists, like their peers elsewhere, grew restless with their elders.

From 1948 onward, Mizrachi, (now called the National Religious Party, or NRP) forged an unbreakable bond with the Labor establishment of Ben-Gurion and his successors, faithfully sat in every cabinet, and oversaw the Ministry of Religion, focusing on education and social welfare while pursuing a dogged course of political moderation. Rav Kook was for them a culture hero and authority figure, an exemplar of tolerance and engagement, minus the radicalism, tension, and longing.

Ha-Po'el Ha-Mizrachi merged with the Mizrachi in 1956, and its twin sensibilities—revolutionary fervor and social justice —went their separate ways. The latter found its place in the socially liberal policies of the National Religious Party and the work of the religious kibbutzim. The former was concentrated in the Bnei Akiva youth movement and its yeshivot led by Rabbi Moshe Zvi Neriah, an alumnus of Mercaz. The 1950s saw the creation of a semiclandestine youth movement, Gachelet, and, later, a youth wing within the NRP, both of which gathered young people who were beginning to see themselves as equal partners in the Zionist enterprise, but on their own terms. Graduates of Bnei Akiva yeshivot began to make their way to Mercaz, primed to absorb as much as they could of the elder Kook's teaching and charisma by way of his only son. Neriah had kept alive in his yeshivot and in Bnei Akiva the incandescence he himself had experienced while studying with Rav Kook in the 1930s. Finally, in the 1960s, Zvi Yehudah lit the match.

On the eve of Israel's nineteenth Independence Day, in May 1967, amid the prewar crisis, Zvi Yehudah addressed his students and gave the speech of his life. He recalled the night of November 29, 1947, following the United Nations vote to partition Palestine, which gave the Jewish people a state of their own, with borders well short of those promised to the children of Israel in the Bible. As the masses thronged the streets in celebration, he could not join in: "Where is our Hebron—are we forgetting it?! And where is our Shechem—are we forgetting it?! And our Jericho . . . our East Bank?! Where is each and every clod of earth? Every last bit, every four cubits of the Land of Israel? Can we forego even one millimeter of them? God forbid! Shaken in all my body, all wounded and in pieces, I couldn't, then, rejoice."[6] The day after the partition vote, Charlap came to see Zvi Yehudah: "We sat, shaken and silent. In the end we recovered, and said as one, *This is from God, to our eyes, a wonder* [Psalms 118:23]." The State of Israel, he told his disciples, is, to be sure, far from perfect: "Yet I say, this is the state that the prophets foresaw." How to realize its redemptive potential? By "the fulfillment of the mitzvah of settling the land . . . and gathering the multitudes of Israel to her." Several weeks later, in the Six-Day War, the heartlands of Judea and Samaria came under Israeli control, and Zvi Yehudah, it seemed, was a prophet.

The breathtaking reversal of fortunes in 1967 and, above all, the liberation of the Temple Mount and Wailing Wall (by military units that included students of Mercaz Ha-Rav) opened new horizons in all directions. The first settlements in the West Bank and elsewhere were largely established by Labor Zionists, who almost instinctively began to encourage settlement, as they had in the prestate days, when settlement was the peaceful and necessary way to conquer the land. Some settlements—in Hebron and the Etzion Bloc (the site of a number of kibbutzim before 1948) were the work of Religious Zionists, but by and large classic Zionism set the terms of the early settlements and their few critics.

The catastrophe of the Yom Kippur War in October 1973 unleashed a deep sense of crisis, shaking the political establishment to its foundations. The near apocalypse of the war's early days elicited a similarly eschatological response in early 1974 with the creation of Gush Emunim, the "Bloc of the Faithful." This was an extraparliamentary movement that promoted settlement "throughout the land," established a young guard within the NRP, and worked, its platform declared, for "fulfillment of the Zionist vision," namely, "complete redemption of the people of Israel and the entire world."[7]

Gush Emunim was a mind-bending mixture of religious fervor, Rav Kook's messianism, the classic Zionist can-do ethos, and the romance of a revolutionary avant-garde (with a dash of the youth rebellion of the 1960s). Its members saw themselves as the true inheritors of prestate Zionism, picking up the flag being dropped by an increasingly urbanized and ideologically placid Israel. By seizing the hilltops, they were rebelling simultaneously against the quietism of the ultra-Orthodox and the compromises of their Mizrachi parents, and their sacred youth rebellion would bring the Messiah and save the human race.

Some senior Laborites, seeing in them a reflection of their own youthful ideals, helped them from within the corridors of power.

The settlement movement gathered steam, as did opposition to it. Tensions came to a head at a spot near Nablus christened after the biblical Elon Moreh (where God told Abraham, "Unto thy seed I will give this land" [Genesis 12:7]). On June 5, 1974, a day after Zvi Yehudah told the new defense minister, Shimon Peres, that settling the land was one of the religious precepts for which one must be willing to undergo martyrdom, he went with Ariel Sharon (then a private citizen and a general in the reserves) and instructed the settlers to reject the alternate site being offered them. At night, though Sharon told the soldiers to disobey orders, they dragged the settlers away. Zvi Yehudah stood before them, opened his jacket, and said, "Take your guns and kill me!" In the end, the ranking general on the scene took him by the hand and led him away. The settlers pledged to return, if not to that hilltop near Nablus then to another.

Zvi Yehudah had often said that Religious Zionism was a bridge, which meant that at times it was supposed to be walked on. Then in his eighties, he decided that when it came to what mattered most, they would be walked on no more. When Menachem Begin was elected prime minister in 1977, one of his first visits was to the new settlement of Kedumin, to which the Elon Moreh activists had relocated, where he pledged, "There will be many more Elon Morehs." And there were.

In an essay of 1939, Hillel Zeitlin astutely observed that one of Rav Kook's major innovations was to project Kabbalistic doctrines onto the concrete social and political movements of his time. But even there, aside from his broad commitment to Jewish nationalism, Kook kept his distance from individual movements, seeing each as playing its role—an ecumenical vision that led to his own political paralysis. Facing new realities, and unable or unwilling to maintain his father's exquisite dialectical balances, Zvi Yehudah took sides.

His father had never written or thought much about statehood, government, or sovereignty as such. For Zvi Yehudah, they were central, and the passage (made canonical by his including it in *Orot*) about "the state of Israel, the foundation of God's throne in the world" was taken to be referring to the sovereignty founded in 1948. Rav Kook had essentialized the nation, and Zvi Yehudah essentialized the state.

Zvi Yehudah died in March 1982. Mercaz Ha-Rav soldiered on, but the center of gravity was moving elsewhere. The *hesder* yeshivot, where both army service and Rav Kook's writings were front and center, continued to grow, especially in the territories. While Zvi Yehudah's disciples differed on how to carry his and his father's ideas forward, they and mainstream Religious Zionists largely agreed on the overall direction.

The one major exception was Yehudah Amital, who had not studied with Zvi Yehudah but began to challenge him during his lifetime. A Hungarian Holocaust survivor who had smuggled an anthology of Rav Kook's writings into a Nazi labor camp, Amital had fought in 1948, later helped create the *hesder* system, and now headed the flagship *hesder* yeshiva in the Etzion Bloc. While he believed that Israel and the Jews were indeed on the path to redemption, he took deep issue with Zvi Yehudah's claim to understand why the Holocaust happened, and in general to read God's mind. Amital further argued that Rav Kook's ethical and universalist teachings were his cardinal doctrines and the key to reading his corpus as a whole. He contended that Gush Emunim, its antithesis Peace Now, and the militarism of Ariel Sharon were all false messianisms marked by a single-minded evasion of moral and political complexity. His was a powerful but lonely voice, and after his denunciations of the Lebanon War of 1982, Amital came to be seen as a renegade.

Meanwhile, a fundamental paradox began to take hold: though the settlements kept growing, with sustained governmental support, the movement, and certainly its religious vanguard, came to feel increasingly alienated from Israeli society as a whole. As Yoel Bin-Nun, one of Zvi Yehudah's most thoughtful disciples, famously said in 1992, they had failed to settle in people's hearts. This became painfully clear in the Oslo Accords of 1993 and then in the Gaza "disengagement" (which they called "expulsion") of 2005 at the hands of none other than their former patron, Ariel Sharon. This isolation resulted from not only their willed geographic isolation but also from their continuing to speak an ideological language that the society around them no longer understood. As the Religious Zionists looked behind them, they saw that they were a vanguard leading nobody—the secular and Haredi settlers were drawn to the territories by economic incentives, and their secular political allies were motivated largely by security concerns and a sense of embattlement.

Rav Kook and the secularists of the Second Aliyah were, for all their disagreements, engaged in the same argument. Even at their most diametrically opposed, they stood at points along a spectrum. Their descendants failed to maintain that essential connectedness; the religious camp became hermetic, and the secular camp dispensed with its own cultural legacy. Rav Kook's successors abandoned his appreciation for complexity, and Aharon David Gordon and Berl Katznelson's successors abandoned their ideological forebears' deep dialogue with Jewish religion and culture. Both camps played out the fate of ideologues who set out to educate their children not as they themselves were taught, but in keeping with their own abstract visions.

The ecstatic messianic fervor that characterized much of the Israeli Right, and nearly all the Religious Zionist camp from the mid-1970s onward, has been ground down by hard realities into a grim combativeness toward enemies from without and within—a combativeness resulting in very large part from Palestinian rejectionism and terror. The Religious Zionists are as committed to the settlement enterprise as ever, but one hears much less talk of imminent redemption. It is still posited as looming on a far horizon, but between there and here, relentless struggle lies ahead. Religious Zionists are increasingly visible and prominent in government, society, economics, and culture—and their self-confidence has in many ways been made possible by the figure and teachings of Rav Kook, especially the latter as made into a more assertive and fighting doctrine by Zvi Yehudah.

Some of Zvi Yehudah's disciples, such as Shlomo Aviner, continue his teaching that the currently constituted State of Israel is itself the messianic advent. Setbacks such as the Gaza disengagement result from a failure of public education to convey the true meaning of statehood. For others, notably Zvi Tau, the redemptive process is as esoteric as it was in Rav Kook's own time. Obstacles and reversals have a dialectical role to play, spurring on the elect, who see through politics and society to grasp Israel's true mission and who slowly but steadily assume positions of power in the military, business, and politics. For these men and many, perhaps most, Religious Zionists, not only is Rav Kook their defining thinker, but his works are also a sacred canon that can brook no contradictions. The universalistic elements of Rav Kook's teachings are ignored or reinterpreted to the vanishing point by increasing numbers of religious nationalists, who read him largely through the dogmatic lenses ground by Zvi Yehudah.

Yet the publication in recent years of long-hidden manuscripts, above all the original journals, demonstrate just how much more complicated a thinker his father was. The manuscripts have been kept under wraps for decades, and many still have yet to see the light. Some have been published in their entirety; others, published by the circles closest to Mercaz Ha-Rav and the legacy of Zvi Yehudah, in ways that cross the subtle but unmistakable line between editing and censorship. The raw journals show the depth of his immersion in the Kabbalah, the radicalism of his thinking and his critique of conventional religion, and the extent to which his ideas emerged from not only attempting to think through problems old and new, but also registering and reflecting on passions and visions that took hold of his soul.

Sadly, Rav Kook never developed an understanding of politics (and its endless deferral of ultimacy) to match his profound grasp of metaphysics and intuitive understanding of the deep cultural and spiritual processes at work in modernity. He was too optimistic about human nature and about religion's ability to attain power without turning idolatrous. The state, as such, fundamentally did not interest him. For him, the nation, not the state, was the terrestrial body through which spirit is actualized and people are realized. The lines identifying the State of Israel with God's majestic seat, included in *Orot* by Zvi Yehudah, became so central precisely because they were one of the few places where Rav Kook actually commented on sovereignty, albeit decades before 1948. Taken with his wartime correspondence with Zalman Pines in which the legitimacy of biblical monarchy was transferred to modern democracy, his comments were read as a warrant for seeing the modern State of Israel as the new kingdom.

Yet modern as he was, he shared a crucial feature with premodern Jewish theorists of Jewish messianism. He simply could not imagine the real, prosaic meaning of Jewish power, nor the possibility that Jews could abuse it. Rav Kook wrote that the Jewish return to politics could only be to a politics devoid of coercion, force, and violence, but of course such a politics is no politics at all. Utterly convinced as he was of Jewish centrality, he never projected Jewish political supremacy. His own ethical

fiber and human sympathy enabled him to restrain and contain the destructive potential of his esotericism, his belief that,
thanks to the Kabbalah, he understood the people and movements around him better than they understood themselves. He
did not realize that essentializing Jewish peoplehood and the
land as he did could create its own forms of moral blindness.

Yet interest in Rav Kook reaches well beyond Zvi Yehudah's disciples and the settlements and far into Israeli society.
His vision of culture as an indication of God's drive for self-
expression helps fuel the contemporary religious renaissance
in literature, music, and the performing arts. He is a constant presence in discussions of tolerance and pluralism, and a
touchstone for much of contemporary Israeli spirituality. He is
endlessly discussed and written about in the academy, treated
as a thinker with whom most every Israeli theologian, left or
right, must in some way engage. He is, for many secular intellectuals, still a chief conversation, or sparring, partner. To try
and unpack the meaning of the encounter between Zionism
and religion at its most tectonic levels is inevitably to contend
with him.

From his first published essay on Jewish nationalism in
1901 and forever after, Kook was exercised by the reported declaration of the First Zionist Congress that "Zionism has nothing to do with religion." In point of fact, no such declaration
was issued, but the statement well captured the uncertain place
of religion in the undertaking of political Zionism. For the
Religious Zionists of the Mizrachi, that qualification enabled
their participation. For Rav Kook, Zionism without religion
was idolatrous and doomed.

His failed attempt at an alternative in the Degel Yerushalayim movement reflected his characteristic mix of insight and
naivete. He correctly saw that integration into the secular Zionist enterprise would permanently deflect the spiritual revolution
that both secular and religious Jewry needed to undergo in order

to save themselves from mediocrity and the deformities of exile. He did not understand that in the frenzy of institution building and the political work of the mandate years the only viable alternatives were to make a separate peace with the Zionists—as did Agudat Yisrael—or to join them—as did the Mizrachi. To proceed in tandem while creating institutions of one's own was not an option, especially since he could not grant secular, political Zionism equal rights with religious tradition, inasmuch as the former is, by his theological terms, the base of the holy and not its equal.

Rav Kook did succeed in laying a theological foundation for marrying Torah study to Zionism, and for an ethos of traditional Judaism engaged with Zionism and with modernity. And although he became a role model for a different kind of rabbi, it was in creating rabbinic institutions that he most foundered. In some ways, the chief rabbinate was one of the worst things that ever happened to him. (And what he would have gone on to do had the British not needed the rabbinate for their own purposes is a tantalizing what-if.) The creation of the rabbinate permanently mobilized the Old Yishuv against him, raised expectations in the New Yishuv that he could not fulfill, brought his deficits as an administrator to the fore, and cast him in a political role for which both his personality and philosophy made him unsuited.

Ever since modernity upended traditional life, Jews have been looking for some substitute for the premodern *kehilla*, the traditional self-governing community—but the chief rabbinate could not take its place. As Menachem Friedman wrote in his indispensable study of religious politics in Mandatory Palestine, the rabbinate's attempt to create a super-*kehilla* structure that would encompass all of Palestine cut against not only the religious free market of the New Yishuv, but also the previous century and a half of developments in religious Jewry itself. The *kehillot* had, in Europe at least, been superseded by

Hasidism and its rebbes and by the great Lithuanian yeshivot, which had produced Rav Kook himself.

There is no denying that in the mandatory years Rav Kook pulled back a bit from his theological radicalism—or thought that he was creating structures whose radical outcomes he could discern from a distance. Of course we will never know how things would have gone if he had simply continued as rabbi of Jaffa, or Jerusalem, or as head of a yeshiva. But once he was chief rabbi, there was no turning back. His own teachings militated against enacting radical reforms—that was central to his critique of Christianity—yet his institutional role forced him into an inescapably conservative mode that pulled against the direction of his ideas. He sought to restore the great law-making bodies of classical Judaism and realize Maimonides' vision of halakhic constitutionalism, and what he got was a chronically underfunded, politically orphaned clerical bureaucracy. Perhaps, as he wrote in St. Gallen, the man of spiritual and mystical unification, of *yichudah*, truly cannot function as a man of action, inevitably divisive as all men of action must be. A lesson we all would do well to learn.

His institution building emerged from his insistence that we must engage the life of our times, that spirituality cannot remain ethereal, solipsistic, and detached from social and political responsibility. And yet we cannot institutionalize the holy. That has become painfully clear in the decades since his death. Today, the chief rabbinate is a patronage mill for the ultra-Orthodox groups that once disdained it, still formally reject its authority, and disdain its founder. (Over the decades, a number of ultra-Orthodox figures, especially those who knew him, privately expressed reverence for him, ideological differences notwithstanding, and some Haredi intellectuals have been drawn to his metaphysics and spirituality, but here as elsewhere, the public face of ultra-Orthodoxy has been resolute in its continued rejection of him and his stature.) It is precisely the institution of the chief rabbinate that stands in the way of the spiritual revolution that Rav Kook sought to promote. Orthodox institutions can reap the rewards of a stagnant monopoly, and secular elites can evade grappling with Jewishness, entrusted as it is to clerics and satraps. The present-day rabbinate is yet another demonstration of the truth of Marx's dictum that history repeats itself first as tragedy, and then as farce.

Assessing Rav Kook's place in the history and future of Jewish thought is not easy. It is hard to find another Jewish thinker who fused as he did the public with the personal, tradition with revolution, and a vision of the cosmos with the tangled webs of human subjectivity, always allowing each side full expression. The intensely personal idiom in which he wrote, the eclecticism of his sources, and the range of issues with which he dealt defy simple categorization. The multiple currents of modernity—nationalism and universalism, reason and romanticism, pragmatism and utopia, discipline and freedom—pulse throughout his life and ideas. In a striking mixture of insight and empathy, he understood that modernity's cataclysmic effects on traditional Jewish life were not simply catastrophes imposed from without or depraved rebellions from within; they were sets of answers, incomplete to be sure, to genuine moral and spiritual problems, to the multiple antinomies of modernity. He threw himself into the task of reconciling them all because within himself he felt them all.

A thread running through his life and thought is a principled affirmation of complexity and the ways in which that complexity, that dialogue of opposites, gives birth, slowly and painfully, to whatever it is that we can know of truth. That affirmation of complexity, grounded in a faith in truth, can save us from the terrible certainty of dogmatism and the terrible uncertainty of doubt.

Rav Kook did not follow his own ideas through to their

radical conclusions. Like other fin de siècle romantics, he longed for vitality beyond structure and reason. Unlike them, however, he was intensely dialectical and acutely aware of the dangers of excess. He tried to find a place for that anxiety in his thought-world. It was the dialectic—the rhythm between radicalism and conservatism—that kept the destructive tendencies of both in check and gave him a place to stand. That appreciation of dialectic and complexity—not to mention the deep and universal human empathy that went with it—is tragically absent from so many of his latter-day disciples. His sinuous, complicated personal meditations have been read as dogma, and the dialectical energy that makes them so thrilling to read has been eclipsed by a new, dogmatic political theology.

The absence of appreciation of complexity is a function of more than just his followers' personal limitations. It is related to another central feature of his thought, and that is his messianism. Rav Kook had no doubt that he was living in messianic times, even in his later years, though toward the end of his life it seems that deep conviction took on the humbler proportions of faith and hope. Looking inward, he did not see himself as the Messiah, but did understand his own expansive and healing consciousness as profoundly redemptive. Looking outward, his messianic perspective provided a field of gravitational energy that enabled him to hold together the seemingly irreconcilable religious and sociopolitical conflicts of his time. He was by no means the only messianic Zionist, but while mainstream Zionism secularized the language of redemption when turning it to terrestrial purposes, he kept its religious charge. For him, the secular and religious meaning of such terms as *land, people,* and *redemption* existed reciprocally. That balance was undone by Zvi Yehudah, for whom secular Zionism had fulfilled its historical purpose, and was done.

Thus, one of the key questions about Rav Kook's place in

future Jewish thought is whether the structure of his ideas is entirely dependent on messianic energy to hold all its contradictions together, and just how long that apotheosis can be deferred. His ideas emerged out of his own restlessness; he tried to resolve the antinomies of modernity because he felt them so keenly. As we look at him today, it is his contradictions that save him, above all his genuine difficulty in reconciling his celebration of Israel with his love of humanity.

Like every great thinker, Kook inherited multiple traditions, clusters of ideas, and terms that he reworked and remade. He infused new meanings into a host of terms—*sacred* and *profane, written Torah* and *Oral Torah, Jewish people, Land of Israel, ethics, nature, will,* and on and on. As Shlomo Fischer has well put it, he was able to sound a very modern language of subjectivity out of the deepest recesses of tradition. His writings speak to a globalizing world, and perhaps to worlds and forms of consciousness we cannot yet imagine. As a theologian, he united process and personality. God and the universe are, in a deep sense, endless processes, but they are not faceless, since we recognize them, as we recognize the truths being put forward by others, in ourselves. Yet precisely because he so profoundly fused past, present, future, and infinity in his life and writings, engaging with his ideas today means honestly recognizing what he did and did not believe, and only then navigating through the vast latticework of his ideas.

Perhaps his greatest legacy is his life, his capacity for thought and feeling, his acceptance of differences, his nobility in the face of relentless and vicious personal attacks, and his respect for the inner life of the individual as one of God's thrones in the world. Vision, tolerance, courage, and perspective were all things that he achieved. They were the fruit of processes, labors, and travails within his complex personality and soul. And those achievements, in turn, perhaps tell us something about ourselves: that we can work to believe in the processes, labors, and travails within our own souls as themselves disclosing and affirming something very real. And yet, who and how he was, how a soul as broad as his came to be, remains a mystery. Indeed, the more you try to grasp him, the more elusive Rav Kook becomes.

And where does that leave us? We can perhaps believe, as did Rav Kook, that everything is alive with God's light and irradiated by it, if only we look generously and with freedom. We can believe that God has created a good world and that the multiple and contradictory stirrings we feel within us regarding art, politics, society, ethics, and aesthetics, as well as that crabbed thing we call "religion," are attempts to honor it. Our search for truth, hope, and kindness comes from an unending desire for peace, rest, and union, from "the ceaseless prayer of the soul," whose infinitude faithfully echoes God's own. The contradictions we feel in ourselves are the world's, infinite and resolved only, if at all, in God, who feels them too. We can—if we take care to remember that we are not God, but creatures riddled with contradictions—still believe in others and ourselves. We can believe that all our multiple and contradictory stirrings are themselves the sign of something good and rich and right, alive in ourselves and in the world.

It seems, though, in light of the spectacle of human history, certainly during the last century, to be more than we can justify or bear to say that everything is rising. That is far from guaranteed, if it is imaginable at all, and it all depends on us.

This volume is a brief introduction to a very large subject—and so the notes are meant simply to provide references for direct quotations. There is a further discussion of sources in the bibliographic essay following the notes.

The oft-appearing word *Reiyah* is the standard acronym for "Rav Avraham Yitzhak Ha-Cohen" and a (providential?) pun on the Hebrew word for *vision*. Citations to *Orot, Orot Ha-Kodesh, Orot Ha-Teshuvah, Mishpat Cohen, Mussar Avikha,* and other works by Rav Kook, unless otherwise stated, follow the standard editions published (and frequently republished) by Mossad Ha-Rav Kook.

Rav Kook's *Eyn Ayah* is cited by tractate, chapter, and paragraph of the commentary; for example, *Eyn Ayah,* Brakhot 3:4 means *Eyn Ayah* to Tractate Berakhot, chapter 3, paragraph 4.

Igrot refers to *Igrot Ha-Reiyah,* the edition of Rav Kook's correspondence published in three volumes by Mossad Ha-Rav Kook. Citations to volume four of the *Igrot* refer to the volume edited by Ya'akov Filber and published by Ha-Makhon al-shem Ha-Ratzyah Kook zt"l (Jerusalem, 1984).

Ma'amarei refers to *Ma'amarei Ha-Reiyah*, the volume of Rav Kook's essays and articles edited by Elisha Aviner (Langauer) and David Landau (Jerusalem, 1984).

Citations to a *pinkas* refer to Rav Kook's notebooks (*pinkasim*) published in *Pinkesei Ha-Reiyah*, volume 1 (Jerusalem: Ha-Makhon al-shem Ha-Ratzyah Kook zt'l, 2008). The numbering of the *pinkasim* corresponds to their numbering in that edition rather than to the nonsequential numbers given them by Zvi Yehudah; for example, *Pinkas* 4:3 refers to the fourth *pinkas* in that volume, paragraph 3.

Rav Kook's *Shemonah Kevatzim* (2nd ed., 2004) is abbreviated *SK* and cited by notebook number and paragraph; for example, *SK* 2:100 means notebook 2, paragraph 100.

"Avneri" refers to Yossi Avneri, "Ha-Reiyah Kook ke-Rabbah shel Eretz Yisrael, 1921–1935" (PhD diss., Bar-Ilan University, Tel Aviv, 1989).

"Frankel" refers to Aryeh Frankel's exhaustive entry on Rav Kook in *Ha-Encyclopedia shel Ha-Zionut Ha-Datit*, vol. 5, cols. 89–422 (Jerusalem: Mossad Ha-Rav Kook, 1983).

"Friedman" refers to Menachem Friedman, *Chevrah va-Dat: Ha-Ortodoksiyah Ha-Lo-Zionit be-Eretz Yisrael, 1918–1936*, 2nd ed. (Jerusalem: Yad Ben-Zvi, 1988).

A number of the books cited in this volume are available at www.hebrewbooks.org and on other websites. Many of the newspapers and periodicals quoted herein are available on the websites of the National Library of Israel (www.nli.org.il) and the Historical Jewish Press (jpress.org.il).

Introduction

Epigraph: *Pinkesei Ha-Reiyah* 8:4, *Olat Reiyah*, vol. 1, p. 11.

Chapter One: "No Ordinary Rabbi"

Epigraph: Kalman Frankel, ed. *Shemu'ot Reiyah* (Jerusalem: Ha-Sneh, 1939), p. 7.

1. Eliyahu David Rabinowitz-Teomim, *Seder Eliyahu* (Jerusalem: Mossad Ha-Rav Kook, 1983), 63.

2. Yehoshua Leib Rados, *Zikhronot* (Johannesburg, 1936), 64.

3. Alter Druyanov, cited in Samuel Mirsky, "Yeshivat Volozhin," in Mirsky, ed., *Mosdot Torah be-Europa be-Vinyanam u-ve-Churbanam* (New York: 'Ogen/Histadrut Ivrit, 1956), 61n6.

4. Shalom Grey, "Toldot Ha-Gaon Rabbi Zelig Reuven Bengis," *Yeshurun* 12 (Nissan 5763/Spring 2003): 156.

5. Zev Rabbiner, *Or Mufla* (Tel Aviv, 1972), 16.

6. Nathan Kamenetsky, *Making of a Godol* (Jerusalem: Ha-Mesorah, 2002), 1087.

7. Rabinowitz-Teomim, *Seder Eliyahu*, 67.

8. Appendix to Kook, *Ittur Sofrim* (1974 reprint ed.).

9. Kook, *Ma'amarei Ha-Reiyah*, 441.

10. Zev Wolf Turbowicz, *Tiferet Ziv* (Warsaw: Unterhendler, 1896), 1.

11. Kook, *Chevesh Pe'er* (1985 ed.), 52.

12. Kook, *Mussar Avikha* (1971 ed.), 17.

13. Kook, *Orot Ha-Reiyah*, 16–19.

14. Immanuel Etkes and Shlomo Tikochinski, eds., *Yeshivot Lita: Pirkei Zikhronot* (Jerusalem: Merkaz Shazar/Hebrew University, 2004), 338.

15. Kook, *Mussar Avikha*, 26.

16. Ibid., 40.

17. Levin, "Zikhronot," *Sinai* 14 (1944): 198.

18. Ibid., 199.

19. Chaim Nachman Bialik, *Kol Kitvei Ch. N. Bialik* (Tel Aviv: Dvir, 1947), 31.

20. Kook, *Pinkas Acharon be-Boisk*, 14:1, in *Kevatzim mi-Ktav-Yad Kodsho*, ed. Boaz Ofan (Jerusalem, 2006), 36.

21. Ibid.

22. Ibid., 14:11, 40–42.

23. Ibid.

24. *Sinai* 29, nos. 7–8 (1951): 109–10.

25. Yitzhak Nissenboim, *Alei Cheldi* (Warsaw: Halter, 1929), 188.

Chapter Two: The New Will Be Holy

Epigraphs: Rebbe Binyomin (Joshua Radler-Feldman), "From the Weave," in Yitzhak Lofban, ed., *Arba'im Shanah* (Tel Aviv:

Mercaz Mapai, 1947), p. 24. Berl Katznelson, quoted in Shimon Kushner, *Ha-Ro'eh li-me-Rachok* (Tel Aviv: 'Am Oved, 1972) p. 68.

1. Quoted in Yehoshua Kaniel, ed., *Ha-Aliyah Ha-Sheniyah* (Jerusalem: Yad Ben-Zvi, 1997), 2:5.

2. Kook, *Pinkas* 13:15.

3. Kook, *Igrot Ha-Reiyah*, 1:240.

4. Kook, *Ma'amarei Ha-Reiyah*, 98.

5. Cited in Frankel, col. 113.

6. Chaim Lifshitz, *Shivchei Ha-Reiyah* (Jerusalem: Makhon Harry Fischel, 1978), 81.

7. Ibid.

8. Quoted in Ephraim Tzoref, *Chayei Ha-Rav Kook* (1947), 119.

9. *Hashkafah*, March 17, 1905, cited in Frankel, col. 115.

10. Kook, *Igrot*, 1:16–18.

11. *Havazelet*, April 18, 1905.

12. Kook, *Pinkas* 13:117.

13. Kook, *Ikvei Ha-Tzon*, 108.

14. Ibid., 111.

15. Ibid., 110–11.

16. Ibid., 134.

17. Ibid., 136.

18. Ibid., 139.

19. Ibid., 145.

20. Kook, *Igrot*, 1:317.

21. Kook, *Igrot*, 3:158.

22. Lifshitz, *Shivchei Ha-Reiyah*, 98.

23. Kook, *Igrot*, 3:270.

24. Ibid., 3:183.

25. Kook, *Igrot*, 1:185.

26. Cited in Azar, "Keter Torah," *Luach Eretz Yisrael* (1912), in Yehoshua Be'eri, *Ohev Yisrael bi-Kedushah*, 2d ed. (Tel Aviv: H.Y.KH., 1989), 4:48.

27. Ibid.

28. Be'eri, *Ohev Yisrael bi-Kedushah*, 2:73.

29. S. Y. Agnon, *Me-Atzmi el Atzmi* (Jerusalem: Schocken, 2000), 190–94.

30. Transcription of unpublished letter, copy in author's possession.

31. Kook, *Igrot*, 1:128–29.

32. Quoted in Benjamin Ish-Shalom, *Ha-Rav Kook beyn Ratzyonalism le-Mistikah* (Tel Aviv: 'Am Oved, 1990), 17–18.

33. Brenner, *Ketavim*, 3:320–26.

34. Kook, *Orach Mishpat*, no. 114, 136.

35. Kook, *Shabbat Ha-Aretz* (1979 ed.), 61.

36. Ibid., 14.

37. Kook, *Igrot*, 1:94.

38. Ibid., 1:103.

39. Kook, *Shabbat Ha-Aretz* (Jerusalem: Levy, 1910), 8.

40. Kook, *Igrot*, 1:245 ff.

41. Ibid., 2:188.

42. Ibid., 2:235.

43. Ibid.

44. Ibid., 1:214.

45. Brenner, *Ketavim*, 3:515.

46. Kook, *Igrot*, 2:56.

47. Mordechai ben Hillel Ha-Cohen, *Olami* (Jerusalem, 1927–29), 4:171 ff.

48. Kook, *Orot*, 119.

49. Ibid.

50. Ibid., 121.

51. Ibid.

52. Brenner, *Ketavim*, 4:1093–95.

53. In Elchanan Kalmanson, ed., *Ha-Machshavah Ha-Yisraelit* (Jerusalem: Levi, 1920), 13.

Chapter Three: The Mists of Purity

Epigraph: Kook, *Shemonah Kevatzim* 3:234.

1. *SK* 1:315.

2. *SK* 1:164.

3. *SK* 1:92.

4. *SK* 1:147; Kook, *Orot Ha-Kodesh*, 3:24–25.

5. *SK* 1:141; Kook, *Orot Ha-Kodesh*, 2:363–64.

6. *SK* 1:660; Kook, *Orot Ha-Kodesh*, 1:269.

7. *SK* 1:135; Kook, *Orot*, 122–23.

8. *SK* 1:89–90.

9. *SK* 2:21; Kook, *Orot*, 84.

10. *SK* 1:329.

11. *SK* 2:326; Kook, *Orot*, 77.

12. *SK* 1:552.

13. *SK* 3:240; Kook, *Orot Ha-Kodesh*, 3:143.

14. Luzzatto, *Choker U-Mekkubal*, (Zhitomir: Shapira, 1855), 16.

15. Luzzatto, *Adir ba-Marom* (Jerusalem, 1995 ed.), 209.

16. *SK* 1:435; Kook, *Orot Ha-Kodesh*, 2:484.

17. *SK* 2:31, 340.

18. *SK* 2:307; Kook, *Orot Ha-Kodesh*, 3:81; Kook, *Olat Reiyah*, 1:6.

19. *SK* 1:208–9; Kook, *Orot Ha-Kodesh*, 1:248.

20. *SK* 2:35; Kook, *Orot Ha-Kodesh*, 2:297–98.

21. *SK* 2:35.

22. Quoted in Ya'akov Yosef of Polnoye, *Toldot Ya'akov Yosef* (Koretz, 1781), Vayechi, 63a.

23. *SK* 1:575; Kook, *Orot Ha-Kodesh*, 3:307.

24. *SK* 1:17, 804.

25. *SK* 1:676.

26. *SK* 1:708; Kook, *Orot Ha-Kodesh*, 3:332–33.

27. *SK* 2:99.

28. *SK* 3:66; Kook, *Orot Ha-Kodesh*, 2:493–94.

29. *SK* 1:132; Kook, *Orot Ha-Kodesh*, 3:13.

30. *SK* 1:807; *Middot Ha-Reiyah*, s.v. "Ahavah," 5.

31. *SK* 1:808; Kook, *Orot*, 156.

32. *SK* 2:157; Kook, *Orot*, 138.

33. *SK* 2:267, 285.

34. *SK* 2:302.

35. *SK* 3:4; Kook, *Orot Ha-Kodesh*, 3:349–50.

36. *SK* 3:352; Kook, *Orot Ha-Kodesh*, 3:119.

37. *SK* 1:133; Kook, *Orot Ha-Kodesh*, 3:14.

38. *SK* 1:75; Kook, *Orot Ha-Kodesh*, 3:xxvii.

39. *SK* 3:134; Kook, *Orot Ha-Kodesh*, 3:244.

40. *SK* 1:186; Kook, *Orot Ha-Kodesh*, 3:191; Kook, *Orot*, 160.

41. *SK* 3:1–2; Kook, *Orot*, 70–72.

42. *SK* 1:598; Kook, *Orot Ha-Kodesh*, 3:151.

43. *SK* 2:150.

44. *SK* 3:68; Kook, *Orot Ha-Teshuvah*, 9:6.

45. *SK* 3:24.

46. *SK* 3:61.

47. *SK* 3:208.

48. *SK* 3:209; Kook, *Orot*, 148.

49. *SK* 3:210; Kook, *Orot Ha-Kodesh*, 3:1.

50. *SK* 3:222.

51. *SK* 3:223; Kook, *Orot*, 78.

52. *SK* 3:234.

53. *SK* 3:235.

54. *SK* 3:236.

55. *SK* 3:237.

56. *SK* 3:279.

57. *SK* 4:17; Kook, *Orot Ha-Kodesh*, 1:157 (partial).

58. *SK* 4:21; Kook, *Orot*, 95.

59. Kook, *Igrot*, 2:293.

60. Kook, *Igrot*, 2:295–96.

Chapter Four: The Gruesome Rights of Spring

Epigraph: Kook, *Shemonah Kevatzim* 5:118, Kook, *Orot Ha-Kodesh*, vol. 2, pp. 515–16.

1. Cited in Paul Mendes-Flohr, *From Mysticism to Modernity: Martin Buber's Transformation of German Social Thought* (Detroit: Wayne State University Press, 1989), 95.

2. Kook, *Orot*, 13.

3. *SK* 5:64: Kook, *Orot*, 16.

4. Ya'akov Moshe Charlap, *Hed Harim* (Elon Moreh: Yeshivat Birkat Yosef, 1997), 62–63.

5. Kook, *Igrot*, 2:311–12.

6. *SK* 5:1; Kook, *Orot Ha-Kodesh*, 1:25.

7. Ibid.

8. *SK* 5:2, *Orot Ha-Kodesh*, vol. 1, p. 1:26.

9. *SK* 5:180.

10. Kook, *Pinkas Acharon be-Boisk*, 55.

11. Kook, *Ma'amarei Ha-Reiyah*, 5–6.

12. Kook, *Igrot*, 1:99.

13. *SK* 5:47–48; Kook, *Orot ha-Kodesh*, 2:488–89.

14. *SK* 5:98: Kook, *Orot*, 21.

15. *SK* 5:267; Kook, *Orot*, 15.

16. *SK* 5:148; Kook, *Orot Ha-Kodesh*, 2:330–31.

17. *SK* 6:40; Kook, *Orot Ha-Kodesh*, 1:91.

18. *SK* 6:12; Kook, *Orot Ha-Kodesh*, 3:286–87.

19. *SK* 6:248.

20. *SK* 6:263.

21. Harel Cohen, ed., *Dodi li-Zvi* (Jerusalem: Nezer David, 2005), xvii.

22. Ibid., 1.

23. Kook, *Orot Ha-Kodesh*, 1:18.

24. She'ar Yashuv Cohen et al., eds., *Nezir Echav* (Jerusalem: Nezer David, 1977), 1:312–13.

25. Kook, *Igrot*, 3:4.

26. *SK* 6:71.

27. *SK* 7:13; Kook, *Orot*, 9 (with a significant editorial addition).

28. *SK* 7:12; Kook, *Orot*, 17.

29. *SK* 7:38.

30. *SK* 7:112; Kook, *Orot Ha-Kodesh*, 2:444–45.

31. Kook, *Orot Ha-Kodesh*, 327–28.

32. Ibid., 337.

33. Ibid., 359.

34. Shimon Glitzenstein, *Mazkir Ha-Rav* (Jerusalem: Kiryat No'ar, 1973), 34.

35. Kook, *Igrot*, 3:122.

36. Abraham Melnikoff, *London Jewish Chronicle*, September 13, 1935, 21.

37. Kook, *Igrot*, 3:82.

38. *SK* 5:76; Kook, *Orot*, 11.

39. *SK* 6:83.

40. Kook, *Rosh Milin* (1987 ed.), 3.

41. Ibid., 111.

42. Kook, *Igrot*, 3:131.

43. Ibid., 3:132.

44. Shmuel Avidor Ha-Cohen, *Ha-Ish Neged Ha-Zerem* (Jerusalem, 1962), 119.

45. Quoted in Stuart Cohen, *English Zionists and British Jews* (Princeton, N.J.: Princeton University Press, 1982), 201.

46. Mendes-Flohr, *From Mysticism to Modernity*, 104.

47. *SK* 8:23: Kook, *Orot Ha-Kodesh*, 2:380.

48. Cited in Menachem Kasher, "Da'at Torah 'al Ha-Shevu'a she-lo Ya'alu be-Chomah le-Eretz Yisrael," *Shanah be-Shanah*, 1977, 219.

49. Ibid.

50. *SK* 6:101; Kook, *Orot*, 14.

51. *SK* 7:60–62; Kook, *Orot Ha-Kodesh*, 2:456–58.

52. Cited in Avneri, 68.

53. Kook, *Igrot*, 3:138.

54. Ibid., 3:143.

55. Ibid., 3:178–80.

56. Ibid., 3:216.

57. Ibid., 3:262–63.

58. *SK* 8:213; Kook, *Orot Ha-Teshuvah*, 15:10.

59. Menachem Mendel Porush, *Be-Tokh Ha-Chomot* (Jerusalem: Verker, 1945), 245.

Chapter Five: Dear, Wounded Brothers

Epigraphs: Kook, *Pinkas*, 9:9, p. 491. Shulamit Hareven, *City of Many Days*, [Hillel Halkin, tr.], (San Francisco: Mercury House, 1993) p. 99.

1. Kook, *Eyn Ayah*, Berakhot 9:361.

2. Kook, *Igrot*, 3:156–57.

3. *Ha-Po'el Ha-Tza'ir*, September 17, 1919, cited in Avneri, 394.

4. *Chadshot Ha-Aretz*, October 27, 1919, cited in Avneri, 394.

5. Kook, *Igrot*, 2:330.

6. Ibid., 4:48.

7. *Do'ar Ha-Yom*, April 19, 1920, cited in Friedman, 166.

8. Kook, *Orot*, 80; *SK* 1:716.

9. Charlap, *Tovim Meorot* (Jerusalem: Lunz, 1920), 9, 13.

10. Frankel, cols. 250–51.

11. Ibid., col. 251.

12. Ibid., col. 250.

13. *Ma'amarei*, 54.

14. *Ha-Tor*, March 4, 1921, reprinted in *Ma'amarei*, 457.

15. Ronald Storrs, *Orientations* (London: Nicholson and Watson, 1937), 486–87.

16. Cited in Kook, *Orot*, ed. Bezalel Naor, 22.

17. Quoted in Aviezer Ravitzky, *Ha-Ketz Ha-Meguleh u-Medinat Ha-Yehudim* (Tel Aviv: 'Am 'Oved, 1993), 153–54.

18. Ibid., 344n138.

19. *Ha-Tekufah* 14–15 (1922): 633, 640.

20. Hillel Zeitlin, "Beyn Shnei Harim Gedolim," *Ba-Derekh*, September 20, 1935, in Yehoshua Be'eri, *Ohev Yisrael bi-Qedushah*, 2nd ed. (Tel Aviv: H.Y.KH., 1989), 5:185–88.

21. Ibid.

22. Kook, *Hartza'at Ha-Rav* (1921 ed.), v, 1.

23. Cited in Avneri, 248.

24. Kook, *Orot Ha-Kodesh*, introduction, xviii.

25. David Cohen (Ha-Nazir), *Mishnat Ha-Nazir*, ed. Harel Cohen (Jerusalem: Nezer David, 2005), 89.

26. Bialik, *Kol Kitvei*, 212.

27. Be'eri, *Ohev Yisrael bi-Qedushah*, 4:105.

28. S. K. Mirsky, *Ohr Ha-Mizrach*, December 1965, 104–5.

29. *Pinkas* 7:50.

30. *Pinkas* 7:79.

31. *Pinkas* 7:86.

32. Jewish Telegraphic Agency, April 15, 1924.

33. Kook, *Igrot*, 4:190.

34. Lifshitz, *Shivchei Ha-Reiyah*, 231.

35. *Ma'amarei*, 306–8.

36. Ibid., 101–4.

37. Moshe Zvi Neriah, *Sichot Ha-Reiyah* (Tel Aviv: Moreshet, 1979), 24.

38. Simcha Raz, *Ish Tzadik Hayah* (Jerusalem: n.p., 1972), 61.

39. Ibid.

40. Ibid., 65.

41. Azriel Carlebach, *Sefer Ha-Demuyot* (Tel Aviv: Modi'in, 1959), 226.

42. In *Sefer Shragai*, 1:234.

43. Haim Cohn, *Mavo Ishi* (Or Yehudah: Kinneret/Zmora Bitan, 2005), 96–102.

44. Cohen (Ha-Nazir), *Mishnat Ha-Nazir*, 93.

45. *Ma'amarei*, 360–62.

46. Moshe Zuriel, ed., *Otzarot Ha-Reiyah*, 2nd ed. (Rishon Le-Zion: Yeshivat Ha-Hesder Rishon le-Zion, 2001), 2:349–51.

47. *Ma'amarei*, 252–53.

48. Reproduced in Menachem Friedman, ed., *Pashkevilim* (Jerusalem: Yad Ben-Zvi and Israel Museum, 2005), 22, 24.

49. In Friedman, *Chevrah va-Dat*, 347n34.

50. Lifshitz, *Shivchei Ha-Reiyah*, 30.

51. *Kevatzim mi-Ktav-Yad Kodsho*, ed. Boaz Ofan (Jerusalem: n.p., 2006), 211.

52. Ibid.

53. Ibid., 213.

54. *Davar*, June 26, 1933.

55. *Davar*, July 7, 1933.

56. Cited in Avneri, 448.

57. *Ha-Hed*, June 17, 1934, reprinted in Kook, *Chazon Ha-Geulah* (Jerusalem: Ha-Agudah le-Hotza'at Kitvei Ha-Reiyah Kook zt'l/Jewish National Fund, 1941), 275.

58. Reprinted in *Ma'amarei*, 268.

59. Reprinted in ibid., 170–71.

60. Kook, *Eyn Ayah*, Shabbat 14:13.

61. Reprinted in *Ma'amarei*, 113.

62. *Pinkas* 12:1.

63. *Pinkas* 12:3.

64. *Pinkas* 12:9.

65. Cited in Benjamin Ish-Shalom, "Beyn Rav Kook li-Spinoza ve-Goethe," in *Kolot Rabim: Sefer Ha-Zikaron le-Rivka Schatz-Uffenheimer*, Jerusalem Studies in Jewish Thought 13, ed.

Rachel Elior and Joseph Dan (Jerusalem: Hebrew University Press, 1996), 537.

66. *Pinkas* 12:2.

67. Reprinted in *Ma'amarei*, 365–66.

68. Shmuel Baruch Shulman, *Ha-Kayitz Ha-Acharon be-Chayei Rabbeinu Ha-Gadol* (Jerusalem: Defus Eretz Yisrael, 1935–36?), 15.

69. Moshe Zvi Neriah, *Likutei Ha-Reiyah* (Kfar Ha-Ro'eh: Chai Ro'i, 1990), 1:477–78.

Conclusion: Afterlight

Epigraph: Hebrew translation in Rivka Horvitz, *Yitzhak Breuer: 'Iyunim be-Mishnato* (Ramat Gan: Bar-Ilan University Press, 1988), 187. (Breuer's essay first appeared in *Nachlat Zvi* (1934/5), pp. 301–11.)

1. Avneri, 330.

2. Agnon, *Me-'Atzmi el 'Atzmi*, 201.

3. Cited by Uriel Barak in *Da'at* 67:98–99.

4. Ravitzky, *Ha-Ketz Ha-Meguleh u-Medinat Ha-Yehudim*, 200.

5. Ibid., 176.

6. Zvi Yehudah's speech, known as "The 19th Psalm," was recorded and has been widely reprinted. It can be heard in its entirety at http://www.meirtv.co.il/site/content_idx.asp?idx=5410&cat_id=3778. The specific passage referred to in the text can be heard at http://www.youtube.com/watch?v=cLywerLqZao.

7. Cited in Gershom Gorenberg, *The Accidental Empire: Israel and the Birth of the Settlements* (New York: Times Books, 2006), 267.

THE LIBRARY of volumes by and about Kook is large and constantly growing. This brief essay offers the merest sampling. The standard edition of Rav Kook's works, published by Mossad Ha-Rav Kook (the Rabbi Kook Foundation) in Jerusalem, runs to nineteen volumes of essays, letters, halakhic responsa and treatises, Talmudic commentaries, and other writings—this in addition to other collections of essays and teachings that have long been in print. These have in recent years been supplemented by the publication of many works that had remained in manuscript, most significantly a number of his spiritual diaries in their original forms, especially *Shemonah Kevatzim*, the eight notebooks written during the heroic period of his theologizing, 1910–19, which were the mother lode for the many works culled and edited by Zvi Yehudah (*Orot, Orot Ha-Teshuvah*, and *Orot Ha-Torah* among them), by David Cohen ("Ha-Nazir"), editor of the theological magnum opus *Orot Ha-Kodesh* (*Lights of the Holy*), and by others. A number of other notebooks have been published in recent years, in censored editions, under the title *Pinkesei Ha-Reiyah*, and uncensored, under the title *Kevatzim mi-Ktav Yad Kodsho*. The publication of the notebooks has settled the long debate over whether Rav Kook was to be read chiefly as philosopher or mystic. The notebooks demonstrated the overwhelmingly mystic and Kabbalistic tenor of Rav Kook's own thought-world, which does not banish the philosophical dimension, but rather embeds it in a richer perspective.

Other notebooks and hitherto unpublished works have been published, sometimes in censored form, leading to new and heated debates over the shape and meaning of the evolving canon of works by Rav Kook. Almost all of Rav Kook's published works, in his lifetime and after, were edited, often intensively, by others. For a fascinating discussion of his editors and their milieus, see Jonatan Meir, "Orot ve-Kelim: Bechinah Mechudeshet shel 'Chug' Ha-Reiyah Kook ve-'Orkhei Ketavav," *Kabbalah* 13 (2005): 163–247. For a very helpful survey of the state of these publications, and of the political and theological stakes of seemingly recondite bibliographic and editorial issues, see Avinoam Rosenak, "Hidden Diaries and New Discoveries: The Life and Thought of Rabbi A. I. Kook," *Shofar: An Interdisciplinary Journal of Jewish Studies* 25, no. 3 (Spring 2007): 111–47.

Rav Kook has been the subject of scores of academic volumes and literally hundreds of studies and monographs (not to mention a large and growing body of popular and even children's literature), almost all in Hebrew. Readers seeking to learn more about him in English are advised to consult Yosef Ben-Shlomo, *Poetry of Being* (Tel Aviv: Ministry of Defence, 1990), perhaps the best brief introduction to him; Zvi Yaron, *The Philosophy of Rabbi Kook*, translated by Avner Tomaschoff (Jerusalem: Eliner Library, 1991), a broad and well-organized survey of his basic ideas; and the essay collections edited by Benjamin Ish-Shalom and Shalom Rosenberg, *The World of Rav Kook's Thought*, translated by Shalom Carmy (New York: Avi Chai, 1991), and by Lawrence Kaplan and David Shatz, *Rabbi Abraham Isaac Kook and Jewish Spirituality* (New York: New York University Press, 1995), the latter of which contains a very helpful bibliography of works by and about Rav Kook. Another essential volume is Aviezer Ravitsky, *Messianism, Zionism, and Jewish Religious Radicalism*, translated by Jonathan Chipman (Chicago: University of Chicago Press, 1996). Other especially valuable studies in English have been written by Shlomo Fischer, Jonathan Garb, and Tamar Ross.

In addition to these writers, my thinking has been shaped in particular by engagement with the works on Rav Kook in Hebrew by Yosef Avivi, Yosef Ben-Shlomo, Yoel Bin-Nun, Benjamin Ish-Shalom, Dov Schwartz, and Smadar Sherlo. I have likewise benefitted from the studies of Rav Kook's halakhic writings by Neriah Gutel and Avinoam Rosenak and from Monty Penkower's research on the Arlosoroff affair.

For Rav Kook in English translation, I especially recommend two volumes by the late Ben-Zion Bokser: *Abraham Isaac Kook* (Mahwah, N.J.: Paulist Press, 1978); and *The Essential Writings of Abraham Isaac Kook* (Teaneck, N.J.: Ben-Yehuda Press, 2006). Bezalel Naor published a valuable and richly annotated translation of the first edition of *Orot* (London: Aronson, 1993), along with other illuminating volumes of studies and translations. Tzvi Feldman and David Samson published other translations that readers may wish to consult.

A full-length scholarly biography of Rav Kook has yet to be written in any language. The last attempt at one in English was Jacob Agus's still-rewarding volume *Banner of Jerusalem* (New York: Bloch, 1946). The writing of the present volume would have been impossible were it not for the researches of Yossi Avneri, Kalman Frankel, and Menachem Friedman, mentioned in the endnotes, as well as Avneri's essay on Rav Kook's Jaffa years, which appeared in *Cathedra* 37 (1986). I am also deeply indebted, as are all who study Rav Kook's life and times, to the pioneering biographical essay by Yehudah Leib Maimon, first published in the memorial volume he edited in 1937, and to the many volumes written and compiled by Moshe Zvi Neriah. An attempt at full-length biography of his early decades is Yehudah Mirsky, "An Intellectual and Spiritual Biography of Rabbi Avraham Yitzhak Ha-Cohen Kook from 1865 to 1904" (PhD diss., Harvard University, 2007).

ACKNOWLEDGMENTS

ואמרת ביום ההוא אודך ה' כי אנפת בי ישב אפך ותנחמני

THE GATES TO RAV KOOK were first opened to me in the fall of 1978 by my teacher and master, Rav Yehudah Amital of blessed memory, the founder and longtime dean of Yeshivat Har Etzion—who is in death as he was in life, a comfort, goad, and inspiration. In our last conversation, shortly before his passing in July 2010, I asked him, as I regularly did, what he had been thinking about of late. He replied with a characteristic provocation: "It's time for the young people to think thoughts." I'm trying.

It was while standing in the *beit midrash* of Yeshivat Har Etzion one early afternoon in those years that I was gripped by the sense that I would one day write Rav Kook's biography. Yet it took many years for the gate to this volume to appear, in the form of a letter from Steve Zipperstein, inviting me to join this series. In the ensuing years, Steve has been as encouraging, thoughtful, supportive, and understanding an editor as one could hope for—and most important of all, a good friend. The coeditor of this series, Anita Shapira, has from the beginning graciously offered her encouragement and rich knowledge. I am grateful to her and to Leon D. Black, without whom this series would not exist. I thank the Jewish Lives team—Ileene Smith, John Palmer, and Aaron Kaplowitz—for their many efforts and their faith in this volume. I am grateful for Kip Keller's terrific copyediting, Margaret Otzel's tireless sure-footed production management, and Nancy Zibman's deft indexing.

This book was made possible by the great generosity and faith of the Alice M. and Thomas J. Tisch Foundation, as well as by the support of Aryeh Rubin and the Targum Shlishi Foundation.

My dear friend Jamie Star has been, as always, a faithful friend and delightful buddy, and I am glad that I have finally written something he may want to read.

A number of friends helped this project come to be: Michael Baris, Deborah Harris, Shaul Magid, Jonatan Meir, Marc Shapiro, Rami Tal, Ann Wroe, Osnat Weinfeld, Carole Zawatsky, and Menachem Butler. Benjamin Balint and Sylvia Fuks Fried generously offered, at crucial turns, sound advice laced with friendship.

My dear friends Stacy Burdett, Shai Held, David Starr, Alan Mayer, Marcie Lenk, Dave Makovsky, and David Pollock, companions on the journey, have helped me more than they know.

Seth Aronson has been my friend for thirty-five years now, and I still marvel at his extraordinary faithfulness, insight, and humility. Jody Sampson has been for twenty-five years a wonder of wisdom, support, and kindness.

I began this book in Jerusalem, where I lived for the last ten years, and completed it in Boston after Ilan Troen, director of the Schusterman Center for Israel Studies at Brandeis University, recruited me to join the faculty. It is a pleasure to thank both him and Sylvia Barack Fishman, chair of the Department of Near Eastern and Judaic Studies, who have welcomed me into a supportive community of educators and scholars. I would like to thank all my new colleagues, in particular Joanne Arnish, Marc Brettler, Jonathan Decter, Sharon Pucker-Rivo, Jonathan Sarna, and Eugene Sheppard, for all their assistance in matters large and small.

Stuart Cohen, Simon Erlanger, and Dvora Hacohen were

very helpful in answering specific queries, and I am grateful to Hillel Cohen for sharing with me his work in progress on the 1929 riots. Moshe Sokolow generously proofread.

The errors and infelicities in this volume are mine.

I owe a special debt of thanks to Rabbi Ari Shvat (Chwat), research director of Beit Ha-Rav Kook in Jerusalem, who unstintingly shared his knowledge—and photograph collection—and read and commented on the entire manuscript. Our differences in interpretation and ideology are more than made up for by our shared love of our work, and the deepening of our friendship has been one of this book's unexpected blessings. And I would like to thank the Nezer David Foundation for the Publication of the Writings of Ha-Rav Ha-Nazir for generously sharing with me photographs of Ha-Rav Ha-Nazir and Rav Zvi Yehudah; thanks also go to Professor Naomi Cohen for facilitating that connection.

I have been immensely enriched by my many conversations with Shlomo Fischer. My friend Ari Ackerman read through this manuscript, and once again his learning and good judgment kept me on track. The support and encouragement of Moshe Idel have meant a great deal to me.

I was for years blessed by the guidance, intellect, faith and deep human sympathy of Rabbi Dr. Emanuel Rackman, of blessed memory.

I have in my years of reading, thinking about, teaching, and sometimes writing about Rav Kook incurred too many intellectual debts to mention. To all my teachers, living and dead, older and younger than myself, I say thank you.

The greatest of them all was my father, Rabbi Professor David Mirsky, of blessed memory. I once wrote about my father that he was "a rare mix of *talmid chakham*, literary humanist, ironist, and, with his gentle mix of altruism, grace, and wisdom, a genuine tzaddik. He was human of course, but we all should be so human." Amen.

My mother, Sarrah Appel Mirsky, has lived a life of rare heart and passion, empathy and love, and I have tried to learn from her as best I can.

My brother Moshe and my sister Zipporah, their spouses, Janice and Micah, and their children, have all helped me immensely, each in their own, marvelous way.

This book has been a long accompaniment to my wife and children, who are understandably relieved that it is coming to a close. It is a special pleasure to thank my wondrous daughter Nehara Shulamit for the times she gave me permission to leave her bedtime early so I could go and write. And special thanks to Nofet Shira, not least for her delightedly renaming the subject of this volume *Rav Toot*, that is, Rabbi Strawberry, an appellation that I think—coming from a bright-eyed little girl—he would have greatly enjoyed.

As for my wife, Tamar Biala, I have no words. Her soul is as much in this project as mine, perhaps more so, and her wisdom, compassion, and grace are somewhere on every page. All I can say is that I hope and pray that I can be as good to her as she has been to me.

INDEX

Jewish Lives is a major series of interpretive
biography designed to illuminate the imprint of Jewish
figures upon literature, religion, philosophy, politics, cultural
and economic life, and the arts and sciences. Subjects are
paired with authors to elicit lively, deeply informed books that
explore the range and depth of Jewish experience
from antiquity through the present.

Jewish Lives is a partnership of Yale University Press
and the Leon D. Black Foundation.

Ileene Smith is editorial director. Anita Shapira and
Steven J. Zipperstein are series editors.